THE
NEW FACE
OF JAZZ

An Intimate Look at Today's Living Legends
and the Artists of Tomorrow

CICILY JANUS

PHOTOGRAPHS BY NED RADINSKY

Billboard Books / New York

To Mom and Dad,
Thanks for making jazz a part of my DNA

Copyright © 2010 by Cicily Janus
Photographs copyright © 2010 by Ned Radinsky

Published in the United States by Billboard Books,
an imprint of the Crown Publishing Group,
a division of Random House Inc., New York.
www.crownpublishing.com

BILLBOARD is a registered trademark of Nielsen Business Media, Inc.
Library of Congress Cataloging-in-Publication Data

The new face of jazz: an intimate look at today's living legends and the artists of tomorrow / [interviews by]
Cicily Janus; photographs by Ned Radinsky. — 1st ed.
     p. cm.
  Includes bibliographical references and index.
  ISBN 978-0-8230-0065-4 (alk. paper)
  1. Jazz musicians—Interviews. I. Janus, Cicily.
  ML385.N534 2010
  781.65'50922—dc22
                        2010005659

Designer: Nicole LaRoche

Printed in the United States of America

First printing, 2010

1 2 3 4 5 6 7 8 9 10 / 15 14 13 12 11 10

I'll play it first and tell you what it is later.

MILES DAVIS

CONTENTS

There are people who fall in love with certain stages of jazz. When they fall, they're so deeply in love that when jazz moves to another stage they feel angry and betrayed by that new stage. I guess this is just the way the world works.

Miles Davis' career was the perfect example of this. He started with bebop; then it was cool jazz; then he moved on to hard bop, modal jazz, and fusion. He faced criticism each time he changed his style. In the fifties, when Miles had his first great quintet, people criticized him for having Red Garland as his pianist and said that John Coltrane played too much. But in the sixties, when Miles moved on to his second quintet, with Herbie Hancock and Wayne Shorter, the people who loved the first quintet got upset. They said they didn't understand what he was doing; that it didn't make any sense. They claimed it wasn't jazz or "real" music. In the seventies, when Miles was playing fusion, one guy said to him, "I love what you did ten years ago, but I can't get into what you're doing now. I just don't get it." Miles responded, "You want me to wait for you?"

This attitude applies nowadays. It's hard for certain people to embrace hip-hop or hip-hop influenced jazz. The new forms just don't have enough of the musical elements that they value. But the one thing that's kept jazz from disappearing is its ability to embrace new elements and influences and still, somehow, keep its essence. Jazz gets into trouble when it resists this change. If we don't embrace this change and encourage young musicians to create music that reflects their time, then jazz is going to become another form of classical music. That means nothing new will be created at all, and we'll end up spending the rest of time glorifying what has happened over the last fifty years. We can't let this happen. Jazz is, and will always be, different from classical music because it can live on forever continuing to be relevant and vibrant at each new stage.

Of course there will always be musicians who carry the torch of the past. This is necessary, because we don't want to forget the music that's been created—after all, jazz over the past fifty years is some of the greatest music ever made in the history of time—but there's always been another section of musicians who are forward thinking. They love what's happened in the past, but they absorb and learn from it instead of spending a lot of time trying to recreate it. If I see a young musician whom I think has potential, and he's trying to figure out what he's going to do, I tell him, "Listen man, don't downplay the time you live in, the time you live in is as valuable as any other time in history. It's up to you to show the world of the future how cool today was."

We need to glorify the moment we live in. Every culture we admire, every piece of art we admire, glorifies the time in which it was created, which should be the first job of any artistic creation. You've got to do this first, and, if you're lucky, and what you've created is good enough, the future will be kind to you. You might last. Your creation might even become classic. But you can't guarantee that. The job in your hands is to reflect the current world through your lens. Mozart did it; Beethoven did it; King Oliver did it; and Louis Armstrong did it. You can hear the time in their music. Charlie Parker didn't know his music would become classic; there was no way to know. He just played from the bottom of his heart. He did it the right way. Coltrane didn't know when he was playing in the Village Vanguard, finding new ways to express himself, that there would be tenor saxophone players trying to imitate him for the rest of eternity. We can't skip that uncertain, scary phase of not knowing if our music is good enough to last. We've got to go through that hard part. This means taking our hits and punches. People are going to criticize us, but if all the critics instantly understand and like what we're doing, then what we're doing probably isn't far-reaching enough.

When my mom would listen to Duke Ellington, she would close her eyes and you could see her remembering those ballrooms in Harlem where she used to dance and do her thing; the music contains those memories for her.

Our music has to do that for us. It has to have a beat that reflects the way people walk now, the way people dress now, and the way the city streets sound now. Young musicians can't worry about the critics. They'll catch up eventually.

After interviewing several hundred musicians who are in the jazz moment today, Cicily Janus found a common thread. It seems that we're all living life while reaching to be heard. In each interview in this book you can find musicians asking their listeners to listen. They're saying, "We're here. Now. Playing for you. Reflecting our time." Cicily found there's a real need for us to have a creative space in our world that is void of the expectations of the past.

By writing this book, Cicily has helped establish a living, collective authority among this jazz community. As artists, we're allowed to speak for ourselves, instead of letting critics and journalists define our art for us. She found that by doing this, natural leaders will emerge. She wants you to buy into them as people so that you can buy into the reality of their art. This book encourages you to be your own judge and discover the new faces for yourself through their words. Usually the musicians say everything they have to say through their music, leaving others to discuss it in words. Here are their words. The words of the actual music makers who work so tirelessly to show us our world through music, through jazz.

MARCUS MILLER

A WORD FROM WYNTON MARSALIS

As an American, I feel that jazz is a great legacy that has been bequeathed to us. It's a way of life, a way of looking at the world, and a way of living. I didn't grow up with the glories of jazz. I only knew it to be about people struggling—the musicians were struggling to earn  a living and the audience was struggling to get more meaning from life. The local New Orleans musicians at the time—my father included—were always struggling to feed their families and to get people to understand this music. In the 1930s, the music was popular, but musicians were barely making a living traveling all around the country on buses. Of course this was through the teeth of the Depression, and musicians were doing better than most. These musicians and their music penetrated the consciousness of this country and laid the foundation of jazz as community music. When the big bands became economically unfeasible after World War II, most of these traveling musicians were out of work. Here come Charlie Parker and Dizzy and Monk and Miles and them, and jazz was reinvigorated as chamber music in clubs (even though Phil Schaap says they played a lot of dances). There was a battle between the older and newer music (now we know that all jazz is modern).

A lot of musicians got involved with dope following Charlie Parker and trying to cope with the pressures of being conscious in an unconscious era. Involvement with dope sucked a lot of love out of the scene and affected the perception of jazz as community. And then rock and roll (a folk version of one small aspect of jazz) became the music of choice in America and a way to exploit younger people by making them think involvement with music could make you hip. It worked and is still working today. Jazz becomes something for a small group of devotees, but it's really an art, which speaks to and embraces this whole country—the world for that matter. We still struggle for an audience, for recognition of what has happened, for a culture ready to be nurtured by this music. This struggling is something we've gotten accustomed to.

We all need this music to penetrate deeper into our way of life. It will make us more thoughtful, creative, and relaxed people. It seems that many in our culture would rather be *perceived* as something than *be* that something. We accept a commercial vision of ourselves that is bereft of substance. That's what wrecked our financial systems. They sell smoke. If someone questions our way of life and tries to seek improvement or create actual change without the right marketing, they risk being misperceived as the enemy.

Our national life would be much richer if we were more culturally informed through our education system. Taking arts out of the education system was a tactical error. We all know that—I should say, people in the arts know this because those who are not in the arts don't. But I suspect they feel something is wrong and just can't figure out what it is. They think the arts are important because they can help you compete with other countries' kids in math and science. That's so backwards. The arts teach you how to embrace your own creativity and enable you to perceive the creativity of others. That makes global communion and communication much easier. Jazz is the one of the most liberating arts to yet grace our planet. And we choose enslavement to fads and machines. Damn! I guess the arts community is not successful at communicating why this music is important. When we talk it seems to fall upon deaf ears.

If we could only understand that everyone's mutual interest lies in correcting these problems, they would be addressed. But with this love of the fast buck and the absurdity of what passes for "young people's music," no one knows when things will turn around or change.

When this music occupies the central position it has earned in our culture, I believe jazz will make us better as people, as Americans. Musicians create community through their art. In this time, our aspirations are as much about audiences understanding the larger sound of jazz as they are about musical objectives. We want people to understand us. But sometimes following the people is not a way to have them follow you. If you fundamentally alter who you are or misuse your talent, you've lost the ability to communicate your true creative perspective. The objective is to come out of this art and life with yourself and with your sense of integrity. This way, we can't be upset when the world doesn't go our way. The world has always gone where it's going to go. It's too big to mess with. Sometimes in this world we lose faith in "what is" for "what can be projected." Jazz is very concrete music. It's just what we do. We have to put our best foot forward with what we have. All we can do is lay it out there for others to hear. If they dig it, great. If not, we have to play better.

AUTHOR'S INTRODUCTION

I assumed, as an avid reader and writer, that the best histories were told after a life had already been lived. If you read most jazz books, you would assume the same. Shortly after I began writing this book, I realized that I had to change either my perspective or my chosen genre. I now believe that some observations of the human experience are best made by taking one's own life and setting it to the soundtrack of others. Age is but a number to mark the time; experience is the true reality.

I guess you would say that I was one of the chosen ones. My experience in this life began when my parents chose to raise me on jazz—modern jazz to be exact. To go into even more detail, Pat Metheny was pretty much the "religious" icon in my house. I knew no different. Later on, I chose trumpet as my instrument of study and made it my life. By the time I left home to begin college, jazz had infused every fiber of my being. Yet four weeks into my freshman year at the University of North Florida, I crashed and burned. I felt as if jazz had gone stale. Of course, this was before iPods and MP3s—I had to actually go to a record store to buy and discover new recordings.

Jazz, it seemed, had failed me. It was mentally exhausting. Even the albums I found the most solace in, such as *Kind of Blue*, were suffocating my trained ears. At that point in time, my experiences alone were not enough to carry me through this depression. While awaiting my college band rehearsal one afternoon, another band was finishing up their time in the room. The director called one last song. A pianist by the name of Oscar Perez, who is now listed in this book, began to paint a picture through the opening lines of the piece. The music showed me a place I knew I had to find but had never seen. I found myself captured amidst a wordless poem and suddenly I felt I could move on. This isn't to say I was completely changed, or my depression was permanently lifted, but that moment offered a glimpse into a side of the one art form I thought I knew that I hadn't seen before.

The tune: "Last Season" by Maria Schneider. In many ways, Maria opened my ears to music again. She painted with subtle colors and textures. She fed my need for change and offered a new dialect of the jazz language. I was forced to resign my preconceived notion of the art form and I had to tell everyone and anyone who would listen about what I had heard.

Since that day, I've looked at jazz in a different light. I've had to seek out music that suits my ears, and there's plenty of it. Yet if someone had not shown me that that side of music existed, how would I have known to find it? Too many in our technologically advanced culture, I believe, see and hear jazz as I once did.

This, I believe, is where we are going wrong as a culture. Somewhere along the way, people mistook their notions of jazz for background noise. We dismiss this art as what we once heard in one place or what others tell us it is. We herald the past as if it's the only way to go when it comes to jazz. But this isn't what it is. Jazz is the equivalent to musical storytelling. Jazz tells the story about the life we're living right this very second. The music changes with the moment, and if you hold onto its past, it has already passed you by.

This book is about that moment in time played out by the very best accessible, prolific artists who are enriching our lives. If we as a culture don't take the time to listen to this moment in this art, we're going to miss out on it too.

Throughout the past year, I learned a lot by taking time off to hear their stories. Although my professional career as a musician didn't last much past seven or eight years after college, I am intimately familiar with what musicians do day in and day out: hours spent practicing, odd hours of the night when actual work gets done, lobby calls and that time of the day when you wish silence would take over and calm your mind.

I am also, by far, not the first one to have taken down an oral history of jazz. Although I am certainly continuing the tradition, I believe my time as a musician has allowed me camaraderie with the players and access to the places in their minds that only musicians know to go. Whereas other writers have chased down only the most notable voices among the crowd, I chose to give a broader perspective on the scene. Many of the artists included in these pages are those who live in your community. Some have won major awards, such as Grammy Awards or NEA grants. Some musicians were chosen simply on their merit and sheer talent-filled ambition. But each of them brought a voice to the table that needed to be heard.

Of course, many were excluded, and I'm sure there are those of you who are questioning their exclusion. I can only answer that there will never, ever be enough pages or time to include every important player and their music out there. It's a big community, and, admittedly, this book barely scratches the surface. I hope the positive effects of spotlighting the artists who are in these pages outweigh the negative effects of the unfortunate but inevitable omissions. Those who were interviewed but unfortunately omitted from the manuscript will be included on our website for the book (www.newfaceofjazz.com) along with reviews and jazz industry news.

As for those that were included, they offered a side of themselves that is rarely seen in method books, trade magazines, or pared-down critiques. They spoke of their fears, hopes, challenges, and reasons for living. Some interviews took ten minutes; for others I spent up to six or seven hours with the subject in a café, in their homes, or on the phone, praying my battery didn't die while we spoke. More than a few of them said they rarely were asked who they were. Some of them ended in tears, but all of them had laughter peppered throughout, as if they'd been granted the title of a seasoned professional in the emotion of joy. Each artist also selected one disc from their discographies that they thought best represented their career to date. Yet the recurring theme that surfaced in more than four hundred of the interviews over nine months, across racial, financial, generational, and geographical boundaries, was that their needs were the exact same.

The *exact* same.

They've placed a dire call for help, a plea for a very basic human connection. They want for others to listen and reach out to them and hear what they are doing. It's much easier, in this culture, to stay complacent in our ways. But jazz is a contradiction to that lifestyle. It never stays the same. It reflects the here and now. It's part of us. Although we've all seen and heard the past, I can guarantee that jazz is vastly different now. It's a new face. Its tradition has sewn its lines in the wrinkle of time while moving ahead and forging a path of its own. And although its face may have changed, the accompanying melody has been sung since the beginning of time. Give jazz a second glance, another listen, another chance, and you too will see that it's the soundtrack we're all missing in our lives.

Michael Abene

COMPOSER, KEYBOARDIST, EDUCATOR, PRODUCER

GOT MUSIC?
Avant Gershwin, Patti Austin,
Rendezvous, 2007

"Just because I'm having fun doesn't mean I'm not serious."

BACKGROUND AND SOUND

As a renaissance man walking among the music industry, Michael Abene has done it all. He has produced Grammy Award–winning albums over and over again. He has played side by side with the top musicians as a keyboardist. He also runs the BMI Composers Workshops with Jim McNeely. From Duke Ellington to GRP Christmas Collections and Charlie Brown, his ability to show all sides of his gift is a gift to us all. He homes in on the intent of the song and draws emotional and rhythmic attachments from his life to seal them with his signature.

HIS STORY

I grew up in Farmingdale, Maryland. It wasn't until high school that I wrote my first arrangement and it was horrible. I guess improvement was just a matter of writing and writing. Eventually I became interested in the concept of orchestral arranging. I was always listening to music, and I enjoyed playing piano, but arranging was the most interesting to me. To see all the parts come together, et cetera. I tried to transcribe Ellington's band, but it was like a jigsaw puzzle to me . . . was fascinating. I would write for all groups, and once I was able to drive I would go out and hear live music like Clark Terry, Oliver Nelson, Jimmy Nottingham, and Papa Jo Jones.

Once I began to write for commercials I was put into situations where you write stuff you'd never though you'd write before. They'd ask for piccolos and tubas, and eventually I learned how to write for strings too. I was homing in on my craft then and getting myself together. The fascination with composing and arranging has never stopped. The process of learning is never ending. My experiences have shaped me from where I was to where I am today. I'm like a kid, a workaholic kid and I'll work until four or five in the morning. As long as I'm working, I'm happy. Sometimes when I'm working on one piece something will click and move me to something else. Regardless, I'm having a great time. Just because I'm having fun doesn't mean I'm not serious. This business is a business and should be treated as such. But I'll never retire. The only way to learn is to constantly listen to others. Hopefully I'm doing my thing right and injecting my little pieces in each work so you know it's me when you listen.

Jamey Aebersold   {LIVING LEGEND}
SAXOPHONIST, EDUCATOR, COMPOSER

HOME BASE
www.aebersold.com

"Jazz musicians never give up."

BACKGROUND AND SOUND
Internationally known saxophonist and educator Jamey Aebersold has been helping musicians of all ages and skill levels learn jazz for more than forty years. He is the authoritative voice on jazz education methods, and his Play-A-Long jazz series and summer camps have quite literally shaped the future of this art form. He has been inducted into the International Association of Jazz Educators Hall of Fame and was awarded the Governor's Award in Indiana in 2007. His dedication to the future of jazz is simply amazing, and the legacy he is building will most assuredly leave the world of jazz in a better place than where he found it.

HIS STORY

I was born in 1939. There wasn't television, radio, CDs, nothing. Entertainment was in the home. My parents were musical; my mother would play piano and sing, and my father played banjo. They listened to dance bands while I was growing up. But when I first heard Elvis I said, "he's never going to make it." I was raised on much higher standards. When rock and roll came here the only object was to make a record. You didn't have to get good enough to do anything. Music fell off its cliff at that time. When I look back, it all happened so slowly. But now that I'm sixty-nine, it all seemed to have happened really fast. When I started at twenty or twenty-one years old I had no idea what would come of it. I used to think that in order to teach you had to do something with your creative side at night. But I didn't think it was possible with jazz education to give people a chance to get out and make a living. I just thought that if we gave kids a dose of it once, twice a week they would learn to seek it out. If it's not presented to them they're going to continue on with whatever the media feeds them. I've always thought of jazz education as being an uphill battle. There's a lack of money, lack of teachers, et cetera, and it's much easier to have a concert band with eighty kids and one teacher then twenty kids with one. You have to break down the barrier, cut that ice, and warm things up. Listen to see who's connected and what's being played through the brain. I think Thelonious Monk said it best when he said, "you don't have freedom unless you've been restricted and chained up for a while." Jazz musicians never give up. They continue to intrigue me. You can't shut off that fire once it's ignited. Sometimes it takes a long time to acquire the freedom through that uphill battle in order to be satisfied with your playing and not be so critical. I just try to make jazz sound as inspiring as possible so others can go back enthused. My own journey has allowed me to do this.

Toshiko Akiyoshi

COMPOSER, PIANIST, NEA JAZZ MASTER

HOME BASE
www.toshikoakiyoshi.com

GOT MUSIC?
Toshiko Akiyoshi–Lew Tabackin Big Band (Box Set), Mosaic Select, 2008

"Because I love what I do, I keep going."

BACKGROUND AND SOUND

Manchurian-born pianist Toshiko Akiyoshi has made waves throughout the jazz world for more than fifty years. Her uniquely woven compositions echo the rich tradition of such greats as Duke Ellington and Oscar Peterson. Over time she has recorded more than eighteen albums with her big band and earned four Grammy nominations. She has also been named as the number one pick for Best Arranger/Composer in *DownBeat* magazine's readers poll. This was the first time in the history of this award that a woman had been named at the top. In 2007 she was awarded the most prestigious of jazz awards, the title of NEA Jazz Master. As of today, her accolades and awards are too numerous to list. Akiyoshi continues to produce a prolific amount of work that exemplifies her heritage and experience into a mastered body of work.

HER STORY

I was born in Manchuria, which today is China. I was there for sixteen years and then I was in Japan for ten years and then came here in 1956. I guess I've been here for some fifty years now. People always ask me where I'm from. Although my birthplace is China, I consider Japan as my homeland and America as my workplace.

Jazz is sort of a fusion of European and African art that was born in this country. So the Japanese culture was never a part of it. I began studying jazz when I was about sixteen years old, around 1946. Back then being Japanese and playing jazz was considered a handicap. Many people saw it that way. I'm not sure how it is today but Lew always jokes saying that I'm demographically challenged.

Around 1974 Duke died. There was a memoir written around that same time by Nat Hentoff. This talked about how proud Duke was that he was black and how much of the music was based on his race. I dealt with the same issues. I remember one of the jazz journalists around then saying, about me, "I question her authenticity." Sometimes you just don't think about it until someone points it out. Because of Duke, I began to look into my own heritage. It's taken me a long time but once I did I realized I was heavily influenced by it, still am. It's helped me be totally different than anyone else playing jazz. I had to look at this as a positive asset instead of a negative one while I tried—and perhaps still do—to repay something to jazz history and the jazz world through this knowledge. Since Duke's death I've been deliberately doing this. All of my writing comes from my experiences as a player and my heritage. I want to show people that this jazz world has been very kind to me. Because I love what I do, I keep going. I have no choice. This is why I'm alive. I think anyone who finds jazz will find that there's a soul in it that will stay with you throughout your life.

Ben Allison

COMPOSER, BASSIST

HOME BASE
www.benallison.com

GOT MUSIC?
Think Free, Ben Allison, Palmetto Records, 2009

"Jazz is defined daily by the people who make it."

BACKGROUND AND SOUND

Ben Allison is more than the sum of the usual parts. He is one of the most industrious and profuse composers working today. Ben has made it his job to reshape the way jazz is felt and heard and because of this his works are in demand around the world. His unique sound can be heard on television, film, radio, live performances, recordings, and theater venues. At the young age of twenty-five he helped create the Jazz Composers Collective. One of the first of its kind, this was a nonprofit organization based in New York and run solely by musicians. Through this group Ben and the other composers produced more than one hundred special events and concerts that featured compositionally based jazz. The continued critical and international acclaim are icing on his cake. The significant weight of each of his works combined with his visionary goals prove all too well that he is an exceptional and brilliant leader in jazz today.

HIS STORY

Jazz is an evolutionary music that will continue to be vital only if it changes and develops. In order for it to remain relevant as an art form it has to reflect the lives and convictions of the musicians who make it today. In 1992 I helped form the Jazz Composers Collective, a nonprofit, musician-run organization that presented new music and helped to build audiences for jazz. During its twelve-year run, the Collective presented more than one hundred concerts featuring more than 250 musicians and premiering more than three hundred new works. The Collective published a newsletter written by musicians, organized an annual festival in New York City, commissioned new pieces, and produced or helped to produce many CDs by its composers-in-residence and guest artists. The Collective was the organizational force behind a lot of what I did for the first twelve years of my career and provided me support—creatively, financially, and socially—in my drive to be a bandleader.

One of the goals of the Collective was to inspire musicians to see composition as an extremely powerful and effective way to get to something musically personal. Composing gives you the chance to "improvise in pencil." You can revisit and rework ideas—and erase if necessary. You can take time to craft a mood and create a sonic world that musicians are then free to explore. However, I also like to leave a lot of room for spontaneous improvisation in my music. I believe improvisation is a truly indispensable part of jazz and without it we might as well not use the word. At its best, composition becomes a springboard for musicians to develop their improvisation language.

It was through the Collective that I learned how vital it is for artists to reach out to audiences and do what they can to build their fan base over time. Many of us don't have the luxury of a corporate machine behind us to help get the word out about our music. This music exists somewhat on the fringe and is not thrust in people's faces in the way that much of mainstream pop music is. We're required to be more grassroots about audience development. I work hard to build my audiences by touring and working with technology to make sure they know what we're doing.

The good news is that jazz audiences of today, at least the people who follow my music, tend to be open-minded and thoughtful people. They're not afraid to go in search of something new and tend to share what they find with other like-minded music enthusiasts. I'm gratified that, although my music has changed a lot over the years, I still have a lot of the same fans I had ten years ago. I also have a lot of young people discovering my music for the first time with every new CD that comes out. In fact, the younger generations seem to represent the largest percentage of people who listen to my music these days.

Jazz is defined daily by the people who make it. It's also a totally international music now. There are great jazz musicians all over the world. They each have their own style and approach. In a sense, jazz can be described as a language with a very large lexicon. And each geographic area has its own dialect that reflects that community. I'm optimistic about the future of jazz.

Karrin Allyson
VOCALIST, PIANIST

HOME BASE
www.karrin.com

GOT MUSIC?
By Request: The Best of Karrin Allyson, Karrin Allyson, Concord Records, 2009

"Music is a worthwhile endeavor to find truth and humor and exercise my intellect."

BACKGROUND AND SOUND
Three-time Grammy-nominated Concord Records artist Karrin Allyson has produced an impressive body of work. Her interpretations of standards and added tenderness to original works have enchanted audiences for

over fifteen years. She has performed with groups ranging from small jazz quartets all the way up to symphony orchestras throughout the world, including Carnegie Hall. Her style and belief in this art is not only about the music; it's about forging the way for future generations in jazz to find their own voices and strengths.

HER STORY

I was a classical pianist to begin with and loved it. I still love classical music. Maybe if I'd had patience for sight-reading, who knows what would have happened. Classical piano was my major in college. I thought that's what I was going to do. I got a bachelor's in piano performance and a minor in French. I was interested in music all along. Then I started to sing along with and play a lot of my favorite pop tunes of the day and loved that aspect of making music. I think it came rather easily to me. I'm not saying by any means that it's easy, because I don't feel that I have the kind of voice or ease of voice that others do. It's just different. I've always found the performance aspect of singing to be less harrowing than classical piano. Then again, I love both so very much. Music is a worthwhile endeavor to find truth and humor and exercise my intellect. The people involved with jazz, the players themselves, are fabulous people as a rule. It's like they're your instant family. There's an understanding, a basic understanding. In my view, it's important for me to become a "musician who sings," not just a singer. To make music interesting you have to be engaged in a conversation with your players; you can't just do your own soliloquy. This is a constant learning process. There's always a carrot dangling in front of you to strive for excellence in your art form.

But life itself is a constant teacher. What you choose to do with your life is how you choose to learn, or at least one avenue you choose to learn from. It's been the same for me in that it's always changing. I wouldn't even separate nowadays or most days from when I first started as a musician. For musicians the unknown is the norm. I seldom feel like, "oh my God, what's going to happen?" Maybe it's that I'm somewhat secure or used to the unknown. Jazz, however, is a very worthwhile pursuit and endeavor. I feel like any art form is. Jazz just keeps me interested like no other music can. I'm in constant pursuit of excellence and am very serious about it. But, I also have a good time doing it. When I sing, I'm singing to you. And "you" is whoever is reading this sentence or hearing our music. I truly am singing to you as an individual . . . my experience, my hopes, and my dreams are out there and if you listen, you might see that they're very akin to yours.

Stephen Anderson
PIANIST, COMPOSER, EDUCATOR

HOME BASE
www.artiststephenanderson.com

GOT MUSIC?
Forget Not, Stephen Anderson Trio, Summit Records, 2008

"I'm very passionate . . . a warrior for my craft."

BACKGROUND AND SOUND

Living in Chapel Hill, North Carolina, which he calls mini-New York because of its emphasis on culture, Stephen Anderson has ensured his success through molding and shaping the way music is heard not only by today's audiences but also by future generations. Named outstanding classical composer at both the University of North Texas and Brigham Young University, he now holds a position among the jazz faculty at the University of North Carolina, Chapel Hill. Recording with the likes of Lynn Seaton and peers at UNT has taught him the dense textures, rhythms, and resonating lessons that now coordinate his hands with his heart to create a balance in both home and career.

HIS STORY

Jazz is a tradition, a history, and a culture. An emphasis on groove—all sorts . . . it means sacrifice to the people who were enslaved. If you dig deep enough with the culture, pain, and sorrow, you see how people transcended. You then begin to see yourself as a part of the musical tradition. We're in a totally different time with new challenges, but we're still a part of that legacy. We should keep this music alive, but when people only want to hear the same things again we'll never learn to appreciate the new. As a composer, my music is constantly evolving. I draw upon my influences and react to them. Why not do what very few people do and merge it with jazz and blues and make it your own? Progressive, not assaulting, not elitist. I'm very passionate . . . a warrior for my craft. I'll fight to do the very best I can. It's important to keep this balance in life. If things get out of balance inspiration stops flowing. It's very sensitive and delicate and if it suffers so do the beautiful things in life.

Darcy James Argue
COMPOSER

HOME BASE
www.secretsociety.typepad.com

GOT MUSIC?
Infernal Machines, Darcy James Argue, New Amsterdam Records, 2009

"There was just a real desire on my part . . . to try to create something that had shape, narrative, and continuity to it."

BACKGROUND AND SOUND
Darcy James Argue is a very visible and outspoken new voice in composition. He has been the recipient of numerous grants and commissions from organizations including Chamber Music America, the Aaron Copland Fund for Music, and the American Music Center. Darcy is also one of the founding members of Pulse, a federation of six New York–based composers that collaborates with guitarist John Abercrombie, trumpeter John McNeil, and vocalist Joy Askew. His big band has collaborated with groups such as the Frankfurt Radio Big Band. Darcy has not only the drive and tenacity to have his voice heard, but also music that reflects his surroundings and charismatic personality. This is a gift he uses with an unabashed fervor to bring new music and original use of sound to the world.

HIS STORY
There's a certain type of person who's drawn to being a jazz musician. When you're in high school, the social benefits of starting your own garage band are obvious, in terms of gaining popularity or attention, being perceived as

cool by your peers. But for kids who are into jazz or classical, there's clearly not the same cachet. With a couple of exceptions, the jazz musicians I've encountered tended to be the freaks and weirdos of their high school. Most of us didn't really feel like we belonged to the mainstream culture where we grew up, or to the hip types of alternative culture that other kids our age were into. We found a certain escape in music that wasn't in any way tied to the culture we were living in.

Growing up on the West Coast of Canada, I always thought of jazz as this incredibly exotic thing. I would have felt differently had I lived in a city where there was a real history and community built around jazz. But in Vancouver, jazz was on the extreme fringe. Maybe this was part of the appeal for me . . . certainly my attraction to this music, especially the big band thing, has always placed me a little bit on the outside, even among other jazz musicians.

There was just a real desire on my part, even then, to try to create something that had a shape, narrative, and continuity to it. That's what the best improvisers do, consciously or not. You listen to a classic Sonny Rollins album and his playing always has this real storytelling vibe. This is the hardest thing to do as a player. I always struggled with my ability to create this sense of story in real time, especially on a standard. But when I played my own compositions, I was more successful. I wrote tunes in a way that made it easier for me to be able to construct the kind of musical narrative I was interested in when I improvised on them. Eventually, I realized that composition was where my own voice was strongest. Writing music was the most distinctive and identifiable thing I did, and it's where I feel I belong.

Patti Austin

{LIVING LEGEND}

VOCALIST, COMPOSER

HOME BASE
www.pattiaustin.com

GOT MUSIC?
Avant Gershwin, Patti Austin, Rendezvous, 2007

"If you want to call jazz, jazz, fine . . . as for me, I call it music."

BACKGROUND AND SOUND

Grammy Award winner Patti Austin's voice has wrapped its fingers around the ears of the music world since she was a little girl. Quincy Jones raised her through the industry with the help of Dinah Washington sitting in as her godmother. Since then, her voice has laid down the beat with such great artists as James Ingram, Michael McDonald, James Brown, Bette Midler, and Paul Simon. Yet this did not keep her back. She now has a tight hold of the reins that allow her to follow the light into the lead.

HER STORY

My dad was my primary influence. He was a trombone player and hung around with Father Hines, Dinah Washington, Billy Eckstein, and Quincy Jones. It was because of him that the house was constantly filled with music. I could get up in the mornings and anything from Stravinsky to Duke Ellington would be on the stereo. This is probably why I grew up thinking that music had no category. And just like my father's taste in music, my influences came from anywhere and everything. This is also why I've never taken on a purist approach to jazz. If you want to call jazz, jazz, fine . . . as for me, I call it music.

But it's unfortunate that the ones who created this form are gone and we don't have the ability to talk to them about what they did. They had tremendous classical, blues, folk influences and could play all forms and created jazz that borrowed from every imaginable place, even politics. Their music made a statement as to these eclectic influences. Bebop came from black musicians who were tired of being pushed out of the system. First time you play a tune through, you played it as written. Second time, you played it with embellishment. Third time, you played it out there, as if it was a part of the racial and political revolution. This is where *my* background came from. Jazz has a connection and relationship with people in the past and now. The influence it can have in your life is very personal. You just have to turn this music around to go your way so you can take it and make it your own. A strong component of your personality has to be there. Unlike classical music, which is all about the composer's vision, jazz is all about the artist's vision. This is what jazz represents: individuality. Because of this, jazz is the perfect form for me.

Kevin Bales
PIANIST, COMPOSER, EDUCATOR

HOME BASE
www.kevinbales.com

GOT MUSIC?
Experiment in Truth, Rene Marie,
Independent. Label, 2007

*"It's been a great bridge for understanding things about the world and life;
it's taught me how to be a better person."*

BACKGROUND AND SOUND

Winner of the Biennial American Jazz Piano Competition in 1994, pianist
Kevin Bales has unlocked the door to success using eighty-eight ivory
keys. Bales is not only a top call player and educator in Atlanta, he is
internationally known for his work as a soloist and sideman with artists
such as vocalist Rene Marie. He has taught in the critically acclaimed jazz
studies program at the University of North Florida in Jacksonville and is
now one of the top piano teachers in Atlanta, Georgia. With a sound and
personality that burns a quiet fire into each note, Kevin Bales has proven
that his command of the language of jazz is strong and will endure.

HIS STORY

My relationship with music has been a little more unique than most of
my peers. I never remotely considered music as a career. I came to music
late. When I was seventeen, I would have never said I was going to be a
professional musician. I was primarily interested in computers, things that
make money. When I started college my mom wanted me to go somewhere
I really didn't want to go and the only place I could get into was Georgia
State. At that point I had a job programming computers, and I was only
going there to appease her. But it was during those years that I met Marcus
Printup. This is when I discovered jazz and really fell in love with it. But
I also discovered the role this music plays in people's lives. It wasn't a
commodity; it was more important, a real healing force in my life. It still
is. It's something that's made me a much better person. Up until then I had
been this guy who was deeply involved in computers and was extremely,

painfully shy and introverted. I couldn't communicate well. For whatever reason music became this place were I could express and let things out.

I didn't know, when I quit my job as a computer programmer, what doing this meant other than it had nothing to do with money. When I went to my boss and my family to tell them I was quitting my job to be a jazz musician they looked at me like I was crazy. My families offered to have professionals help me. I might as well have told them I was going into interpretive dance. From my point of view, I could always go back and become a programmer any day. Just like every other musician though, you want to quit one day but then you realize you can't. It's not an option, being a musician is hard but doing anything is hard. I can't imagine being a good father, husband, or human being if I didn't have the music in my life.

As musicians we forget what a privilege it is to be doing what we're doing. I teach a large number of private students right now and I feel like I'm teaching life enrichment instead of music on most days. These people are guys who own their own companies, financial officers and surgeons, and are at the top of their game in the world. But all they want to do is make music. This music, as it is for my students and others, became and still is a force that heals me. It's been a great bridge for understanding things about the world and life; it's taught me how to be a better person. When I play, there's a certain amount of nakedness. You're really listening to an expression of a person's story. I'm being honest, transparent in that moment, and it's a very intimate thing. I'm not interested in what category or genre I'm playing in; I'm just trying to be Kevin Bales. The fact that I'm able to do this and that it ever reaches any person at all is a real measure of my success.

Wayne Batchelor
BASSIST, EDUCATOR

HOME BASE
www.waynebatchelor.com

GOT MUSIC?
Blueprint of a Lady, Nnenna Freelon, Concord Records, 2005

"We have to communicate in a real way in order to get anything of real value that's ever going to last."

BACKGROUND AND SOUND

Internationally known bassist Wayne Batchelor began his career at London's Guildhall School of Music. He has since toured, performed, and recorded with greats such as Nnenna Freelon, Take 6, Jonathan Butler, Will Downing, and George Benson. His kind demeanor and solid talent have only complimented his already firm grasp on the jazz world.

HIS STORY

I was born in London and my family is Jamaican, so both these cultures were big influences on me as a child. I was often taken to reggae parties where I would see grown-ups dancing, and everyone, especially when I was really small, looked like trees. They were tall, moving to the music in the background. I took it for granted that Bob Marley was all I was listening to during those parties, and I remember being enchanted by his music. When I was older I got into Weather Report, then Wayne Shorter through them, and then Miles through Wayne, and then Monk through Miles. I thought Monk, who was a huge influence on me, sounded like the quintessential jazz musician. He didn't sound like anyone else I knew, and I learned that the great musicians have a distinctive sound. I realized that I had to have my own unique sound that has intent behind it and is true to who I am. I needed to follow the beat of my own drum. When I find myself listening to music, I really like those who have a song for everything they do, the ones that tell stories in their music and transcend genre. This music stands the test of time. Words aren't enough to explain music. We have to communicate in a real way in order to get anything of real value that's ever going to last. Anything that's lasting has to be real, tangible, and grounded in reality. I believe in objective reality and anything that's been of value has this objectivity. It seems we have so much crap running through our heads that's been forced on us. We get lazy, and into bad habits of not focusing. I'm not just speaking about musicians; in general, our culture has a problem with art. In ancient Greece everyone was educated in a broad range of philosophy, art, and the world around them. Now we educate people to make as much money as they can. This is a very specific education and doesn't leave you open to investigate what's going on in the world. When that's forced on you, the arts go out the window. We have to revamp our thinking and introduce the arts in a different way. There are all sorts of mediums though which people can express themselves. If you take arts out of the schools, your tastes and judgments are not developed independently. You are left at the mercy of companies that force commerciality upon you. Take a step back from this and look at it with a much more holistic view and you'll see what's wrong. There is a problem with the dumbing down of culture in general from the arts and education to heath and finances. Consequently America buys and digests seventeen billion dollars of legal pharmaceuticals a year, and we've been conned into credit card scams by large corporations. You have to ask what they're asking... how do you control three hundred million people? You dumb them down. It is up to us as artists to communicate things that are of value.

I don't believe in forcing art on someone, and I won't force my art on anyone. I'm just going to play with intent and meaning. Things are not always what they seem to be and I'm definitely not what I appear to be on the surface—you just have to listen to me play to hear what I'm saying.

Jim Beard

KEYBOARDIST, COMPOSER, PRODUCER, EDUCATOR

HOME BASE
www.jimbeard.com

GOT MUSIC?
Revolutions, Jim Beard, Sunnyside Records, 2009

"There's an insatiable curiosity that found its way into me early on, and it's still there."

BACKGROUND AND SOUND

Internationally acclaimed pianist and composer Jim Beard walks among the very best musicians of our time. He has toured the world time and again with heavy hitters such as Pat Metheny, Steely Dan, and Wayne Shorter.

He has won multiple Grammy Awards for solos on albums, including his work on *Some Skunk Funk* with the Brecker Brothers. His work as a producer and composer can be found on albums by such cats as Mike Stern, Bill Evans, Eliane Elias, Chick Corea, and Al Jarreau, and in books (such as *The New Real Book*), on radio, on television, and in movie scores. Jim has also taught at esteemed schools of music such as the Aaron Copland School of Music and the Sibelius Academy in Finland. His five solo albums have received international acclaim and top ten status within the jazz charts. His music narrates his story by providing a lush harmonic ride throughout each tune and this is what defines the story of his success.

HIS STORY

A long time ago I decided that when I'm taking part in any music project, I have to be involved with the people I'm playing or working with on a personal level. Whoever I'm writing with, performing with, or whatever, I've got to know who they are. I have to respect them, tolerate them, and learn what buttons they have installed on them really quick. It's important to know which ones you can push and should not push. It's essential—critical even—that you know these things. You can hear someone's style of music just by listening to something they've done but . . . this doesn't mean you can work with them. I can work with a musician for just a little bit and feel that I know them. By learning this lesson through music, I feel it's helped me be a better father to my kids and helped me learn about cultures, places, and history. The first time I played with a group and it really clicked, I was fairly young and it was in Indianapolis back in the early eighties, a club gig for five nights. There was real communication going on and it felt extremely purposeful. It seemed that a lot of the things I was curious about regarding decision making prior to that all of a sudden made sense. I had made the proper ones and I was going to stick with them. Unfortunately, not all musicians are lucky to have these experiences.

Playing with musicians that want to communicate raises the bar a certain level. Communication, empathy, and bonding with other musicians are essential to jazz, but it's not always about those things for me. It could be about doing your job correctly and taking care of business. Sometimes, the last thing you want is someone who's mimicking everything you do and (musically) saying . . . "look at me and communicate with me." That's when you want to say, "shut up and do your job." Restraint doesn't seem to play a big role in a lot of players I come across these days. I find that unfortunate. When you work with someone who's doing his or her job fabulously, it's great. Music can conk you over the head and make you fall in love with it. It's this that makes me want to keep going. There's an insatiable curiosity that found its way into me early on, and it's still there. I haven't asked it to leave, and as long as it's there, I'm going to keep doing what I do.

George Benson

{LIVING LEGEND}

GUITARIST, VOCALIST, COMPOSER, PRODUCER

HOME BASE
www.georgebenson.com

GOT MUSIC?
Livin' Inside Your Love, George Benson, Warner Bros., 1979

"Music is a great way to talk to people."

BACKGROUND AND SOUND

Entertaining and influencing millions of fans and musicians for more than four decades with his brilliance, Grammy Award–winning guitarist George Benson is a living story of success. But it hasn't been the easiest road, as talent only gets you so far. He has worked for over six decades on becoming the musician you see today. Building his music upon honesty and soul-shaking love, George Benson is a tremendous power in the industry. He has shared the stage with Miles Davis, Wes Montgomery, Ron Carter, and Freddie Hubbard, to name a few. What he has done for the jazz world reaches well beyond an archive of solos and album releases. He brought the beat back to the heels and heads of listeners of all genres. Hits such as "On Broadway" and "Give Me the Night" can be heard in places ranging from high school marching band repertoires all the way to Top 40 radio stations. His groove is distinct, creative, and sharp, and each decade seemingly thrives off the mercurial rise of his original voice. A mature flow and sense of style continues to endure as he influences new generations with his vivacious spirit.

HIS STORY

I was born and raised in the ghetto. We didn't have a lot, but I was a happy kid. My stepfather met my mom when I was seven years old. When he came into our lives, he brought with him records that featured Charlie Christian with the Benny Goodman Sextet, as well as George Shearing records. I was mesmerized with that at seven. It gave me a tremendous foundation and insight into what good music and swing was all about. I fell in love with it.

There was one man who came on the radio who was different from all the rest: Nat King Cole. Nat would sing stories instead of just the blues and I began to gravitate toward him. To this day, he remains at the top of my list as one of my main influences. There was also Charlie Parker. I didn't find out about him until I was a teenager. To me, he was the greatest instrumentalist of our time. He had harmony, dexterity, and purpose, and a great sense of rhythm. All of his performances were memorable. I never got to see him play, but my father used to tell me that he saw him play and hung out with him. I didn't believe him. Later, when I moved to New York, I ran into a lot of people that saw them together. I gave my father more credit after that.

I've listened many of the great musicians of this world (Vladimir Horowitz, Errol Garner, Wes Montgomery, John Coltrane, et cetera). The best of the best. There is the one thing I will give myself credit for: I never get lost in the rhetoric of our time, I tried to rise above it. I believe you can't be great unless you really know what great is. I listen to a lot of singers, too. When I came up it was the blues singers like Ray Charles, Charles Brown, and Little Willie John that influenced me. Then the organist Jack McDuff took me under his wing. He helped me see what jazz could be. I learned a lot about what people liked when I was with him. He introduced me to players like Jimmy Smith—another best of the best. These experiences helped shape the George Benson that you know today. They inspired something in me that said, "Alright, George, it's your turn to sing."

My musical experiences have changed over the years, and my opinion of music has changed as well. I recently went back and found an old high school yearbook. Beneath my picture it said I wanted to be a guitar player with a big band. Ha! I took the Basie band on the road for a year, and I haven't stopped since. I keep moving on with the times. To make the fans remember me is my challenge and my goal as a performer. As a musician, I have a lot of options to make people feel happy or relaxed. I can change people's moods with my music. I can create harmony with people in diverse ways in different countries, different stations of life, and different economic positions. Music is a great way to talk to people. The records I've made speak volumes as to who I am. They really tell the story. Most people use music as a reference point in their life's journey. They say they know me through my music, and I would say they're pretty close.

Shelly Berg
PIANIST, COMPOSER, EDUCATOR, AUTHOR, CONDUCTOR

GOT MUSIC?
Blackbird, Shelly Berg Trio,
Concord Records, 2005

"If it's worldly success I look forward to, then I've missed something important along the way."

BACKGROUND AND SOUND

Shelly Berg has been widely acknowledged as one of the best educators in jazz for more than a quarter century. He spent two years as the president of the now-defunct International Association of Jazz Educators and eight years as the Department of Jazz Studies chair at the University of Southern California's Thornton School of Music, and he was the McCoy/Sample Endowed Professor of Jazz Studies at USC until 2007. And this is when he entered the picture at the University of Miami School of Music as their dean. Exhausted? This is only the tip of Shelly's iceberg. As an arranger, composer, accompanist, and soloist he has released two albums on Concord Records, performed on numerous others as a sideman, and worked with groups ranging from the Royal Philharmonic to KISS and the Basie band. Lou Fisher Music Publishing Group has published his book *Jazz Improvisation: The Goal-Note Method*, and he has written at least eight more books on jazz theory and his Chop Monster series for beginners. He has won numerous awards and fellowships for his prolific works. Despite this busy schedule, his performance chops are solid gold and keep him going at the end of long days. Yet his students are the ones who benefit the greatest, because they're in the hands of a giant of jazz.

HIS STORY

People with talent or brilliance or genius sometimes have a set of expectations that are set in motion. These expectations are then encouraged by others . . . people say you're going to be famous and a star and change the world. The pressure this puts on an artist is intolerable. I wanted to be a household name. I guess if I go by this then I haven't obtained success. But, along the way, I've learned that this isn't a measure to go by. I've achieved a certain degree of artistry that I can impart to my audience. I think I've impacted a couple of generations of students and by that I've impacted the world of music. I've obtained a healing and positive effect that has come from the most wonderful friends I've made a long the way. I've also raised three of the most wonderful human beings and I have a deep love with my wife. I guess there's nothing I've wanted to do that I've strived to do and haven't had the chance to do. Unequivocally I can say, by this, that my life has been a success. But, it doesn't mean it's over. If it's worldly success I look forward to, then I've missed something important along the way. We all have to be careful of what we wish for. Had I become that household name I would be gone, around the world, and my life would have been greatly different. Had I become the next John Williams, I'd be locked in a room writing all day. Instead, I get to play and teach. Every time I play, a part of me is being reborn, and every time I write, a part of me dies. I've been fulfilled and fueled in life, and that's all I can ask for and continue to strive for.

Pat Bianchi
ORGANIST, PIANIST, COMPOSER

HOME BASE
www.patbianchi.com

GOT MUSIC?
East Coast Roots, Pat Bianchi Trio,
Jazzed Media, 2006

"If more people took this on as a challenge and tried to understand it they would see that life and music intertwine in one way or another."

BACKGROUND AND SOUND

Jazz organist Pat Bianchi has established himself as one of the very best to have ever graced this niche scene. He has performed around the world with some of the biggest names in jazz history, including George Benson, Christian McBride, Mark Whitfield, and Terell Stafford. With his own groups he has released two albums that continue to receive praise from the critics. Pat's contributions to the revival of the organ in modern jazz are quite remarkable and should be noted as a vision of the future of this art.

HIS STORY

I come from a long line of musicians in my family. Both grandfathers were musicians that gigged all the time. At some point I expressed interest in the keyboard. I would sit down with tapes and records and a toy keyboard as a child and try to figure it out. This was long before I actually took lessons. My family saw the interest lingering, so when I was eight years old one grandfather bought me an actual Farfisa Organ and the other one gave me the amp. At some point I was told that I had to train classically. The whole idea of playing Bach and Chopin never appealed to me. I did it more out of having to do it. Chopin and Bach were thrown to the side and my focus turned to playing tunes with my family. There did come a time where things died. I guess the excitement wasn't there as much. I'm not sure what I did during that time, I guess normal teenage stuff. When I was seventeen I heard a recording of Joey D. It was his *Live at the Five Spot* recording. It changed my outlook for playing the Hammond organ. Just like that I started getting back into jazz gigs and playing standards.

By the time I hit my second year at Berklee, I was listening to Joey D all the time. He flipped me out and renewed my excitement. Around 1995 or 1996 I signed up for a mailing list for the Hammond organ. It was arranged so that it helped with the technically difficult aspects of playing it. One point along the way there was a discussion about playing bass lines with your feet as opposed to your left hand. I had never played it with my left hand. I got a group e-mail from someone called "Authority." I argued back and forth for a few weeks and one day a friend of mine who was on the list said, "You realize you're arguing with Joey D?" . . . I was just being a smartass, and then I felt two inches tall. I sent him an e-mail apologizing and said he was right and then walked out with my tail between my legs. I called him later on and he busted my chops for about an hour to make sure I got the point and that was the start of an ongoing friendship. This changed my life forever.

Obviously music has been a source of growth for me. I've learned lessons of humility along with the history of what's come before me and where my place is now. Ideally this is how I want to be as a person. When one finally realizes the potential of what they're stumbling on and the true thing that's motivating for you, the sky's the limit. It's just a matter of taking and making the effort to put the work into it. It's not instant gratification. Too bad the whole music industry is all about this instant gratification and marketing powers that be. They've already decided who's going to be the new greatest thing based on money and marketing. If the record industry had put a fraction of this money behind jazz it would be popular again. It would have more respect and there would be more possibilities to grow as an artist in this country. It's something you have to place importance to, enjoy, and listen to. If more people took this on as a challenge and tried to understand it they would see that life and music intertwine in one way or another. You can't put it off and wait for another time or dream about it.

David Binney

SAXOPHONIST, COMPOSER

HOME BASE
www.davidbinney.com

GOT MUSIC?
Third Occasion, David Binney,
Positone Records, 2009

"We all should keep in mind that we need to leave ourselves open to possibilities."

BACKGROUND AND SOUND

As one of the leaders in the "alternative" jazz scene, David Binney's innovative work has garnered worldwide praise. His distinctive compositions are fresh and accompanied by thoughtful solos throughout. It's this aspect of his voice that's paved his way into the orchestras of Gil Evans and Maria Schneider. As a rising legend in modern jazz, he has tirelessly worked on his development as an artist by never losing sight of his creative vision. David is truly an inspiration to all artists who want to achieve their dreams.

HIS STORY

Indirectly, jazz has mapped my whole life since I was twelve years old. It's a language that's fascinating and interesting and one that's opened up a vocabulary for me to say whatever I have inside emotionally. Beyond that it becomes the issue of what its done to my life. When I was thirteen it took over my life in the sense that I focused on music so heavily that it dictated what my schedule was and how much energy I put into other things in my life. Now, it keeps on dictating what my life is, maybe even more than it ever has. I don't do much that's not related. I travel so much now that when I'm home I don't do much except to stay in and work on music and practice and write. I live it. I feel strongly about what I'm doing and it's what I should be doing. This is a huge thing, and in order to do something really well, it's the way I need to do things. Music is that important to me, and there's only so much you can do in your life. Trying to do too much would be a disservice to what I've tailored my whole life to. Why dilute it now? I've suffered so much to get this far . . . so I have to do more before

I start to get away from it all. After all, if you haven't lived it, it's a lot more difficult to explain it.

I've been on the road for years now and I have been known to push things on the road. I was always the guy who would hang out the latest and get the least amount of sleep. I would go out with people I just met, either friends, students, et cetera. A lot of these experiences and stories are part of my music too. Hopefully this comes through in what I'm doing in anything in life, whether an artistic endeavor or not, as something that is more interesting to a listener than it would be without those experiences. I hope I can cause the listener to be more curious and want to know something more about what they just engaged in. In the jazz world there's an argument about how much we care and think about the audience. I'm in the minority that would argue that I think about the audience heavily. Even in the midst of improvisation. I'm not sacrificing anything musically to be highly aware of the audience. It actually helps the deepness of the music. I question myself a lot, and ask if I would enjoy my music if I were in the audience. This has to happen for me. What happens a lot in the jazz world can be technically amazing but not deep or aware in any way for the people that are listening. I'm listening and feeling the audience when playing and recording and I think it's reaching people and this is my goal.

I'm probably doing one of the least accessible forms of art. I am always checking out new stuff. It's not often jazz that I listen to. I listen to pop, alternative rock, country, classical, everything. I just don't find much in new or modern jazz that's interesting. Although there are some great things happening in jazz too. It's not a lot of stuff though.

Musically I think of myself as being open to every idea and possibility. I've been the guy among friends who gets along with people in widely different worlds. My friends come from all walks of life, and I like to be in the middle of what's happening. We all should keep in mind that we need to leave ourselves open to possibilities. If we all had openness, in all aspects of life, we would be better off, I think. This is important to me and is what makes music interesting. I just do what I want to do to the fullest. I haven't veered from this at all. I've known since I was younger that there were going to be times where there was a lack of acceptance, but now it doesn't get me down. I like living in the space where you can completely make a living without being acknowledged by the "business." It can work in your favor. Don't let the things like rejection waste your time and energy. I've always done exactly what I wanted to do and I've never compromised what I wanted to do. This only comes from living in this space. I want to do more, but if it all ended right now, I'm satisfied with what I've done so far. It's certainly not about the car and has nothing to do with where I live. I've lived a very frugal life. This is not how I measure my success. Success is doing what you do truthfully and honestly to the best of your ability. Doing what I've done just makes my journey a little more interesting and positive.

Nate Birkey

TRUMPETER, VOCALIST, COMPOSER

HOME BASE
www.natebirkey.com

GOT MUSIC?
Almost Home, Nate Birkey,
Household Ink Records, 2008

"Music isn't meant to be just an indiscernible soundtrack for life."

BACKGROUND AND SOUND

Nate Birkey is an often overlooked and quiet force among the heavy hitters in New York. Unlike other musicians in this modern climate, Nate utilizes an understated and austere style to express himself. His various groups have released more than seven recordings of original music and brilliantly recast standards. His art is vocalized through a reserved intensity that translates into one of the most inimitable voices in jazz today.

HIS STORY

Music is all encompassing in my life, not only jazz, but all of it. It's been such a huge part of my life since I was a kid that I don't ever really turn it off. Some people comment on the fact that I don't listen to music as much as some because I don't always have it on in the background. They find it curious that I don't constantly have music on at home, or have earbuds in when I'm on the subway or walking around. To tell you the truth, I don't even have an iPod that I carry with me. I don't listen to it like this because I have it inside of me at all times. It's in my head and I find myself frequently walking around singing or humming or working out the music in my head. I get sort of uncomfortable when I do try to use a portable device while walking around the city. I end up listening so intently to the music that I can't concentrate on what's going on around me. When I put music on, I really, really listen to it. Music isn't meant to be just an indiscernible soundtrack for life. My environment inspires a lot of the music I write, and I like to listen to the sounds around me. In New York there's an almost inescapable barrage of sound that has influenced me and changed the way I approach a song.

Finding this voice—my voice has been a process that's taken more than twenty plus years as a musician. Finding who I am as a musician means I have to get rid of a lot of superfluous things and find that melody that hasn't been written or played yet. This can be tricky as we only have twelve notes to deal with. I have to remain curious and open to new things, and this is what music is all about for me—listening and absorbing what is going on around me in the clubs and on the streets, as well as what's going on in my own head. Jazz is such a spontaneous and creative music that if you're not receptive, you'll miss the experience that this music has to offer.

Jim Black

DRUMMER, COMPOSER, PRODUCER, EDUCATOR

HOME BASE
www.jimblack.com

GOT MUSIC?
Houseplant, Jim Black's
AlasNoAxis, Winter & Winter,
2009

"Every day is another chance to be more of yourself."

BACKGROUND AND SOUND

Seattle native Jim Black has become one of the most diverse and technically apt players of our time. He has played the part of sideman

to an infinite number of players around the world and is the leader of his group, AlasNoAxis. His diverse influences include far-reaching Balkan rhythms and innovative electronic textures and are abundantly showcased on his albums with his group. Because of this there isn't a single clichéd moment in anything he does. With wholly original concepts and technique, Jim is one of the revolutionary voices around today.

HIS STORY

I was one of those pots-and-pans kids. My parents would put them away and I'd pull them back out. As early as I can remember, I wanted to play drums, and I began banging on plastic buckets along with the Jackson 5. I was always in love with listening to music, so wanting to play and become a musician was a given. Many years later, I've made a very, very self-generating life style: creatively, artistically, and socially. I have friends around the world that are extremely close to me through this music.

It doesn't have to do with jazz per se, but it is through the all-inclusive word "improvisation"—found at the root of all music—that we continue to work and play together. All sounds, all styles—musicians are reaching out for more musical connections than ever before.

My music could be viewed as a type of tribal music because you tend to play with your friends and play with people who hear music the same way as you do, not only using and transcending the ideas of fixed styles, but including anyone from anywhere, crossing all borders of nationality and race, let alone age and gender. Of course, when poked about who has the right to play and represent this music, namely in this case what we are calling "jazz" nowadays, my brain starts to hurt. These arguments are beyond tired and dated, and should be buried forever if we are going to be living in the global, present tense world of music and improvisation, forever connected at the speed of electricity worldwide where almost anybody, anywhere can listen, watch, absorb, and even learn to play music twenty-four/seven. Well-worn, stylistic, canonized definitions of jazz just don't cut it anymore, let alone our stereotypes of who looks and acts the part to play it.

I grew up in a pleasant but slightly vacuous culture in Bellevue, Washington. What would I say was the music of my people? It was whatever played through my stereo system. Whatever I could check out of my public library. Whatever live music I could get my eyes on. It was whatever my friends played for me. Our influences can come from everywhere and that's the beauty of it. Just through hearing sound and trying to identify with it is all there is to it. Music is an aural tradition; we literally hand it over from one person to the next, in as many and any ways as possible. You are inherently unique and born with a flexible musical identity that you have to discover, the sooner the better. Everyone has to follow their own path of self-individualization to realize how unique their power and sound is. We need more great teachers, funding, and open minds to aim high and keep up with our world musical culture. Music is one of the greatest of all art forms, and teaching should never be a default lifestyle for musicians who cannot financially survive otherwise. If you have the wherewithal to stand in front of a group and show them how it goes, then you better know what you're doing and love doing it. Teaching should be something that's healthy for all involved. Teaching makes me question myself daily and work harder at understanding my art.

It's amazing how territorial we can become and how bent out of shape we can get as a culture due to music. Everyone has a different relationship to music, and what means so much to you may mean nothing to somebody else. That's a hard fact for most people to swallow. As an artist, though, there is nothing more liberating than to realize there is no such thing as an inherently higher or lower form or class of music—it's value is absolutely in the ears and mind of each listener. People should be listening to everything—all music needs to be out there, represented, recorded, and performed live. If we don't, we'll just grow only smaller, more divided minds.

Every day is another chance to be more of yourself. As a fellow human being, the music I make is just about me asking tough questions of myself and being honest about who I am and how I fit into the world. This is all that matters because people respond to honesty. Every night on stage has to be like I'm giving blood. It would be insulting to somebody to not give them one hundred percent of myself and dumb it down for them just to make it easier to understand. This understanding is more about someone being curious enough to take the time to listen with their ears first, see if it makes an impact somewhere inside the body, and then sort it out with their brain later. After years of experience, I realize that all music is only made of five basic elements—form, color/tone, rhythm, melody, and harmony . . . but it's always going to be about the mood and the vibe first—not the components inside.

Ron Blake

SAXOPHONIST, COMPOSER, EDUCATOR

HOME BASE
www.ronblakemusic.com

GOT MUSIC?
Shayari, Ron Blake, Mack Avenue Records, 2009

"Our ambition is the one thing we have that's free."

BACKGROUND AND SOUND

Virgin Islands native Ron Blake has inhaled the jazz community around him for more than twenty years. A graduate of Interlochen Arts Academy, he went on to study at Northwestern University, where he received the Presidential Award for Outstanding Academic Achievement. His teaching career has involved positions at University of South Florida in Tampa as well as Julliard and New York University. He has also held positions in the bands of Roy Hargrove, Christian McBride, and *Saturday Night Live.* An undeniably influential strength in jazz today, Blake has spread his flavorful and eclectic blend of texture and sound throughout the jazz world.

HIS STORY

We have spent so much time being consumers in the past several decades that we have not given much thought to the value of things that are lasting— that is, things which reflect who we are as a culture. Now, though, there is some hope. There are more schools across the country offering degrees in jazz studies or which are incorporating jazz education in the curriculum.

The increasing efforts to introduce jazz (listening classes) as a part of US and world history would also raise awareness.

Now, there are musicians who are really making a difference, and who aspire to a level where the passion they (we) have for jazz is communicated to the listener. When I reflect on music that's being released now, I hear amazing things: artistically, creatively, and compositionally. Yet, I also feel that I am not hearing things (sometimes) that connect us to the spirit of the music. I hear a lot of intellectual pursuits—which is great on many levels—but self-indulgence should not replace self-expression and the ability to communicate.

Listeners need to identify with the music on a more visceral level. Musicians have to continue to recognize and employ those elements that engage our audience. We should share our excitement of performing in a band; listening and interacting to create balance amidst variations on themes, rhythm, and harmony; or the expression of a lyric that is captured by an instrumentalist through effective nuance and phrasing. There's a time and a place for all that this music has to offer as it continues to reach new audiences. After all, our ambition is the one thing we have that's free, and no one can take that away from us. The role of the artist and entertainer is to discover the balance. And it should be a goal that jazz musicians can realize without having to abandon their integrity. There are intangibles, beyond description, that made jazz work then and make it work now. I incorporate those things in my music; it is my vision both on a personal level and as an artist.

Seamus Blake
SAXOPHONIST, WOODWINDS, VOCALIST,
EDUCATOR, COMPOSER, GUITARIST

HOME BASE
www.seamusblake.com

GOT MUSIC?
Live in Italy, Seamus Blake
Quartet, Jazz Eyes, 2009

"I've loved music so much I've weathered it."

BACKGROUND AND SOUND

Seamus Blake lends us his voice in many forms—thinking outside the box is his specialty. He has had the distinction of winning the Thelonious Monk Award and graduating from Berklee College of Music in Boston. In addition to his own body of original recordings he has graced the recordings of such contemporaries as John Scofield, Kenny Barron, and Christian McBride. Rattling cages with his pronounced and sultry sound, he defies genre boundaries to yield effects that fall both inside and out of traditional jazz. Seamus's insight into the art of sound has earned him a limb on the family tree of greats in jazz.

HIS STORY

It was my mom who bought me tapes of Ella and Billie Holiday and a smathering of random things, Spyro Gyra and Grover Washington Jr. She is very intelligent but wasn't really a jazz fan at the time. She came home one day with the Cannonball live in San Francisco album. It's still my favorite because it's live. He was especially buoyant, jubilant . . . happy during that period. I listened to it until the cassette actually died. That obsession continued on when I was a student at Berklee. I could feel daily progress. As a kid, it didn't matter who it was and what it was, I was into it if it was jazz. I was open and fresh then.

So many great players attended Berklee at the same time as I did. It was almost unparalleled to have that talent around. My roommate was Kurt Rosenwinkel. Roy Hargrove, Brad Meldhau, Jeff Parker, Mark Turner, and Donny McCaslin were all there, too. Not too many stayed to graduate, but it's not a guarantee that a piece of paper from Berklee will get you a gig anyway. What's important is that you love what you're doing. If you don't, then you go on to something else. I've loved music so much I've weathered it. Even though my tastes have changed, it's music that keeps me going. It's what keeps me going. Certainly not the money . . . I do it for the right reasons.

Terence Blanchard

TRUMPETER, COMPOSER, EDUCATOR

HOME BASE
www.terenceblanchard.com

GOT MUSIC?
Choices, Terence Blanchard,
Concord Jazz, 2009

"If an idea pops in your head, no matter how ludicrous it sounds, don't ask why, ask why not and move on."

BACKGROUND AND SOUND

New Orleans native and Grammy Award–winning trumpeter Terence Blanchard has single-handedly redefined the notion that a musician is just someone who plays music. Terence's achievements and massive body of work include more than twenty-five scores for films and theater, ten solo albums, and Golden Globe, Emmy, and Grammy nominations, as well as winning the Grand Prix Du Disque award (the French equivalent of a Grammy) in 1984. He is a member of Roy Hargrove's group as well as Christian McBride's group. As a leader he makes a point to bring in the youth of the art so he may mentor them through the earlier stages of their careers. Yet throughout his lifetime he has been able to bowl over audiences in all genres by reaching beyond the bell of his horn and into their hearts. As an advocate for the continuation of jazz in all forms, he is moving the genre forward with his limitless imagination and open mind.

HIS STORY

Somehow down the line, the word "jazz" became synonymous with the word "history" and it became the music of the past in some people's minds. Part of this is the musician's fault because we're not keeping up and being creative with our times. We can't just rest on our history. We have to move forward and create something that's relevant to the social times in which we're living in. These younger musicians that are doing it now are out there, doing their thing. The problem is that the history itself hasn't taken a look-forward approach. It's constantly a look-backward approach. And we're referring and comparing these younger musicians to the older ones instead of taking stock of what they're doing that's unique. This has to cease. If someone in jazz has something to offer that's basically relevant to the times in which they're creating their art, we have to accept it. Some of these guys are not going to come through the ranks by being compared to these other musicians that have come before them. There's nothing wrong with that. If we piece all these things together there's still hope for jazz. I'm very optimistic because I know very young, talented, gifted musicians who are doing some extremely creative things. The industry itself will eventually catch up to what's going on with these guys. They're not going anywhere nor are they going to disappear. They're creating great music and we need this. The issue of not having any young musicians playing jazz should be laid to rest because there's a proliferation of them who are entering the scene.

One of the reasons I'm part of the Monk Institute is because I hope to try to bring some of these uniquely talented musicians to a place where they can develop their art. They should understand that there's nothing wrong with thinking up something that's a little different than the norm. This is what innovation is all about. Some of these guys can really play, and they break the rules with their unorthodox ideas. You know what this sounds like to me? It sounds like the origins of the music. We run the risk of choking the creativity when we enforce rules about specific things within the art. I'm not talking about learning to play changes or learning how to play your instrument in the basic sense of the word; I'm talking about people who are well beyond that . . . more specifically, the personality and individuality I see among these artists. These are young people who have a burning passion and desire to express themselves and they're made to feel guilty because they don't play a certain way. This shouldn't be an issue if they're contributing something positive to the art form.

Because of this some of us are now realizing that we have to become the leaders. I've been fortunate enough to be on the bandstand with some great musicians that have come through the ranks. There are a lot of people who are doing the same thing, too. We're beginning to realize that our role is important. This is why I think the future of jazz is very bright. We just have to get through this period of trying to forecast what the future is going to be. We all know that throughout the history of jazz we've never been able to accurately do that anyway. Art Blakey told us, some years ago, that if we're not careful we're going to have bands that play the music of Duke Ellington and Count Basie and Charlie Parker, et cetera. These bands won't push the music forward, and this music will become a museum piece. Although this music is great with great artists who play it, these artists gave a lot to not only the world of jazz but to the world of music. We now have to be responsible for our generation and contribute to the world, too. We have to be brave enough to go out there and try something people may not like. But this is being honest with ourselves. We have to constantly search for this and put our fears aside. If an idea pops in your head, no matter how ludicrous it sounds, don't ask why, ask why not and move on. We're all trying to get the absolute truth about what life is all about. When you're honest, this is when your art will touch the souls of those around you.

Luis Bonilla

TROMBONIST, COMPOSER, EDUCATOR

HOME BASE
www.trombonilla.com

GOT MUSIC?
I Talking Now, Luis Bonilla, Planet Arts/Now Jazz Consortium Label, 2009

"Once you get to know yourself, then you'll have the tools to be able to get to know others."

BACKGROUND AND SOUND

Costa Rica and California native Luis Bonilla is as diverse a player as you'll find on the scene today. He has toured, arranged for, and performed with McCoy Tyner, Dizzy Gillespie, Lester Bowie, Tom Harrell, Mary J. Blige, Tony Bennett, Marc Anthony, and Billy Childs. He is on faculty at Temple University in Philadelphia and the Manhattan School of Music in New York. His solo albums have received critical praise as being reflective of both jazz and Latin persuasions. Link his influences with substantial skills and an entertaining personality on the horn and you are left with a man who creates and expresses completely in tune with the core of this music.

HIS STORY

I've always been clear about what I wanted to do. Now, I'm more clear than ever. But times are changing for some. There are many nervous people that feel like "uh-oh, it's a whole new ball game out there." It is; they're just out of it and probably weren't in the game to begin with. I see an opportune time for those of us who have always plugged away, continue plugging away, remain open to new and different ideas, seek balance and truth within ourselves, as well as possess a strong sense of practicality in our daily life. So it's no surprise when I see this nervous look in someone's eyes. This only makes me feel that much more confidant that I've made the right choice for me. I certainly don't see myself as an anomaly or exception or genius in terms of having "it" figured out. I'm just not afraid to take risks. Deep down inside everyone just wants to know we're the same. Just as we think we may be better than someone else in any given situation, we may also feel we'll never be good enough for others. For example: "I'm better than that person. That gig should be mine!" Or, "I'll never be good enough to play with people like Herbie or Wayne." Either situation, you're judging yourself. Only in the first example the mirror is a little farther away, making it convenient to confuse seeing someone else in that image other than you. Somehow we never want to imagine we're going to be that person, but it's so right up in your face that it's your breath fogging that mirror up. Recognizing this is paramount to our growth as an artist or individual. The beginning of this process is to open up your mind and grab hold of a more tranquil sense of getting to know yourself. Once you get to know yourself, then you'll have the tools to be able to get to know others.

Carmen Bradford

VOCALIST, COMPOSER, EDUCATOR, PRODUCER

HOME BASE
www.carmenbradford.com

GOT MUSIC?
Home with You, Carmen Bradford
and Shelly Berg, Azica Records,
2004

"This path has taught me that if you want to get something done you have to do it yourself."

BACKGROUND AND SOUND

Carmen Bradford is a walking inspiration. Her story resounds with perseverance and a love for music. Her soulful style is thickened by the sounds of Motown, R&B, and jazz greats such as Ella Fitzgerald. And despite the difficulty of this business, Carmen has managed to balance jazz with work in musicals, in commercials, and on the stage, all while educating future generations. A heartfelt musician on the highest level, her beauty pours from her voice into the ears of listeners everywhere.

HER STORY

I somehow always knew that jazz wasn't going to be the easiest career. This path has taught me that if you want to get something done, you have to do it yourself. As women, we tend to be all about details, going overboard on things that aren't of any importance, the stuff no one gives a damn about. We should, instead, be someone who cares about ourselves. Part of this lack of caring is because we tend to forget that we can say no. We're so afraid not to get it that we sell our souls for having some self-pride, and this then becomes a constant struggle. We have to keep our heads together if we want to make it. In the end it's only about being able to take care of yourself and your family while keeping a roof over your head and still doing what it is you want to do. Thinking enough of myself to give myself the time to achieve what I need to achieve while making others feel good is success to me.

Randy Brecker

TRUMPETER, COMPOSER, PRODUCER, EDUCATOR

HOME BASE
www.randybrecker.com

GOT MUSIC?
Randy in Brazil, Randy Brecker,
Summit/MAMA Records, 2008

"All of my life experiences, good or bad, go into everything I do."

BACKGROUND AND SOUND

Four-time Grammy Award–winning trumpeter and composer Randy Brecker has coated the ears and souls of musicians in all genres for more than three decades. Philly native Brecker cut his teeth as a professional in Horace Silver's and Art Blakey's bands. Over the years since then he has toured extensively with Frank Zappa, Stevie Wonder, Steely Dan, Tom Scott, James Moody, and Blood, Sweat and Tears, among others. Once Randy and his brother Michael formed the Brecker Brothers, his name skyrocketed among players and listeners alike. As a major influence on several decades of young musicians, Randy has tirelessly worked to leave his mark in and around all forms of music.

HIS STORY

My father was a child of immigrant parents and chose law as his profession. But he was always a musician/composer/piano player first. I think he was very happy that we followed in his footsteps. He taught Mike and me a lot when we were young. Plus, he had a wonderful record collection. We started listening to jazz really early on; it's just something that's now a part of my being and every breath. Growing up in Philly was like growing up among a potpourri of different genres, idioms, and styles. People like John Coltrane, Dizzy Gillespie, Benny Golson, the Heath Brothers, Clifford Brown, et cetera—many amazing musicians came from or resided there or are still living there. But it was also a great blues/organ trio/pop/funk music town, and I brought this diversity to the table when I started branching out in writing and playing, and eventually it became the impetus behind the writing for the Brecker Brothers.

I think Mike was about eight and I was around ten when he started on clarinet.

He didn't want to play the same instrument I did. We were lucky in fact that our father spurred on our interest and bought us a set of drums. Mike was also a great drummer, and he was quite adept on the piano, too. My sister was a classical pianist who doubled on bass, and Mike and I would switch off who played drums. In time we had a family band.

In this respect it was the music that kept our family together. Mike switched to alto in the ninth grade. This was around when I was in the eleventh grade, attending the Stan Kenton band camps. Marvin Stamm led the band I played in, and there were others, like Cannonball Adderly and Joe Zawinul, who were there as guests. I knew about this time that this is what I wanted to do. These guys reached out to all of us as kids and were very helpful, open, and friendly. Cannonball took me under his wing then and was always very supportive.

Around this time, Mike laid off for a couple of years before switching to tenor around the eleventh grade. He was playing basketball at the time but then got serious about the horn. He never looked back. From then on, I was just trying to keep up with him. He was one of the most difficult persons to follow on a solo, and I don't think I would wish that on anyone. We played together for about ten years before we formed the Brecker Brothers, and we had a blast the whole time we played together. Mike was really serious as a musician, but this didn't mean that he didn't have a great sense of humor when it came to music and life. He held John Coltrane in very high esteem. I think Coltrane's influence is behind many young saxophonists since he set an example for all of us that was very hard to follow. Mike followed it with a very spiritual outlook toward the music. He would practice all day long, as did Coltrane, and learned something new every day up until the day he passed. A good testament to this is that his last record, which was done when he was really, really ill, is probably his most realized and best record. I still don't know how he found the strength and spiritual energy to carry it off, but he did. I was very proud of him; he was in a class of his own. He put all of his influences together to create a unique style and set a standard that will be quite difficult to surpass.

Finding your style and voice is hard as a writer . . . as a player it's even harder.

When I write I try to find my own voice. This is the most important thing to do. All of my life experiences, good and bad, go into everything I do. I've always kept an open mind about sound this way. I didn't set boundaries on myself or limit myself to only one style. I had to find what made me unique. Sometimes this requires you to forget what you've learned. I pick out what is good in anything I hear and play and write from that perspective. I go hear young musicians all the time who have all the technique they want and influences at their fingertips. It's the youngsters (as Art Blakey said) who are keeping things alive and slowly moving the evolution of this music along. It's a two-sided coin. Hopefully over the years this Internet and downloading and technology will help in some way. Everybody is striving to make the playing field fair, finally. We're hoping that musicians and music will benefit from this new scenario and business model, but it's difficult readjusting during this process, and it seems there's just no way of getting around the adjustment process. It's just funny how things work out this way, where the record companies screwed us for all these years—now they are screwed! The music itself, the musicians, and the business . . . all are kind of in a quandary as to what will happen in the future . . . but it will pan out . . . all things do.

Bobby Broom
GUITARIST, COMPOSER, EDUCATOR

HOME BASE
www.bobbybroom.com

GOT MUSIC?
Bobby Broom Plays for Monk, Bobby Broom, Origin Records, 2009

"For me, jazz has been a spiritual journey."

BACKGROUND AND SOUND
Chicagoan Bobby Broom has slid his fingers across the frets of the jazz scene for more than twenty years. He works extensively as a leader for his

own groups throughout Chicago and also as a sideman for Sonny Rollins. When he is not performing or touring he is passing the torch to the future generations of jazz musicians at DePaul University School of Music. He has held clinics through the Thelonious Monk Institute, Duke University, and the Ravinia Festival in addition to Chicago's Roosevelt University. With a remarkable range of expertise, Bobby has become a leader among jazz guitarists today.

HIS STORY

For me, jazz has been a spiritual journey. Through my experiences in music I see my responses and reactions to life—how I operate in my relationships to others, myself, and the situations I'm faced with. I can relate a lot of my everyday life to thoughts, feelings, insights, and revelations I might get from playing on the bandstand.

I've encountered a kind of strange and elusive bliss through playing music. It's this elusive state that I'm trying to reach during performances and extend to the listener. I want to reach this and extend it to the listener. Being in jazz has allowed me to continue pursuing this while I also try to improve in my personal and musical life.

Ed Calle
SAXOPHONIST, WOODWINDIST, COMPOSER, EDUCATOR

HOME BASE
www.edcalle.com,
www.professorcalle.com

GOT MUSIC?
In the Zone, Ed Calle, Mojito
Records, 2006

"If I stand up, it's because I lean upon the shoulders of giants."

BACKGROUND AND SOUND

Ed Calle exudes a glowing personality throughout the jazz community. A native of Venezuela and now an American, he is creating the very music he dreamed of as a child. The lineage and understanding he communicates throughout his music speaks with a familiarity that is both comforting and inspiring. This is why Arturo Sandoval, Eddie Gomez, and many more consider him to be one of the very best. Ed further extends this rhythm of perseverance as an educator by approaching students with a broad perspective of life. He is now a doctor of higher education leadership and takes this role very seriously. He believes in lifting the future of not only this music but also our country to a higher ground. It is this omnipresent love for life that gives him a broad passion for music and the art of communication that seeps from his soul.

HIS STORY

I was just a kid from Venezuela. I didn't understand this music at all when I heard it. I couldn't figure out what [Michael] Brecker was doing, the language was so different; I had no idea what to say. I had to try my best out of respect. But when listening to people like Brecker or Leibman, it's obvious where their sources are. I have so much respect and sheer admiration for these people. They not only do brilliant things and surprise you; they've been there and are willing to help you out.

James Moody was sitting next to me at the Grammy Awards and he's singing patterns to me, saying check this out, that out . . . he had played for Quincy Jones that night and played the lick we were talking about and just looks at me and smiles. I've been fortunate to hang out there. If I stand up, it's because I lean upon the shoulders of giants. Anything I accomplish has more to do with the research. Guys like Kirk Whalum and Lonnie Laws are so much in my playing I should send them a check! Those people who shape you day by day are the ones sent by God. We're all striving for excellence, but look at the power of music and the genius it requires. Yet people don't think it's important. Maybe we've expressed it in a way that people don't know this. Sometimes we don't hear our own life because we're too much in the middle of what we're living. My life has been this unbelievable tapestry where everywhere I turn everyone is an astonishing musician. Jazz inspires other musicians to have the life calling to play jazz. It's the top American contribution. The greatest gift I've ever received was becoming an American citizen, and with no disrespect, I say I'm a citizen of the world. Jazz is a loving, all-encompassing, and embracing society for all to listen and see around the world.

Michel Camilo

PIANIST, COMPOSER, EDUCATOR

HOME BASE
www.michelcamilo.com

GOT MUSIC?
Live at the Blue Note, Michel
Camilo, Telarc, 2003; *Caribe*,
Michel Camilo Big Band, Calle 54
Records/Sony-BMG, 2009

"Music is the most intimate language of the soul."

BACKGROUND AND SOUND

Award-winning pianist Michel Camilo's hands have covered the world.
With talent in both classical and jazz, he has been able to conquer the
business by winning awards in multiple genres. His Grammy Award,
two Latin Grammy Awards, Emmy award, and four additional Grammy
nominations, as well as his latest accomplishment in the form of an
appointment as the Jazz Creative Director Chair for the Detroit Symphony
Orchestra, speak for themselves. He has performed around the world as a
soloist, bandleader, and sideman, from the Royal Albert Hall with the BBC
to the Blue Note Jazz Club and Carnegie Hall. His legacy has also been
established as an educator through many clinics, workshops, and schools,
such as the Duke Ellington School of the Arts. Berklee College of Music
has also awarded Michel an honorary doctorate in music. Yet his love for all
music seems to be the driving force behind his diverse and brilliant career.
As a player, his influences range from his family to Art Tatum and Oscar
Peterson. The melodic focus of his compositions brings intensity in both
emotion and technique. His sincere voice on the keys is accompanied by a
strong Dominican heritage. His music conveys a gratifying message about
the perseverance and passion he has for life, his loves, and his career.

HIS STORY

I was very fortunate to grow up in a family full of musicians. Every time
we gathered it was one big musical party. Composers, singers, songwriters,
et cetera, but that's why I started on this path so young. I think I was four

and a half years old; a year later I had already composed my first song. I couldn't write it down. My parents noticed the difficulty I was having and hired a professional to come into the home to take down my notes. By the time I was seven I had thirty compositions, but it wasn't until I turned fourteen that I heard jazz. I turned on the radio and heard Art Tatum one day and that did it for me. He played with an incredible flow of ideas, and I immersed myself into his musical world, which I found out later was called jazz. It was practically nonexistent where I lived, and it took a big effort to find it. I was the first man down there playing this. During the revolution of 1965 the Marines invaded the island. Even though there was animosity against anything remotely American, I made the decision to stick with jazz. The artistic community as a whole liked it. To me they were the thinkers of the island, and they welcomed me into their venue to play once a week. They connected with my creative quest.

The hardest thing is to find out who you are through your instrument. This is how you really contribute your voice, otherwise you end up being a clone and no one will be able to pick you apart from the others. That's not good because the jazz career is a long road. It pays off in a big way to go the road less traveled, and most guys don't have the patience to do this, but I believe in a long career. Most of the jazz masters did too. You look back and see your contribution, efforts, sacrifices, and it's worth it. In the meantime be conscious of your goals. I've always considered my music world as a triangle where my classical training coexists with my love for jazz and my Latin musical roots. I try to inspire the next generation to keep growing. At the end of the day success is temporary, and you must keep building and expanding your vocabulary of knowledge. Release the stress in your life and let your creativity flow through you. It's that creativity that the jazz musician must translate into music, and music is the most intimate language of the soul. Each one of my songs has a message, inspired by a moment of my life, a moment triggered by that particular melody. It's not random. It's an open book and me inviting the listener in to check out my life. These experiences are what I gather from being alive, and I consider myself lucky to be alive everyday.

Frank Carlberg
PIANIST, COMPOSER

HOME BASE
www.frankcarlberg.com

GOT MUSIC?
The American Dream, Frank
Carlberg, Red Piano
Records, 2009

"Art grows out of the culture that nurtures (. . . or sometimes batters) it."

BACKGROUND AND SOUND

Frank Carlberg, a native of Helsinki, Finland, is one of the most diverse composers/pianists in jazz today. Through commissions from such groups as Chamber Music America he has experimented with themes that delve into poetry and classical chamber music. He draws on his native folk music, the eclectic works of his peers in the arts and those he admires in traditional jazz to create richly inventive materials that serve up a profound genre-breaking message. He is on faculty at the New England Conservatory of Music and Berklee College of Music. Frank is also an outstanding member of the Douglass Street Music Collective and a partner of Red Piano Records, an artist collective label.

HIS STORY

Jazz has a central role in my life. I've chosen to live in America because of jazz. For me it represents freedom/discipline, celebration/struggle, love/anger, beauty/friction . . . These seeming contradictions only makes the music stronger . . . more complete. Art grows out of the culture that nurtures (. . . or sometimes batters) it. Jazz initially grew out of the African American experience. However, because of its strength and universal themes it spread like wild fire and caught the attention of people all over the world.

Is jazz alive and well, you ask? Every art form goes through phases. In the eighties and especially in the nineties, much energy was spent on nostalgic movements. People wanted to replicate earlier periods to make jazz a museum music, to enshrine its history at the expense of its future. I've always felt that the mission of jazz is to celebrate individuality and to look forward. Part of the nineties' conservatism had to do with the fact that we were approaching the end of the millennium and that people were scared and looked for comfort in nostalgia. Mister Marsalis's fancy suites were reassuring. Then the year 2000 rolled around and the world didn't come to an end. We could look forward again with a bit more confidence, and that's where jazz is right now.

There are challenges to the artist that are specific to our time. The abundant information available to the creative musician can easily lead to lack of focus. Fairly recently jazz consisted of a handful of parallel developments. Now the various paths/options are practically unlimited. A consequence of this diversification is also that sometimes we care less. When Ornette Coleman came on the scene many people were upset and offended that he played a plastic saxophone and made away with chord changes. Some people felt that Ornette mocked the tradition, or that he didn't show the music proper respect, or that he didn't care to practice on the musical elements that had been part of a musician's training. Although these criticisms were clearly misguided, it did show that people really cared deeply about art. Cecil Taylor, Thelonious Monk, and many others met with similar reactions and criticisms. It is hard for me to imagine such strong reactions in general today. This is not something specific to only jazz. We are not likely to have another scene like the premiere of *Sacre* in classical music either.

American society is set up in a brilliant way, especially from the perspective of the forces of power. We are allowed to say anything, to express anything. This gives us as individuals an illusion of freedom and power. Yet it is very unlikely that anyone is listening no matter what we say. So the society will supply us with a soap box but not with an audience! In Russia during the Soviet era, the citizen's right to express him or herself was heavily curtailed. Yet, in spite of this oppressive environment many people found subtle and brilliant ways to express thoughts and ideas. The imposed limitations led to waves of creative defiance and courageous resistance. Maybe at a time in the not too distant future jazz can once again become a vehicle for social change in America, as it has been in the past through the music of Duke Ellington, Billie Holiday, Charles Mingus, Max Roach, Charlie Haden, Archie Shepp, et cetera.

America has continually failed to recognize the great contributions that jazz has made to its cultural legacy. Part of the reason for this slight, undeniably, is the fact that jazz was and largely still is embedded in the black experience in American history . . . and we all know to a greater or lesser degree the exacting tolls of that experience. . . . But more recently, certainly since the advent of bebop and its inheritors, it has had to do with another fact, that as the music has grown more complex, the listening audience has found it harder to digest. And herein lies a significant cultural divide between America and Europe. In America we want our encounters with culture to be instantly gratifying, while in Europe young people are still taught (to believe) that experiences in the arts and culture have inherent value whether we "like" something or not. That difference is also reflected in the level of public support for the arts there is in these respective societies. That said, it is a miracle of perseverance, dedication, and love that jazz thrives and endures as it does, a testament to both the strength and vitality of this beautiful art form and to the deeply committed men and women (wherever on the planet they may be) who keep jazz alive and fresh and rife with possibilities.

Keith Carlock
DRUMMER, EDUCATOR

HOME BASE
www.keithcarlock.com

GOT MUSIC?
Krantz Carlock Lefebvre, Wayne Krantz, Keith Carlock, and Tim Lefebvre, Abstract Logix, 2009

"You're born with the talent that is God given, and it's up to you to develop it."

BACKGROUND AND SOUND
Grammy Award–winning drummer Keith Carlock has been promoted as the number one drummer of our time by such publications as *Modern Drummer*. But the accolades do not stop there. He has toured with musical icons Steely Dan, Sting, Wayne Krantz, Harry Belafonte, Chris Botti, the Blues Brothers Band, and the late Grover Washington Jr. The driving yet creative machine of rhythm behind Keith Carlock helped him go on to

produce countless recordings. He has held workshops around the world, and students of the drums flock to him at trade shows and clinics in hopes of learning his techniques and methods. His monster chops and ability to predict and complement the next toe-tapping second of each musician's thoughts, along with the sense of melody that he creates through the timbres of percussion, are remarkable.

HIS STORY

You're born with the talent that is God given, and it's up to you to develop it. Along the way you learn how to get it out there and be heard and to create the buzz about you. But, you must also realize this is a business and treat it as such, without losing your drive to just want to play great music with musicians who push and challenge you. You have to work hard and be able to interact with people in a way that's positive and know what it is you want to do musically. For me, working with the artists that I've been fortunate to play with was always a dream for me. I knew also that I had to be in a place like New York for these opportunities to happen. This meant climbing out of my comfort zone and taking risks. I moved to New York City from where I grew up in Mississippi, after going to college in Texas. The people I wanted to play with and the records I was really into were all coming out of New York, so naturally I was drawn there. Once you're able to get out and play and work, you have to nail each opportunity you're given. This means preparing and knowing what the gig calls for and pleasing the boss or whoever has hired you. The word will eventually get out and the buzz starts to happen. One gig leads to another if you nail it and bring something to the table. You can't sound like someone else or copy your favorite players; you must have your own voice and sound and way of approaching the instrument. That's something I've always wanted to have in my own playing and strive for. All the greats have that unique element. This will help you bring out some kind of emotion and passion behind your voice that connects to other people musically that's unique to you. I also think it's very important to be adaptable while letting your personal sound come through. When I play something that's structured, I have to do it as well as I do something that's improvised. Having the confidence to know that you're making mature choices in all the right moments, combined with everything else, is what separates the men from the boys.

Regina Carter
VIOLINIST, COMPOSER, EDUCATOR

HOME BASE
www.reginacarter.com

GOT MUSIC?
I'll Be Seeing You: A Sentimental Journey, Regina Carter,
Verve, 2006

"I believe we attract our own reality."

BACKGROUND AND SOUND

Regina Carter has reintroduced the value of the violin among the jazz community. She has performed or recorded with many notables, including the Atlanta Symphony, Wynton Marsalis, Marian McPartland, Billy Joel, Lauryn Hill, Mary J. Blige, Steve Turre, Cassandra Wilson, and Kenny Barron. Carter has also been a recipient of the MacArthur Fellowship for exceptional creativity and the International Society for the Performing Arts Distinguished Artist Award. In 2006 she also received an honorary doctorate in humane letters from Albion College in Albion, Michigan. On a mission for change in the arts, Regina is marching her way to become a leader and mentor for women and men alike throughout the music community.

HER STORY

I wish there was as much prominence placed on the arts in the United States as there is on sports. Artists and musicians often garner more respect and support in some countries than they do here. It's a shame that being an artist is at times considered the more trivial profession. I've had family members ask, "What is it you do all day?" When people ask me what my "real" job is, they don't understand that being a full-time musician is as demanding a commitment as any other career.

My calendar always looks good on paper, but in real life it never works in a way that I could explain all that I do. I'm a business and a product. I spend a good portion of time answering work-related e-mails, doing interviews, scheduling rehearsals, et cetera . . . If I'm working on a recording, figuring out what I want to record is a lengthy process; it takes time developing a concept, and that idea is constantly changing. I'll listen to a lot of music to see if there's something I want to play or record for a current project. I handle my own money—paying bills, the band, taxes, et cetera. There are rehearsals, school, my family and home, and life in general. I have to fit in everything, just like anyone else.

One of the special rewards of being a musician is that I've had the chance to travel a good portion of the world and be exposed to other cultures. There's so much to learn about the world. When you become immersed in someone else's culture and come back to your own, you look at things differently. Your way suddenly isn't the only way; it's just a way. All of your experiences broaden your perspective.

To share these experiences with people that don't have the opportunities we do is our responsibility as artists. I've learned that I can do this by incorporating music and sounds from other cultures into our own music.

I believe we attract our own reality. What we believe at our most core level is what we attract into our lives. This is what helps me keep my sanity among the noise and to live the kind of life I want—a comfortable life. Doing what I want to do is incredible and a blessing.

Frank Catalano
SAXOPHONIST, WOODWINDIST, COMPOSER, EDUCATOR

HOME BASE
www.catalanomusic.com

GOT MUSIC?
Bang! Frank Catalano, Savoy/
Columbia, 2008

"This music is a direct reflection of the energy you put into it."

BACKGROUND AND SOUND
Chicago native Frank Catalano zaps through bop and funk with rebounding energy. His accolades began at the age of ten, when he first attended weekly jam sessions with Chicago legend Von Freeman, and he was picked up by Louie Bellson as a teenager. His influences range from Miles to Griffin,

and it is not just out of admiration—it is because he sat in with them and learned firsthand the tools of the trade. Pleasing audiences time and again, he displays breathless energy as a constant measure to his talent. With more than 100,000 CDs sold and a major-label record deal, he has proved his reeds are likely to keep blowing as long as there is music to be played.

HIS STORY

I grew up on the west side of Chicago in a large Sicilian family. Money was scarce and tempers often flared. When you acted out, instead of a lecture, you got a crack in the face. Music became my escape. I began playing saxophone at age eight, and by age fourteen I had already jammed with Miles Davis, Eddie Harris, Johnny Griffin, Betty Carter, Von Freeman, Ira Sullivan, and Elvin Jones. I went on the road with Charles Earland at the age of sixteen and was signed to Delmark Records at age seventeen. One year of jam sessions with Von was worth a thousand classroom lessons anywhere else in the world.

This music is a direct reflection of the energy you put into it. I know it could be gone at any second because it almost ended when my right middle finger was cut off in a freak accident. I don't take it for granted, and it led to a saxophone accessory that I invented and had patented. I need to play it as much as I can. There are always going to be people who want to keep this music in a box. Regurgitating isn't art. You must believe in the energy. If you try to sound like someone who had their heyday in the forties, you're not playing from your own soul. You've got to sound like yourself. Everyone in this world has a personality; we don't have to fit in a box. I knew I wanted to make music as my profession ever since I picked up the saxophone and I know that's why God put me on this Earth. If you have to think about something too much, it's probably not the real deal. I create good vibes and hand out energy with my heart and soul. It's my hope that through this music, people can come together.

Chris Cheek

SAXOPHONIST, COMPOSER

HOME BASE
www.chrischeek.net

GOT MUSIC?
Vine, Chris Cheek, Fresh Start
Records, 1999

"When we play, we're just trying to find what's real."

BACKGROUND AND SOUND

St. Louis native saxophonist Chris Cheek has swept the scene and claimed his stake as one of the best and most melodic players today. A graduate of Berklee College of Music in Boston, Cheek moved to New York in the early nineties and quickly established his authority by touring and performing with groups such as the Brian Blade Fellowship, Paul Motian's Electric Bebop Band, and Luciana Souza. He is also a member of the widely recognized and followed underground fusion band Rudder. As a leader he has produced five solo albums and toured the world with his group. Chris Cheek's indisputable clout as a soloist is matched only by his distinguished tone and style.

HIS STORY

As time goes on, I feel more and more fortunate to have a life in music. It's been and continues to be a constant source of discovery and renewal. Through my experiences in music, I can now see how this infinite reservoir quite literally sustains people and keeps them going. For many of us, music is our health insurance and our retirement plan. That's not to say that things seem any more secure or stable, but music, and jazz in particular, shows me the joy in spontaneity and the satisfaction to be able to go back to that well.

What's fascinating about improvising is that I have a constant challenge to face the moment and react to what's happening and then try to make sense of it all and come up with something good. To have this shared experience with a band, and better yet, bring the listener with us, that is the best. The great thing is that it's never the same thing twice. Each new day brings a new reality and opportunity, and when we play, we're just trying to find what's real.

Music has helped me in life by showing me that it's okay, even advantageous, to encounter this uncertainty. Some of the best musical moments happen when someone or even everyone gets lost, and if you let go of what's familiar and comfortable you're bound to find something different and wonderful. Sometimes what the critics call a mistake the player may see as a new idea. There's always something to look forward to, a chance to start over, to improve, explore, and change. I've been lucky to have a wonderful, supportive family, and although it's difficult at times to be separated from them, the world of jazz has taken me to places I could have never imagined as well as connected me to people who are a real inspiration in my life. It's helped build friendships that I'm truly grateful for.

Corey Christiansen
GUITARIST, COMPOSER, EDUCATOR

HOME BASE
www.coreychristiansen.com

GOT MUSIC?
Roll with It, Corey Christiansen, Origin Records, 2008

"Talent can be overrated, but a work ethic cannot."

BACKGROUND AND SOUND
Corey Christiansen has worked in almost every facet of the music industry. During his years with Mel Bay he worked as a senior editor and chief guitar clinician, and he wrote several books on guitar methods and jazz instruction. Corey has held positions at his alma maters, the University of South Florida and Utah State University, and was the pioneer for Indiana State University's guitar program. Corey has tightened his strings around the world with James Moody, Christian McBride, George Duke, Danny Gottleib, and many others. Fierce ambition and skill have brought him to the stages of notable venues, such as the Smithsonian Institution in Washington, DC, the Umbria Jazz Festival in Perugia, Italy, and the Classic American Guitar Show. His dreams are swiftly being realized as he continues to build an international audience for himself.

HIS STORY

I grew up in Smithfield, Utah. This is primarily a small farming community. Needless to say there weren't a whole lot of other kids my age who were into records or music. But my family was really into exposing all of us to great music of all styles. My father was a professional guitar player, and we were playing together dating back to my preschool years. I knew from that time, probably from three to four years old, that I wanted to be a professional musician. I never really had any other goals, unless you count the time I wanted to be a trial lawyer. I wanted to be a trial lawyer, I suppose, for the same reasons I wanted to be a jazz musician. It's all about improvisation, dialog, interaction, and conversation with others. Throughout the years I've strived not to turn my back on anything that's been an influence to me. All of my music is owed to somebody else. I'm a thief. I steal from people I love in an unselfish way and hope my music pays tribute and respect to them. But jazz only happens when different music, influences, and cultures come together. It's our responsibility to create a new scene where there wasn't one before.

I've always had a sense of how to make this work for me, not just as art but as a business, too. I went through a period of my life where I couldn't make or keep friends. I didn't understand that this was due to other kids not being interested in what I was interested in. I had to learn through this, how to really be into what other people are doing when they're around, and was lucky to figure this out at a really young age. Improving ourselves and proving ourselves as musicians in the very pure sense is a selfish and unselfish profession to be in. Van Gogh once said, "Your profession is not what brings home your paycheck. Your profession is what you were put on earth to do." He's right. But talent shouldn't be regarded as the end. Talent can be overrated, but a work ethic cannot. No matter who you think God is, he loves to see people strive for perfection. Jazz is just one of the art forms where the artists constantly strive to take the art to the next level. When I play, this is when I feel close to God. Jazz musicians, musicians of any kind who strive for excellence can achieve this feeling too. Maybe I won't ever completely know until this life has passed why I do this, but it's what I have to learn to do and be good at so I can pass it along to someone else. It's nice to do something every day that marks improvement in my life.

John Clayton

BASSIST, EDUCATOR, COMPOSER

HOME BASE
www.johnclaytonjazz.com

GOT MUSIC?
Brother to Brother, Clayton
Brothers, ArtistShare, 2008

"The musical instrument . . . is nothing more than an amplifier for the music that's in you."

BACKGROUND AND SOUND

Some musicians play, others teach, and still others influence the sphere of music around them for the generations to come. Some do it all. Grammy Award winner John Clayton would be the latter. He is one of the prominent fathers to the next generations of jazz, and his lines are heard through almost everyone in the field. Running the education programs at both the Vail Jazz Party and the Lionel Hampton Jazz Festival, his collaborations with other musicians in jazz today—including Diana Krall, YoYo Ma, the Clayton-Hamilton Jazz Orchestra, Queen Latifah, and more—have produced some of best sounds and albums around. It is John's ability to swing while painting a smile through his virtuosic technique that makes him so desirable among listeners and peers alike.

HIS STORY

I must have been seventeen or eighteen years old when I was out at a club. I remember two guys, who obviously hadn't seen each other in days, weeks, hours, who knows, but they walked in and hugged, kissed each other. Nobody saw it and there was nothing socially uncomfortable about it all. Yet I remember thinking this: these guys were the family I wanted to be a part of. A family of people who are so comfortable in their skin and express themselves with smiles, hugs, et cetera. You don't see bankers or computer techs doing this everyday. It's so much the way of the jazz musicians world I knew right then that this was it. That was the life I wanted and now have.

There were two major influences in my life and career. One, my mom. She played piano and organ and still plays at home. Number two, Ray Brown. He was, in many ways, like a father to me in ways my father perhaps was not one. I love my dad; that's not the issue. Ray knew what I was about in terms of being a hungry young artist. Although my father never got in the way of it all, and he did support me. No one ever closed the door in my face. I would sit around and listen to their records and transcribe and basically steal from them. I admit it, why not? I don't try to pull it off as if it's mine. At the end of the day your own voice surfaces when you play. You have to dig deep to clearly see who my influences are. Your own voice is nothing but a compilation. The older you get the more comfortable you become in your own skin.

When you get to be my age you don't try to prove as much and you can say, I'm ugly, and yeah, I'm fat, and I don't care. Just get comfortable in your skin with what it is that you do. No matter what you play, whether it's a scale, a piece of music, or a transcription from someone else, the musical instrument you're playing on is nothing more than an amplifier for the music that's in you. It's up to you to fill your heart and soul. It's up to the artists too. We *get* to do this. It's a lesson I've learned, and I'm humbled by it. If people want to know something about me, it's that I appreciate the fact that I *get* to play music. It's not a given factor. It's not something that, unfortunately, too many people are blessed with.

Jeff Coffin

SAXOPHONIST, COMPOSER, EDUCATOR

HOME BASE
www.jeffcoffin.com,
www.jeffcoffinphotography.com

GOT MUSIC?
Mutopia, Jeff Coffin Mu'tet,
Compass Records, 2008

"My success isn't about just being able to make a living as a musician; it also has to do with continually striving and growing to be a better person.."

BACKGROUND AND SOUND

Jeff Coffin is one of the most diverse talents on the scene today. As the saxophonist for Dave Matthews Band and Béla Fleck and the Flecktones, and as the leader for his own group, the Jeff Coffin Mu'tet, his sound rests at the height of progressive jazz. Influenced by the great vocalists of the past, he has channeled his ability to spread language and positive emotions through music. As a brilliantly executed talent, he is adaptable to any genre he is residing in at any given moment. He is a voice to emulate in his positive message and undeniable wisdom behind the art.

HIS STORY

I've been very lucky in my career, but at the same time I've also worked very hard to get where I'm at today. I think being lucky and fortunate, in my case, go hand in hand and have led me to where I am today. My success isn't about just being able to make a living as a musician; it also has to do with continually striving and growing to be a better person. I am grateful to be able to express myself through the medium of music (or photography or composition), and I hope that others will be inspired to follow a similar path with their own personal expression. Our expression can, and should, change constantly, because as people we are constantly changing. I also enjoy giving to others through my abilities. A lot of musicians I play with strive to give back in great amounts, even if it's behind the scenes. If I'm going to be successful in all areas of my life, including my relationships with family and friends, I have to be giving back. This is one of the many reasons I teach and do clinic work. The process of teaching and the process of learning go hand in hand. The word "education" comes from the Latin root "educato," which means "to draw out." What a beautiful concept to share. For me, helping and encouraging people to be curious about life and their ideas and passions is a big part of giving.

Because of much hard work and the openness of others, I'm fortunate to play with very successful bands that still create an incredible intimacy on and off stage. This is something I've always been drawn toward. When I'm playing with Dave Matthews Band, there's a similar intimacy on stage as there is with the Flecktones or the Mu'tet, regardless of crowd size. I'm fortunate because I get to do what I love in so many areas, I get to give a lot back to others, and I can provide for my family. I'm not resting on my success, nor am I trying to search for a way to get through this that's "easier."

I do what I do because I love it and I'm willing to do the work necessary. After all, if I'm doing and/or using my craft just for money, it will be a very shallow grave, and that's not one I'm willing to lie in. The path must have a heart for me to go down it.

Mark Colby
SAXOPHONIST, COMPOSER, EDUCATOR

HOME BASE
www.markcolby.com

GOT MUSIC?
Reflections, Mark Colby, Origin Records, 2009

"The integrity of this music is a powerful thing and a force for good."

BACKGROUND AND SOUND
Selmer artist Mark Colby's slick sound has been heard throughout the jazz community for more than twenty-five years. He has been on the faculty at DePaul University's Jazz Studies Department and on staff at Elmhurst University since the mid-1980s. His performance schedule over the years has included stints with the late Maynard Ferguson, Jaco Pastorious, Gerry Mulligan, Frank Sinatra, Bob James, Charlie Haden, and Mose Allison in addition to more than two thousand commercial gigs throughout the greater Chicago area. He has opened up several decades of listeners and students to the world of jazz, and he is a true asset to the already rich history of jazz, not only in the Chicago area but around the world.

HIS STORY
I had to do this and can't envision doing anything else in my life, and I've been this way since I was a child. I grew up hearing music through my father's collections and his own music. My dad was a professional drummer and vibe player in New York. This made my childhood quite ideal.

When I was about eight years old he brought home a clarinet and had me take lessons with one of the guys in the band . . . I fell in love with it. My father would play Benny Goodman, Artie Shaw, and Tommy Dorsey.

My sister, who was older than I was, would listen to modern jazz like Horace Silver, Miles, and Art Blakey. Once I began listening to the music my sister played, I knew I had to hurry up and switch from the clarinet to the saxophone. I felt this was where my heart was, and there was something about the saxophone that spoke to me.

As soon as I put it together that the music I heard around the house was the music I wanted to play, I started playing it free of the page. This only made me want to listen more and inspired me to pick things off records. I learned to improvise way before I knew anything about chords or scales, and my education definitely didn't come out of a book.

I believe it's the emotional aspect of this music that's the most important. If I'm not emotionally involved, then there's no point. You can learn from a book, but until you actually play the book, it doesn't mean anything. I found out through teaching that I really enjoyed passing on my love and passion for this music to young people. In fact, it changed the direction I was going. I treated it as if it was a calling I had to pass on.

Now I teach my students that the people who get recognition from the pop world are here for the moment and then gone, and they're not really leaving much of a legacy. It seems that people give in to the lowest common denominator and say it's good enough. We've strayed away from really good music, and as time goes on it seems that this has created a diminished demand for clubs and live music. This is what it's important for anyone who really wants to do this to devote themselves to being the best they can be. The cream always rises to the top. You just have to make sure it's about the music first, and you have to be a jazz musician one hundred percent of the time. It's not enough in today's society to be in the media. Because of this it's been my mission to bring this music to as many people as possible in the schools and public. The integrity of this music is a powerful thing and a force for good. I personally don't care what era the music is from, if it's good, it's good. It's all relevant music, and people will always want to play it.

Todd Coolman

BASSIST, COMPOSER, EDUCATOR

HOME BASE
www.toddcoolman.com

GOT MUSIC?
Perfect Strangers, Todd Coolman, ArtistShare, 2009

"The idea that work could be something that one dedicated oneself to, like music, impacted me."

BACKGROUND AND SOUND

Grammy Award–winning bassist Todd Coolman has gained international recognition for his clinics, workshops, and performances. He has toured with Gerry Mulligan, James Moody, Art Farmer, Lionel Hampton, and Benny Goodman. Since 1978 he has laid the foundation for not only his peers but also students of the art. Currently he is on staff as the director of Jazz Studies Program at the Conservatory of Music at Purchase College. His keen instincts and the darkened sound he lays down as groundwork for each musician he plays with keeps the jazz world coming back to him for work time and again.

HIS STORY

Jazz found me, I didn't go looking for it. My private instructor on bass when I was in high school was helping me study traditional and beginner bass lessons in classical music. It was real basic. One day, during a lesson, he handed me a vinyl LP. He said, "there's a bass player on this record that plays the bass in a manner different than what you've been studying. I thought you'd be interested in hearing it." That LP was *Night Train* by Oscar Peterson. Ray Brown was the bassist. I think I was fifteen at the time.

I had never heard this stuff before. The moment it started it was a transformative experience, entirely captivating, riveting, and it captured one hundred percent of my attention and passion in that one instant. No field of interest that was typical of a boy that age, like sports or the outdoors or cute girls, hit me like this. This was a tsunami. I began to go to places like the Jazz Showcase in Chicago. They had a Sunday matinee where underage kids were admitted. The very first week I went, I saw Dizzy Gillespie with Roy Haynes, and after that week I went the following two Sundays as well. One Sunday was Bill Evans with Eddie Gomez and Mary Morrell, and the following Sunday was Ornette Coleman with Don Cherry, Charlie Haden, and Ed Blackwell. I recall that during the drive home after the third consecutive Sunday set I attended, I asked the guys I was with, "Which one of those sets was jazz?" It never occurred to me that they could all be jazz and at the same time be so dissimilar.

During the time I was growing up, everyone I was around in Gary, Indiana, worked in steel mills. They were a miserable lot, to be sure. As soon as they got home they had to sit down and read the newspaper or have a beer. I made the association that work was something you're supposed to hate. It was something one had to do in exchange for money to feed their family. But when I saw those jazz performers, the one thing that stuck out was that they genuinely enjoyed what they were doing and enjoyed their coworkers. There was a certain intensity and focus on the task that I had never observed in the more mundane world of a day laborer. Everyone else in my life had an automated life. The idea that work could be something that one dedicated oneself to, like music, impacted me. The musicians were intense and fun loving, and the audience seemed to be interested . . . there was something going on that the audience needed, and there was something needed by the musicians in an almost altruistic way. Seeing Cannonball was like going to a Sunday church service—it was uplifting, evangelical in nature . . . very moving . . . very powerful. I knew from that moment on that there was something in this for me . . . something worth exploring.

Today, as a jazz musician, I don't view jazz musicians as being in any way mysterious or exotic or separate or odd or elevated. We just have elevated skills in certain artistic areas that are somewhat uncommon. If I meet a guy who's a welder and he's really good at it and "into it," I don't have any trouble relating to him. He's a human being just like me. He pursues a skill with great passion and fervor just like I do. My neighbors know me as Todd, not by what I do. But jazz has affected me. I have learned a lot about humanity and contentment and have a certain grounding. I hope to inspire people to do something meaningful since I think everyone has something to say . . . you just have to listen for it and appreciate it. I'm ordinary in many ways, but very fortunate and grateful to have this vocation and skill that I can practice and hold in high esteem.

Dan Cray
PIANIST, COMPOSER, TEACHER

HOME BASE
www.dancray.com

GOT MUSIC?
Over Here Over Heard, Dan Cray Trio, Crawdad Production, 2008

"Jazz is always going to be quality music that takes thought and time."

BACKGROUND AND SOUND

Pianist Dan Cray is shaping a name for himself throughout the jazz community with his successful trio. His works as a composer have been featured on numerous radio stations and commissions; most notably he composed the theme song to *Gossip Girl* and Michael Keaton's film *The Merry Gentleman*. He has toured throughout the world with some of the very best artists of our time, including Kurt Elling, Eddie Johnson, Bobby Broom, Orbert Davis, and more. Dan has been a finalist in several prestigious competitions, including the 2004 American Pianists Association Cole Porter Fellowship and the 2003 Montreux Jazz Festival Solo Piano Competition. His work is deeply reflective of his Chicago roots and brings out the soul of his environment. He represents some of the very best of the youth in jazz today.

HIS STORY

Imagination is kind of dying in a sense. We're living in a hyper-reality where you don't have to come up with your own stories or use your imagination because it's all there for you in this virtual world. Games are hyper-realistic, and I'm not even sure if kids today have the kinds of toys that you need to make up stories for, like G.I. Joes and Barbies. Everything is now virtual. There's so much to choose from today. It seems that no one has time to put in the mental process to sit down and listen to something. But this isn't about where jazz "went wrong." This is about the culture and what it deems important; across the board, we're lacking in terms of substance.

I can't think of anyone in the pop world that is undoubtedly an artist now like Michael Jackson was, for example. Which songs produced for today's culture are going to live for thirty or forty years? Unfortunately, pop music has become just another product of the over-industrialization of the economy—music has been reduced to the cheapest thing to produce. You can plug these people in to sing computer generated "hooks," they're big for a few years, and then they're discarded for someone younger. If it keeps going like this, the only music we're going to have will be utter shit. I don't even know if people play any instruments at all on a lot of the tracks anymore. It's just a producer with some loop. But no one seems to care too much about this. People just eat it up like they do the crap food and everything else that's been reduced to this point. This is capitalism run amuck. It's discouraging for me because there's something that's getting lost in this rush to make everything cheaply—the quality has been sucked out of everything. When you try to throw jazz into this environment, it doesn't stand a chance. Jazz is always going to be quality music that takes thought and time. At least I hope so. Too many people care about this music to make it into something it's not.

Chris Crenshaw

TROMBONIST, COMPOSER, EDUCATOR

HOME BASE
www.myspace.com/chrittycren

"The way I approach music is the way I approach my life."

BACKGROUND AND SOUND
Georgia native Chris Crenshaw grew up with music all around him. He has attended Valdosta State University and Julliard School of Music and

was the winner of the Eastern Trombone Workshop Solo Competition in 2004. Influences such as Wycliffe Gordon and Wynton Marsalis have had a profound effect on him and led him to the successful career he is in now. Chris has no issues with bringing everything he has to the table when called upon to solo. Holding back just is not his style. His Southern roots and gospel-tinged approach to music sit well with the souls of all who hear him.

HIS STORY

Jazz is the first amendment of the constitution, a freedom of expression. With any other kind of music there's a form or maybe one or two ways of doing something. But with jazz you can come from left field, like Don Cherry or Ornette Coleman. They came out of left field and ended up back right where they belonged and appealed to a lot of people. With this music we can look back to where we came from; it's a historical vehicle. It allows me to say what I want to say, how I want to say it, and when I want to say it. The raw aspect of jazz is emotional, and we're all in the same boat when we play. I'm not more than anyone else because I'm trying to get it all together too. This isn't necessarily a shortcoming or fault. There's no need to put anyone on a pedestal, and that's what's going to come out of my horn. I'm a positive person, always trying to shoot for something great. Family is important, as is music and life. They go hand in hand. The way I approach music is the way I approach my life. I just get it on and try to find the best way possible for me to get through to others. It's a good approach for anyone.

Bill Cunliffe
PIANIST, COMPOSER, EDUCATOR

HOME BASE
www.billcunliffe.com

GOT MUSIC?
The Blues and the Abstract Truth, Take 2, Bill Cunliffe, Resonance Records, 2008

"The things you do to become a good person are relevant in becoming a good jazz musician."

BACKGROUND AND SOUND

Grammy-nominated composer and pianist Bill Cunliffe has emerged to become one of the most sought-after composers and players today. He has toured and played with vocalist Frank Sinatra and Buddy Rich's Big Band, as well as James Moody, Freddie Hubbard, and Joshua Redman. In 1989 Bill won the Thelonious Monk International Jazz Pianist Award, and since then his career has covered a gamut of genres as both a player and a composer. Great orchestras, including the Henry Mancini Institute Orchestra and the  Cincinnati Pops Orchestra, have commissioned him for original works that range from chamber music settings to chorale arrangements. As an educator, he molds the future of jazz one student at a time with his reality- and experience-based methods at California State University in Fullerton. Bill is a great example of how an open and free vision can reach both traditional and modern jazz audiences.

HIS STORY

I never really heard jazz I liked until I was a junior in college. Oscar Peterson was the one who set me off. Listening to him led me to others, like Miles, Wynton Kelly, Herbie Hancock, et cetera . . . there was a pleasure for me in their music that came from combining the predictable with the unpredictable. I try to achieve that myself when I play. I like adventures that happen with the music that aren't always dependent upon blowing solos but also from the composition itself. The interaction of the composition and improvisation brings out the human element of jazz.

I also think that the things you do to become a good person are relevant in becoming a good jazz musician. You have to do unto others in this music. The best way for *you* to sound great is to enable others to do so through listening and responding to them, establishing your humanity with them.

I try to help my students get through the difficulties of life and not make the same mistakes I did. When we find connections between the music and the real world, the students see what is relevant for them and work harder. I want to show them as much respect and love as I can; this forges a stronger connection between us. It's also important to focus on optimism and the good things in life, because what you focus on grows. When I felt inadequate as an improvising musician I tried to sing what I was playing. This helped me to shift my focus to my heart, which is my emotional and connective engine. I love what I do. I'm not always concerned with breaking new ground, so I concentrate more on feeling the music, rather than thinking too much about what is supposed to happen. You just have to do what the music tells you to do.

Eddie Daniels   {LIVING LEGEND}

CLARINETIST, SAXOPHONIST, EDUCATOR, COMPOSER

HOME BASE
www.eddiedanielsclarinet.com

GOT MUSIC?
Homecoming, Eddie Daniels, IPO Records, 2007

"If we know what goes into an art form such as jazz, we can then follow it, enjoy what the artist is doing and who knows, maybe be inspired to carry on the tradition."

BACKGROUND AND SOUND

Grammy Award–winning clarinetist Eddie Daniels was not always the jazz and classical clarinetist he is today. He began his career with the Thad Jones–Mel Lewis Orchestra as a tenor player and later switched to clarinet. Years later he is still going strong. He has played around the world in both jazz and classical genres and with virtually everyone who's anyone in the business. His exceptional ability to cross from classical to jazz to pop and back is a sought-after trait among many, but pulled off with this level of skill by only a handful of musicians alive today.

HIS STORY

It's all about education . . . learning the art of listening and then appreciation. If we know what goes into an art form such as jazz, we can then follow it, enjoy what the artist is doing and who knows, maybe be inspired to carry on the tradition. Then we have listeners who are also players, just like going to the French Open. At least eighty percent of the people who attend also play tennis, which makes them very informed. . . . that's the answer. . . . being informed about something, because that means you have learned something about yourself while learning something, and hence bring much more to the table. Being an informed, introspective participating audience or critic makes for better interaction, and more fun. Some of the critics in jazz that I read are uninformed and therefore pass on wrong information, bad judgments, or critiques and contribute to the death of the art form. It's about knowing what art is, what goes into its creation, and feeling what it's like to be a participant, and the big one . . . opening a window for those who don't know!

Michael Dease

TROMBONIST, SAXOPHONIST, COMPOSER, PRODUCER, EDUCATOR, FOUNDER OF D-CLEf RECORDS

HOME BASE
www.mikedease.com,
www.dclefrecords.com

GOT MUSIC?
Clarity, Michael Dease, Bluesback Records, 2008

"At the end of the day, it's the spirit of a person that touches us, not the vocation."

BACKGROUND AND SOUND

Although he is a new face in New York, Grammy Award–winning trombonist Michael Dease has become one of the more seasoned and mature musicians on the scene within a relatively brief amount of time. In seven short years he has recorded more than fifty albums as a sideman, including Alicia Keys's Grammy-winning album *Superwoman* and others with Jamie Cullum, the Dizzy Gillespie All-Star Band, Mark Whitfield, the Claudio Roditi Quartet, and Paul Simon. Performances in venues around the world, including Dizzy's Coca-Cola Club, the Jazz Standard, and the Village Vanguard, only solidify his position among his peers. A staunch educator in jazz, Michael has been invited to be a clinician and teacher throughout the United States and is a regular lecturer at Northwestern

University. Assisting with the production of albums through labels like Half-Note Records and Jazz Legacy Productions led him to form his own label, D-Clef Records, in the spring of 2009. With his gift for producing and ear for great music, this label and his talents as a performer are sure to weather the stormy front the business often hands off to its newcomers.

HIS STORY

Just like we as musicians work on our technique to perform at the highest level, or our memory to recall songs and ideas, we have to work on our character and integrity to help us improve and be our best as humans, not just musicians. Traveling the world and exploring the cities as jazz musicians introduces us to people from all walks of life: junkies, diplomats, plumbers, musical icons, and weekend warriors. At the end of the day, it's the spirit of a person that touches us, not the vocation.

Jazz musicians have some of the most colorful personalities as well, not all of which may appear positive. We have to learn from those as well, although the clearest memories I have are encouraging, friendly, and saturated with wisdom. As encouragement, bassist John Lee once tapped me on the shoulder as I was preparing to solo after Roy Hargrove and whispered, "Just play like yourself, dude. You're ready." A friendly moment was when I met trombonist Steve Davis at a music store for the second time. He paused and called me by my name, although we had only met once, briefly, six months ago. James Moody drops wisdom with everything he says, does, or touches. My kernel of his wisdom came when he heard my warm-up and asked me to copy it down for him. As I tried to verify his request (to my surprise), he stopped me in my tracks and told me to never stop learning—everybody has something to offer. He later told me that Dizzy told him the same thing, and that he was simply paying it forward. That is the unifying thread of these, and the thousands of similar incidents I've had over the past fifteen years. We're all trying to be better people.

Marko Djordjevic

DRUMMER, COMPOSER, EDUCATOR

HOME BASE
www.svetimarko.com,
www.myspace.com/svetimarko

GOT MUSIC?
Where I Come From, Marko
Djordjevic, Firma Entertainment,
2007

*"I am blessed to be playing a lot and to be inspired to keep practicing
and improving."*

BACKGROUND AND SOUND

Well ahead of his time, Serbian-born drummer Marko Djordjevic
(pronounced George-vich) has created not only a niche for himself but a
definite fuel that is needed within the modern jazz community. An honors
graduate of Berklee College of Music, Marko now has more than forty
albums and thousands of live performances under his belt with greats such
as Matt Garrison, Aaron Goldberg, Wayne Krantz, and Lionel Loueke. It
is obvious that his name is fast becoming synonymous with greatness and
diversity. As the leader of his group, Sveti, his distinctive accent as a player
and composer is aptly brought to the table with each performance. It is this
breakneck pace he has set for others to follow that ensures his longevity in
the business.

HIS STORY

It's difficult to make enough time to do the stuff that doesn't really interest
me. I am blessed to be playing a lot and to be inspired to keep practicing
and improving. To me, this is happiness. But I realize that if I don't do the
legwork, I don't get to play with my band, Sveti. It's not easy to gather the
time and energy and put the legwork into your art. But it needs to be done
and we all know it. It's the only way to get your music heard.

The way things are going in creative music, even people with huge names
are in the position where they're actually in charge of at least some of their
legwork. Maybe my view of the past is simplistic, but it seems there were
many more live playing opportunities, and less competition, so musicians

were able to be musicians. They would play at night, rest up during the day, and practice in between. They could afford to not think about anything except for the gig they're doing and the power in the music really reflected their focus.

Some countries like France or Holland subsidize artists, so a lot of them don't have worry about making their daily bread. On the other hand, if you compare the output of relevant, creative music from those countries to the things going on in NYC, this town is miles ahead, generally speaking. So is this really a solution? Ultimately, when talking about creative music, it all comes down to love and inspiration. In my experience this wins out over everything else. I am fulfilled, energized, and at peace when the music is happening. Yet a lot of commercial music these days is just a sound track for an agenda. The agenda is to create a perfect consumer or customer. Our role as creative people and critical thinkers should be to offer something other than the mind-numbing stream of sounds and images we are assaulted by every day. Use music to inspire, refresh, enlighten, elevate—not to brainwash some kid into thinking that buying an iPhone is the end-all-be-all of the human experience.

Dave Douglas
TRUMPETER, COMPOSER, EDUCATOR

HOME BASE
www.davedouglas.com

GOT MUSIC?
Moonshine, Dave Douglas,
Greenleaf Music, 2007

"You can't separate jazz from the rest of music and life."

BACKGROUND AND SOUND
Guggenheim Fellowship recipient and Grammy-nominated trumpeter Dave Douglas is one of the most inexhaustible and innovative musicians of our time. Innumerable organizations and musicians have commissioned Douglas for new works. These range from the Library of Congress to Stanford University and the Philharmonie Essen. With more than twenty-eight recordings and thousands of live performances, his contribution

to the creative music world is invaluable. Douglas is also the founder of the Festival of New Trumpet Music and is a true champion of his peers. Belonging to another creative realm, his sound and crystallized vision of his goals as an artist have set an example for creative lives around the world.

HIS STORY

I think our first influences are often overlooked . . . the people around you, your parents, siblings, and others. My father certainly got me going in music. All of the different kinds of recordings he had touched me. My brother gave me a Herbie Hancock record when we were living in the Philippines when I was about twelve or fourteen years old. I could tell I loved the music but I didn't quite know what was going on. I said I've got to figure out what this is and I haven't stopped since. The music has taught me everything from morals and ethics to how to work with other people. It's taught me how to be and grow into being the best human being I can be every moment despite obstacles and without any excuses. This is something you're not called to do in many professions. With other jobs you can go home and take the hat off and that's the end of it. With music, everything you do is all the time as part of the process. I guess I got into a much harder job than I thought. It's taken me a lot of years to realize that when I go on stage what comes out of me is a part of what I'm living. This isn't something you can fake for an hour and then go do something else. Hearing these extraordinary personalities through music is what makes it so great. But you can't separate jazz from the rest of music and life.

It's my goal to have my music be understood and have others feel the joy I get from the music. Part of my experience is having the mind to recognize the wonderful things going on and how things change. I have to be able to handle the challenges and see different and interesting formations as challenges rather than impediments. I'm aware of each moment. When I get up every day there are certain things I do every morning. I brush my teeth, bathe, and get dressed. We all have to do this day after day and it's all basically the same, so what makes any of us really get up and get going? It's witnessing the variation in that day-to-day routine that keeps all of us going. This is the improviser's outlook. I have to contribute the most I can. My goal is to have my music be understood and have others feel the same joy I get from music. I guess success is knowing that we're all on the search for this and one day finding it.

Bill Dowling
TRUMPETER, EDUCATOR, COMPOSER, ARRANGER

HOME BASE
www.billdowling.com

GOT MUSIC?
Playhouse, Bill Dowling,
Frayed Hat Records, 2009

"Everything I learned, I learned through all the great gigs I've had."

BACKGROUND AND SOUND

With power behind his years of experience and force behind his sound, Bill Dowling is sitting right where he needs to be. Having played with such greats as Paul Anka, They Might Be Giants, Duke Ellington, and Aretha Franklin and now sporting a release of his own, his sound is sharp and cutting edge brilliant. His voice is one that speaks of tenacity and adaptation in any situation and one we can all learn from.

HIS STORY

Everything I learned, I learned through all the great gigs I've had. And Bobby Shew. I give him full credit for my career. He was the one who gave me my second set of chops. But this music, when I play, is about that personal freedom. It's the most intimate portrait of an artist anyone will ever hear. Pure music. Other genres are about something else, selling or suggesting something you're supposed to think about other than the music. In the end it's not, at least for me, about concentrating on becoming a better trumpet player, it's about becoming more focused and turning into a well-rounded player. One day, you'll realize that yes, this is great, and it's not what you thought it was going to be. It's not a competition; it's about the music, and when it becomes something else, then you've lost the music.

Richard Drexler

BASSIST, PIANIST, EDUCATOR, COMPOSER, MINISTER

HOME BASE
www.richarddrexler.com

GOT MUSIC?
Señor Juan Brahms, Richard
Drexler, Song-o-saurus, 2004

"The music has to come from your heart and go beyond yourself."

BACKGROUND AND SOUND

Richard Drexler is not only one of the best sidemen in the industry, he is a hard-working and prolific leader, composer, and educator. His works are not limited to jazz or even classical—they combine the best of both worlds to bring a new voice that breaks through tired genre lines. Richard has also toured extensively with the Woody Herman Orchestra and the Jeff Berlin Trio. He is someone who not only understands the roots and the history of jazz but also employs his own spin on the music to make sure it moves onward and upward at all times.

HIS STORY

Growing up, I never really knew anything about jazz as I was only around classical music. Both of my parents were university music professors, and the environment in which they raised me in was a nurturing one. They never forced any music upon me; I was just around it all the time. But when I met John Campbell, he told me that the bass was just a big violin, which I played at the time, and then said, "listen to this Ray Brown guy and copy what he did." I knew from then on that I had to play the bass. In addition to the love for the bass, I found with jazz that I had the freedom to let my influences come out when I play and compose. Because of this I narrowed my concentration on jazz so I could be a part of music that is personal and special to me. And it took me a while to realize this, but with jazz, when you solo, you're playing something that no one's ever played nor will somebody ever play again. Nobody can play a Richard Drexler solo except for me, and this personal expression is something I find very gratifying.

The purpose of all music is to quiet the mind thus making it susceptible to divine influence. Entertainment or dance music is fine, but I hope there would be a deeper spiritual level to it. I'd like to think that when I play I make the universe better. In whatever minuscule part I have, I want to create love and unity for people with whatever gift I'm blessed as well as whatever is good in my life. I believe in the transmissions of spiritual benefits and blessings through person-to-person contact, and this, I believe, is truly transported through music.

Most musicians I know are aware of the spiritual aspect of what we do. I know now that I can get to know people much better when I've played with them than when I've only had conversations with them. Who you are eventually comes out from the music somewhere, and just the fact that you're reaching inside to find something to create means that you're vulnerable to open yourself up. When you play jazz you have to think beyond what's in your mind. It's impossible to do this, so the music has to come from your heart and go beyond yourself. This music is clearly my mistress, and a jealous one at that, but I have no regrets. I'm just someone who followed a dream.

George Duke   {LIVING LEGEND}

KEYBOARDIST, VOCALIST, PRODUCER, COMPOSER

HOME BASE
www.georgeduke.com

GOT MUSIC?
Dukey Treats, George Duke, Heads Up Records, 2008

"Music, whether a pop song or purely instrumental, is the first wireless medium to reach people as a true analog and spiritual connection."

BACKGROUND AND SOUND

George Duke has been claiming his stake in the scene since the early seventies. Jean-Luc Ponty, Frank Zappa, and Nancy Wilson are only a small sample of the greats who have shared the stage with him. George has gleaned his voice from the giants and taken heed of what it means to share your music with the world as a way of expressing yourself. This Duke of all things jazz has claimed his own territory in every subgenre from fusion to the gritty home-cooked sound of the blues. These territorial rites of passage throughout jazz history have most certainly landed him at the throne of living heroes.

HIS STORY

The moment I went to see Duke Ellington I was totally amazed. As a four-year-old all I could see was that he was doing something with his fingers while playing the piano . . . that turned out to be conducting. It absolutely intrigued me, that and the fact that he spoke well and his name was Duke. I wasn't sure if he was a relative of mine, but his music spoke to me, and the people that were around were clapping and happy. I wanted to do that too.

Over time I realized that this experience was one of the things that shaped me forever. Music, whether a pop song or purely instrumental, is the first wireless medium to reach people as a true analog and spiritual connection. Therefore, musicians bear a great responsibility to bring their music to people. If you have a piece of art on the wall and no one sees it, then it doesn't mean anything. So whether music is classical, jazz, pop, or whatever, it has to be your way of communicating with others. If it doesn't communicate, then it doesn't fulfill its destiny. I'm not sure why some people don't bring it back to this level so others get into it. It's very possible to do this on a deep level and bring it back to where it belongs. People have connections to this music whether they realize it or not. Jazz is the story of our connections to Africa. It represents the soul of those who started it. If we're going to continue its beginnings, it has to remain honest and contain a spiritual nature and treated as though it's a gift from God.

But in order to treat it as so, you must find out who you are before you can really play. I had to learn how to let my guard down and be honest musically. I still play what I play even when the situation between mainstream jazz and smooth jazz arose from nowhere. A certain group of people began to take a position on what jazz should and shouldn't be.

But the divide really came when those groups of musicians from the seventies that began to play like Earl Klugh and David Sanborn (both of whom are deep musicians but just made this music a part of their arsenal). Next thing we know a new format came out of this time like a quiet storm. Some jazz guys were offended by what they did . . . others became bitter. It's been this way since then, especially since smooth jazz has become this funky and slightly elevated elevator music.

But not all of us are bitter, as we all know it's the real guys who put in the work. Who knows if it's going to change . . . we should keep in mind that the smooth jazz guys really are playing their hearts and being honest with their music. It's all they can play, and if this is an honest replication of what their intent is, then they've reached their goal. Why can't they stand on the same stage with "traditional" jazz musicians and have a larger built-in audience? There's nothing wrong with that. Your art shouldn't go beyond the heart as its journey and walk, in which everyone has their own timing. It's about going through that walk and discovering who you are on the way.

Kurt Ellenberger
PIANIST, COMPOSER, EDUCATOR

HOME BASE
www.kurtellenberger.com

GOT MUSIC?
The Name of the Wind, Ütaké,
Mindful Sounds Records, 2009

"Jazz in particular sinks or swims on its truthfulness."

BACKGROUND AND SOUND
ASCAP Award–winning composer and pianist Dr. Kurt Ellenberger has stretched his ink and keys across the jazz community in many, many ways. His roll call of peers with whom he has shared a stage with include Danny Gottlieb, Kenny Wheeler, and Benny Eckstine. His solo works have received praise from publications throughout the world, including the *New York Times* and *Jazz Education Journal.* As an educator he has introduced countless students to themselves through the music, and he is the author

of several articles regarding music theory and a book on jazz improvisation titled *Materials and Concepts in Jazz Improvisation* (Assayer Publications). His solo piano work has been featured on CBC radio as well as NPR. All of this is enough to keep anyone busy for a lifetime and places him in the upper echelon of musicians and educators in the business.

HIS STORY

Jazz reflects the performer's personality in a spectacular way, and we all have to face that when we look in the mirror. I'm constantly confronting imperfection and fears, which hopefully results in a more meaningful and truthful artistic expression. Am I playing tired old jazz "licks" and clichés? Am I trying to sound like someone else to please the crowd and get another gig? I can't stand anything that's fake or contrived, nor do I like boastful, self-centered personalities . . . and this business is rife with both. The performer has to explore their own relationship with the music including (especially) the flaws and shortcomings. This has to be raw, honest, and visceral, otherwise it doesn't compel me.

Jazz in particular sinks or swims on its truthfulness. I try to reflect this in my music by maintaining that core honesty in everything I do. But like most musicians, I've struggled with it—if you want to make money, you have to deliver what the bandleader and audience wants, which rarely aligns with the artist's own temperament or proclivities. Is it better to eke out a living playing or do something else where I can contribute, be productive, and earn a reasonable salary? Luckily I enjoy teaching and academic pursuits, so this was a good choice for me.

Making a living playing puts you in a position of constant compromise—that route got very tedious for me. You tend to focus on the things you're making money at, which makes it very easy to lose your artistic direction. In the end, you become what you do, so make sure that what you do is contributing to your development, because it will certainly influence it profoundly.

Kurt Elling
VOCALIST

HOME BASE
www.kurtelling.com

GOT MUSIC?
Night Moves, Kurt Elling, Concord
Records, 2007

"Our job is to express the hopes, fears, aspirations, and the thrill of being a human being."

BACKGROUND AND SOUND
Grammy and Jazz Journalist Award–winning vocalist Kurt Elling is the one of the most in-demand musicians in modern jazz. For more than twenty years, Elling has served as a major contributor of our time in the vein of jazz "vocalese," which is the art of writing and performing words over the improvised notes of other jazz soloists. Elling's voice is timeless and well applauded throughout the world.

His traditional quartet features collaborations with the great pianist and arranger Laurence Hobgood. In addition to his own works he has performed with notables Marian McPartland, Benny Golson, Dave Brubeck, Christian McBride, and many more. Elling's approach to each show refines the art of listening by giving a new light to each tune for the listeners to focus on. It is this hallmark trait that brings his audiences in year after year.

HIS STORY
The more things change, the more they stay the same. The way people communicate and the rapid growth of communication can drive and change a culture. It can certainly provide a lot of stress for people because the deadlines are moved up; everyone expects immediate answers and there's

no escape. Your phone is with you at all times . . . and these are all potential improvements but they're also potential endangerments. But there have always been challenges that fit specific time frames. Yet it's the musicians who have been on the front lines of creating a more humane environment. We're the ones who express the fears and concerns and the joys of the human family. This is true in just about every culture. I can't imagine that there's anything that's called a culture without music. If we take music out of the forefront, people tend to think the word "culture" means "high-class status" or "wealth." This isn't the case with music. Music can be high class, but it can be difficult to listen to, like jazz. Our job is to express the hopes, fears, aspirations, and thrill of being a human being. Musicians have to continue to look forward and continue to be sincere and honest in their own ambitions with the music. We're always going to express this. Musicians, specifically musicians who do not deal with lyrics, have, if any, more of a chance to express that which cannot be put into words. They have this opportunity to do so. The music is so much more pliable to the listener because there is that play on emotion. The song then can be interpreted as sad, but then that sadness can spread itself and fan out and take on so many different shades of sadness. For one person it will actually be sad, to another it could be melancholy, and to another it will be thoughtful, et cetera . . . that's the inexhaustible nature of one solo performance. To touch so many emotions with so many different reactions and reflections is a very profound gift to give people. This is why someone like a Wayne Shorter or a Keith Jarrett is such a profound musical experience. There's a flexibility and openness of what is possible to have as an emotional reaction that they bring to their music. What they're playing is so deep it's that much more universal.

In my own career, there have been quite a few things I've had to work through to get to this point. The most pertinent thing I or anybody else has to get through is their own ambitions. I didn't have any conservatory training; I just fell in love with the sound. I wasn't really plugged into a scene right away so I was going mostly from the records I'd heard. I also didn't grow up with people who listened to jazz. I had to discover and learn the process along the way, as well as the history of the sound. I also had my own hang-ups and prejudices to deal with. This probably continues to be the biggest thing I've had to overcome.

When I started I was so on fire to be a part of the scene. I've been given the great gift of musical vision of what I'm noted for. This seems to be a particularly challenging vision for a lot of people to come up with. There are so many people who want to sing jazz, but their vision is so derivative or undeveloped. It's almost as if there haven't been archetypes in the past for them to check out, which of course is ridiculous. We have an incredible wealth of historical cats who took care of business and charted the way. My heart goes out to these people because they have a love for the music and they have, maybe, a moderate gift or in some cases a very profound gift in the sound of their voice . . . but they don't know, necessarily, what to do with it. They don't know how to develop it, et cetera. This has been my greatest asset. I feel like the guy who understands what has come before. You can't just listen to records and enjoy them if you want to produce new music. You have to listen to the great records and you have to comprehend them in a hundred different ways. You have to know how to figure out technically how to reproduce them inasmuch as you can a sound that say, Frank Sinatra made . . . then you study how he stood on the stage, and then how he breathed, and then how did he count a tune off? You have to consider it all as philosophical. What was it about each of the great singers that made them great? If you can identify with it strongly, then you can adapt some of it to your own sound. You have to digest their information to such a degree that it becomes a part of you. Then you have to have these incredible discussions with yourself . . . and you have to do it when you're pretty young and while your brain is flexible and your sound is pliable and your ambition is great enough. You have to know why you're driven enough to *really* do this. This is true in so many ways for those who hope to become artists in one way or another. Each one of us is given a challenge and a gift, and from where we stand one of the things that defines a great artist is that the rest of us look like ants compared to that artist. But . . . from inside you have somebody with a great gift that's much more developed and experienced that has more work they have to do because of the insight you're given from the start.

Keith England
VOCALIST

HOME BASE
www.keithengland.com

GOT MUSIC?
Standards: New and Used, Keith England, Swing Set Music/ RCEG

"I need to deliver the song in my heart."

BACKGROUND AND SOUND

Keith England is living a life composed of many idioms within the music business. He was a successful rock vocalist with the Allman Brothers, but it wasn't until the face of jazz presented itself that he truly saw how he fit into the tangled equation of his passion. His style is savvy, cool, and connected. An ambiance is created around his endearing qualities that turn his sound into a timeless tune for the ears of jazz fans everywhere.

HIS STORY

My father was a jazz musician. He turned me onto Mel Tormé, Ella, et cetera. But Ella was the one who really influenced me, even in my rock singing. Although I had a successful career in the rock genre, I feel jazz is a different instrument altogether. It's like I've played a Stratocaster all these years, and jazz came along and handed me a cello. In a very real way, jazz is an opportunity that presented itself to me. I'm always looking to expand my horizons. I wasn't bored with rock by any means; I just had to find a way to realize the instrument I'd been given. It forced me to stretch my thinking, my physical and emotional awareness of myself, and there's no better way than doing this through jazz. I had to look for ways to develop my art as opposed to using it as a vehicle to deliver the sound and style. I've learned how to make the audience feel my song to the best of my ability. I've always been impressed with vocalists who can convey the sense that they meant every word they sing. Their songs are intricate and exquisite. I'll always try to put more of me into everything I sing. I've never allowed myself to be a phony because of this. Even though some people may say

I mean well when I sing, I'd like to think of it as me becoming the essence of the song. As a performer and artist you can't be artificial. My only choice though, is to hand the music over to everyone who's willing to listen and hope they like it. Everybody has to make a living and have a nice life. Before I can think of having that life, I need to deliver the song in my heart. To take that song and deliver it to everyone else's heart, that's what I'm going for.

Peter Erskine

{LIVING LEGEND}

DRUMMER, EDUCATOR, COMPOSER

HOME BASE
www.petererskine.com

GOT MUSIC?
Standards, Peter Erskine, Alan Pasqua, and Dave Carpenter, Fuzzy Music CDs, 2007

"One of the greatest things I've learned from music is what not to do, what not to play, and how not to fill up all of the space."

BACKGROUND AND SOUND

By the age of four, Grammy Award–winning drummer Peter Erskine was already marking time. Decades later he has been hailed as one of the greatest living drummers of our time. His career has spanned a veritable who's who list of the business, including Joni Mitchell, Weather Report, the Stan Kenton Orchestra, Maynard Ferguson, Chick Corea, Steely Dan, Michael Brecker, the London Symphony, the Berlin Philharmonic, and the Bob Mintzer Big Band, among others. His discography is hundreds of discs long, and he has recorded numerous instructional DVDs and written several books and articles on drumming technique, jazz, and education. His original compositions and film scores have graced television, stage, and even audiobook soundtracks. Peter was recently named as the drumming consultant to the Royal Academy of Music in London and currently acts as the director of drumset studies at the University of Southern California's Thornton School of Music. The magnitude of his impact on the world of rhythm and in jazz has yet to be fully realized, but he is truly going to be one who changes the course of modern jazz drumming forever.

HIS STORY

One of the greatest things I've learned from music is what not to do, what not to play, and how not to fill up all of the space. It's informed my life in more profound ways than I could have imagined. It's occupied my dreams, my thoughts, and every choice I've made as a human being. What I try to do as a drummer is to play compositionally. I'm communicating while trying to find the arc and horizon to the story. I hope that when people listen they'll hear this shape. Whether it's profoundly architectural or simple, there's a concrete sense of space I'm trying to translate my hopes into. A lot of the fun behind music is the unexpected discovery of notes. You can find little bits of heaven being created right in front of you, and when you're young it's things like these discoveries that form your musical personality, your grammar, your accent, and your identity.

In my first private lesson with Professor George Gaber, I was twelve and he sensed that I had a performance anxiety thing. He put a piece of music in front of me and said, "I want you to play this, but if you play any of it correctly I'm going to get up and walk over there with this timpani mallet and hit you." I managed to play every note wrong, upside down and every wrong way you could imagine. He said, "Okay, now go to the window and look outside . . . you see the clouds up in the sky? Is the sun still shining? Is the Earth still spinning? You played that piece as bad as it could have possibly been played. What happened? Nothing. Now let's begin." This was wise and showed, in simple terms, that doing what we do should be fun. Our country, as a whole, needs to wake back up and realize how important this is in our lives and our children's lives. Life and music are essentially fun, and we all need this. We can learn how to be a team player with music, and how a voice can be picked up from someone else and then handed off to the next person. We need these bits of music to call upon when we're happy or sad. If people knew about this music they could create little private soundtracks to their lives. What we don't need is to be plugged into an iPod all day long. This life is magical and rich enough by itself; we just need to invest in it.

Tia Fuller

SAXOPHONIST, COMPOSER, EDUCATOR

HOME BASE
www.tiafuller.com

GOT MUSIC?
Decisive Steps, Tia Fuller
Quartet, Mack Avenue
Records, 2010

"You must move through life and space and not fear what's ahead."

BACKGROUND AND SOUND

Throughout the past decade, Tia Fuller has become an inspiration and beacon to women in all genres of instrumental music. Not only does she act as a leader for her own quartet, but she also plays with notable talents such as Beyoncé and Sean Jones. Students of hers at the Stanford Jazz Workshop, Kansas State University, and University of Colorado Boulder jazz camps have witnessed and testified as to her ceaseless dedication and passion. Yet it is her faith in the music's ability to bring others together that speaks through her music. Her first solo albums, including *Healing Space* and *Pillar of Strength*, echo this positive attitude and further demonstrate her continuous growth as an artist. Her strengths lie in her soothing style. Tia's natural yet hardworking gift shines upon all who cross her path.

HER STORY

I come from a musical family with roots strongly rooted in jazz. My father is a great bass player and my mother, a vocalist. Between the two of them they exposed me to the music but didn't force it upon me. This was always of my own will even though I was encouraged to practice on a daily basis. Knowing there were so many great possibilities as a musician was encouraging too.

I knew I could teach, perform, produce and more from an early age. Of course I did other things throughout my life but music prevailed. By the time I was eighteen or nineteen I had set a good foundation for myself.

Through this career though, I've learned that playing this music is like being in a sandbox as a child. When you're there anything goes. You can create anything you want at any given time and still stay within the box. But even without the box it would still be beautiful. This art is really a selfless vessel for a spirit to flow through.

As musicians we have to recognize our purpose as we have a great responsibility and obligation to help others. We must be a light to them and heal them while at the same time inspiring them. This is not just for us, it's for humanity. I'm very emotionally attached to this music. My inspiration is all around me when I play; it's everything about life and what comes with it. And so far, I've been blessed with so many opportunities throughout this life. But it's a constant climb and I'm still going at it. It's sometimes hard for me to grasp that I'm working harder now on various aspects of my life than I ever have. I guess it's all about perspective. I have to see all the other opportunities in front of me and realize that this is what creates a fulfilling purpose. No, of course it's not what I thought it would be. I thought once I got to a certain point I'd be cool and have everything in place. This isn't necessarily so. I still think it's important though to have a crystallized vision of where you want to go. Then, it's up to you to take aggressive and decisive steps toward this vision on a daily basis. Most importantly, you must move through life and space and not fear what's ahead. This becomes harder the older we get. Our fears become magnified so you have to have faith in the steps you take and that vision you have for yourself.

Vincent Gardner

TROMBONIST, COMPOSER

HOME BASE
www.vincentgardner.com

GOT MUSIC?
Vin-Slidin', Vincent Gardner,
Steeplechase Records, 2008

"When you're playing, it's one moment in life you can be selfish, sterile, and absent all at once."

BACKGROUND AND SOUND

Vince Gardner is a young fireball on the scene today. His experiences include extensive touring with the Lincoln Center Jazz Orchestra, acting as a leader for his own group, and earning a degree from University of North Florida. Influences such as J.J. Johnson and Slide Hampton soar past his bell as he makes his own contribution the sound of modern jazz. This original yet embedded traditional voice brings him to the top of his game.

HIS STORY

J.J. Johnson hooked me early on. His technique and style were different than anyone I knew. I don't think there's anyone out there who played and articulated the way he did. I would sit there and figure out and copy him the best I could. For four to five years, I only listened to and played J.J. Johnson. But, it wasn't until after I graduated from high school that I got serious about jazz. At Florida A&M University, I surrounded myself with other students that were serious about jazz, even though I wasn't studying it formally. I played a lot of gigs, but wasn't really able to practice because I was in the marching band, which also gave me my scholarship. After I had enough of that, I went to the University of North Florida, where I was really able to practice and grow as a jazz musician. Once I got started though, I had to learn through trial and fire on gigs and I was told time after time that I sucked on almost everything. I had no idea what a true jazz "environment" was like in those early days of my career. But in jazz there's humanity in it without the expectations of reality. When you're playing, it's one moment in life that you can be selfish, sterile, and absent all at once.

This is what I think keeps people in music. It's that loss of reality while living in a moment. There's nothing contrived or construed about it. My goal as a player is not to play what my influences played, as it's only up to me to develop my style. I just hope that when you listen to me, you hear only honesty and kindness when I play. This is what makes me feel good as a player and a human being.

Melody Gardot
VOCALIST, COMPOSER, GUITARIST, PIANIST

HOME BASE
www.melodygardot.com

GOT MUSIC?
Worrisome Heart, Melody Gardot, Capitol Records, 2007

"If you truly know yourself enough to trust it, never ignore the feeling in your gut of what is your own personal best or what your instincts are telling you."

BACKGROUND AND SOUND

It is not about an influence or where she studied or even the middle of the road to fame she is traveling at this moment. It is about an indigenous tone. To say that Melody is brilliant would be an understatement. She has lived a lifetime in a moment and stored her experiences in a voice that carries a silent weight between its notes. You can hear this on her albums *Worrisome Heart* and *My One and Only Thrill*. Many have come to caress her lines as though they were woven into the clothes on their backs. Soothing mellow tones flow beneath her spell as Gardot surrounds us with beauty and the grace of her heartfelt words.

HER STORY

It would be pretty selfish of me to tell people that the reason I make music is so that they'll get me. It's not about understanding who I am. Actually, I don't know if anyone's ever really going to understand me. I certainly wouldn't try to do it with my music. I think about the reasons I make any noise at all, and my motivation to speak versus why I sing and write aren't that different. The striking thing is, a lot of the time, I don't want to say anything and the music isn't saying much either. I don't use a lot of lyrics.

I think there's a lot to be learned by quiet in general, a lot to be learned by taking moments of pause. If I really had to describe myself, I'd say I'm simplistic with a sense of modesty. There's no need for exhibitionism. There's such beauty in playing one note. You don't need a whole lot to realize who you are. Singing jazz and playing it, it's simple, not overthought. Being happy, not contriving anything from it, even the lyrics, that's where I come from. I tap into a place within myself that's comfortable enough to do this. It's harder for people to play less than it is for them to play more. This applies to people who really know themselves. If you truly know yourself enough to trust it, never ignore the feeling in your gut of what is your own personal best or what your instincts are telling you. This is almost like saying believe in yourself, but it's not. It's more than that. It's taking the time to break down after your performance and figure out what it is that you're doing as a musician and what you're striving for.

My bassist always says you're only as good as your worst day. We do a lot of gigs where we think, wow man, that isn't it! We're terrible. We're sitting there, beating each other up and we're so inside, hearing what we're doing, knowing what we're capable of. This is when you must know yourself to trust yourself to do your own personal best and continue to reach for it. Raising that bar everyday. It's then when you know what is great to you may not be what others are doing. It's important, in any case, to hold on to your flame and know your standards and never let them drop.

Tyler Gilmore
COMPOSER, PRODUCER

HOME BASE
www.tylergilmoremusic.com

GOT MUSIC?
Ninth and Lincoln, Ninth and Lincoln Jazz Orchestra, Dazzle Records, 2008

"You have to understand your vision in order to build the overall character of a piece."

BACKGROUND AND SOUND

Composer Tyler Gilmore is actively pursuing a vision most others in this art neglect. His grounding in hard work and keen foresight is most often seen in veterans of the art. He is the recipient of the 2010 ASCAP Young Jazz Composers Award, the ASCAP/Columbia College 2009 Commission in honor of Hank Jones and the 2008 ASCAP Young Jazz Composer's award. His influences, including Maria Schneider, Bill Frisell, and John Hollenbeck, often speak through his works with the vocabulary of experts and the boundless

energy of youth. With a focus in jazz that's steadfast and memorable, his works will undoubtedly transcend the generations to come.

HIS STORY

I grew up in Riverton, Wyoming, drawing comic book characters. I lived in a flat, rural space that was quiet. It left me with a lot of thinking time. Drawing, for me, held structure, shape, and a visual interest, but music always had a fourth dimension and immediacy of emotion that drawing didn't have. Naturally, I turned toward the music and started playing jazz in class in ninth grade. I remember the feeling of performing and the excitement it held. Jazz evolves with each performance, and I take it very seriously.

I've been very career focused since then. Trying to make a work connect in an overall way is difficult. Sometimes I get a vision of a piece and it inspires me. Creativity can spark anywhere, anytime. This happens most easily when my mind/body connection is at its most healthy. If you can see this vision, get inspired and create it. You have to understand your vision in order to build the overall character of the piece. What I imagine in my head isn't quite there yet, but I'm influenced by it. I don't want to stay here. Really I just want to grow and be able to paint the picture of what I see. I have to trust myself to trust my intuition. I've too often followed the beaten path when it didn't feel right only to later go in a direction I'd originally wanted to go. Music is just an exploration of the psyche in this way. I think sound, like our sense of smell, has a naturally direct link to our brain's basic system. It has the potential to affect us in ways no other art form can. With that in mind, I try to find structures and textures that more honestly communicate my experience. I'd like to see jazz dominated by people who are artistically honest, but the only way to be honest is to create music for him- or herself. It's scary to trust oneself in this way, but it will always be rewarded.

Will Goble
BASSIST

HOME BASE
www.willgoble.com

"For me, it's about acknowledging that feeling of rhythm."

BACKGROUND AND SOUND

With a love for music that is unplugged with infectious groove, Will Goble is a new cat on the prowl. His mentors and influences are the best. Currently a bassist for Marcus Roberts, Marcus Printup, and Jason Marsalis, he has had the opportunity to study in the school of hard bop and swing. This has fueled his start in the business and should lead to a long and healthy career.

HIS STORY

Unlike most players, I started fairly late. When you're sixteen, you're hardheaded. I think because of this, I didn't spend a lot of my time cerebrally analyzing every element. My main focus was how well I was locking up with the rest of the group. I had to frequently ask myself, how does this feel? If it's not comfortable, then how are other musicians going to respond? For me, it's about acknowledging that feeling of rhythm. This can exist in a ballad or groove in a way that gets down to the human element of the art. Even if you get someone who doesn't know jazz to listen to John Coltrane, they can hear his soul coming through his solos because of the rhythmic feeling. I'm lucky because the mentors I've had, like Marcus Roberts and Jason Marsalis, have taught me how to think of rhythm first without sacrificing foundation. Because of this, I'm still able to acknowledge myself in my playing.

Wayne Goins

GUITARIST, EDUCATOR, COMPOSER

HOME BASE
www.waynegoins.com

GOT MUSIC?
Standard Fare, Wayne Goins, Little
Apple Records, 2005

"If people took the time to help you, you have to finish that line."

BACKGROUND AND SOUND

Wayne Goins is one of the hidden gems of modern and traditional jazz. Although he stands on his own as a superb guitarist, he is more known for his roles as an avid supporter and educator. For more than two decades he has showed students of all levels that jazz is more than just notes on a page . . . it is an art based around the feeling you create when you perform. Shaping lives through his compassion and spirit, he continues his legacy today as the Director of Jazz Studies at Kansas State University.

HIS STORY

I didn't start out playing jazz. I was just a blues guitarist living on the south side of Chicago. When I was a teenager, like most, I got into the heavy rock of the seventies, like Led Zeppelin and Aerosmith. I don't know exactly when it was that I first heard big band music, but I know it was Ellington. I must have stumbled across one of his albums or something. I loved it and wanted to be a part of that so bad. Being in a combo or small group was cool, but when I finally got to play in a big band it made me feel like I was a part of something bigger than myself. I was in a big machine that cranked out a powerful sound, and I knew I had to be a part of the engine that created that machine . . . the power a big band has is like nothing else in this world. By the time I graduated high school, I was completely immersed in the music, and I was playing as much as I could. I know musicians say this all the time, but since then I cannot imagine what my life would be if I weren't a musician. I think I would just die.

I've always known that this was a dual-sided coin. I wasn't just a guitar player. I was also meant to teach. I've been around in a classroom in one capacity or other since I was in kindergarten. The classroom is my oxygen, my natural environment, and my water. To have this ability to play, knowledge of the music, and the insight into what makes music work for me is a gift. If I can't help somebody else see that light, then I'm not a full person. I'm just trying to catch and infect others with this love and passion so they can pass it right on down the line. If people took the time to help you, you have to finish that line. Honestly, I think jazz musicians are the inventors of the pay-it-forward concept. This explains the whole history of jazz. We're just paying forward our debts for the ones that came before us just as they did. They worked at this and worked hard for their careers. It was nothing for them to spend seven to ten hours in a shed. Trying to get students now to adopt not only this work ethic but the pay-it-forward ethic of the old school cats has been the hardest thing I've done. They just don't understand that if you commit to being a jazz musician you have to completely and fully immerse yourself in the tradition. This is a life decision. You have to have that singular mind. If you don't understand how serious something is or the significance of someone's history how could you possibly respect it? This younger generation has so many distractions they don't commit to one particular thing. Maybe it's asking too much these days . . . but this is a fight I have to fight. If you're totally giving into their mentality, something, maybe even jazz, will be lost forever. As a matter of fact, we're watching it vanish right in front of our eyes. I'm not willing to accept the fact that we have to settle for this less focused, less disciplined, and less concentrated versions of our students or ourselves. Needless to say I'm hard on my students, or at least some of them. If they want what I have, this love and passion, they've got to walk the walk I've walked. You've got to walk through jazz. You can't go around it and still live the life.

Jazz is this important to me. It's introduced me to everybody that's ever been important to me. It's taken me everywhere in the world that I'd ever wanted to go. It's allowed me access to the most important, powerful, and loving people. It's been all I've ever wanted to do. I'm on a mission, a role that's already been laid out to show everyone I know that this music is everything to me because it is my purpose for life.

Aaron Goldberg

PIANIST, COMPOSER

HOME BASE
www.aarongoldberg.com

GOT MUSIC?
Worlds, Aaron Goldberg,
Sunnyside Records, 2006

*"It's easy to get caught up in life's frustrations . . . ambitions not fulfilled,
dreams unlived . . . but any kind of great music can help you experience and
embrace the moment."*

BACKGROUND AND SOUND

Turning the beat around on his classical training, Aaron Goldberg has risen
to the top as one of the very best young players today. His skill is established
and his passion is obvious. A graduate of the New School, Goldberg
regularly gigs throughout Boston and New York. His compositions speak
with a lyrical sense of style grounded in harmonic wit. Lucky for the jazz
community, Goldberg is a constant voice whether he is performing as a
leader or as a sideman.

HIS STORY

There was a period of time in my childhood when I was losing interest
in the piano, and the reason had nothing to do with the piano. The music
that was in front of me wasn't sufficiently stimulating. I was unmotivated
to practice. But I didn't give up. I kept searching for music that moved me.
Like many people, I didn't grow up in a household that embraced jazz, and
I had to encounter it in some other way or by chance.

As a musician your first encounter with jazz may not be the one that
moves you, but you must continue to listen, practice, and play. There's so
much out there that will or could move you. But you must keep searching
for that feeling. The piano can communicate the full range of human
emotions. But at the end of the day I would like my listeners to walk
away with a sense that life itself is beautiful. We're all so mind-bogglingly
fortunate to be here in the first place. I want to be able to give my audience
some kind of energy and strength along with motivation to search and to
enjoy their time here.

It's easy to get caught up in life's frustrations . . . ambitions not fulfilled, dreams unlived . . . but any kind of great music can help you experience and embrace the moment. As improvising musicians we have a skill set that allows us to take people on a journey. Every moment offers something new, and really it's pretty hard to get depressed when you realize this. There's hope and a kind of life affirmation within. As introspective and introverted as jazz music can sometimes seem, especially to those unfamiliar with the language, its purpose is always simple: the communication of love, hope, and gratitude. You don't have to have an intellectual understanding of it in order to feel waves or sparks of emotion just let it sweep you up. Try to appreciate it and learn from it. Don't be afraid of it's newness or its complexity, and just allow yourself to feel whatever it is you'll feel, and that's when you'll fall in love with this music.

Dennis González

TRUMPETER, GUITARIST, COMPOSER, EDUCATOR, VISUAL ARTIST, POET, PRODUCER

HOME BASE
www.dennisgonzalez.com

GOT MUSIC?
The Gift of Discernment, Dennis González Jnaana Septet, NotTwo Records, 2008

"People accept my imperfections because they are imperfect."

BACKGROUND AND SOUND
Dennis González has created visual, literary, and musical art around Texas and the lower Midwest for the last few decades. The jazz trio he leads with his sons, Yells at Eels, has created music that has become the center of attention for audiences in Texas throughout the last decade. From world to reggae, to Latin to hard bop, his range of influences is expansive. For the past twenty-five years he has performed throughout the world with luminaries such as Max Roach, Roy Hargrove, Cecil Taylor, Reggie Workman, and Sabir Mateen. In addition to everything

else, he has successfully produced radio shows on local affiliates of NPR, college stations, and others stations that reach as far as Slovenia. Whereas most artists who delve into this range of work would be mediocre at best, Dennis excels on all planes, and his work boasts something for everyone, regardless of their taste in the arts.

HIS STORY

There are so many things jazz has taught me . . . from living in the realm of the Spirit to transcending the tribulations of life as a human being, from connecting with my audiences to learning how beautiful we all are in our differences, the way sound and tone affect us, the abstract and concrete ways in which music moves us.

When I first started playing, my music was very "out," hard for the average audience to understand. I truly believed that this "superior" form of music, esoteric as it is, should be understood by all. My place in music is to share with people, to learn as others have taught me and listen. It's humbling to know that listeners want to hear what I have to offer and that they would make the time and have the inclination to come out and hear me play and to buy my recordings. So I simplified and solidified my musical vocabulary, made it understandable.

Now, I'm relearning to connect in a very personal way with my audience. When I started losing my hearing, I would play the concert and retreat to my corner, as I was embarrassed that I couldn't understand what people, smiling and happy, would tell me. But I missed the spiritual and personal connection and decided to seek help with my hearing loss. It's made all the difference. People accept my imperfections because they are imperfect, and that is one of the intriguing things about us as humans . . . how we choose to see our mistakes.

I want people to hear themselves in my music so I may provide a soundtrack for their lives and be a meeting place where that person and I connect and communicate, where the energy of that life force crosses over into me, and my energy into him or her. I want music to be a dream, but a waking, living, lucid dream they can use to reshape their spirits into a positive, uplifting experience. I would love for them to see themselves as I see them from the bandstand, if it's a live experience—breathing, living beings full of life and beauty. If they are listening on a recording, I would love for them to take away with them some melody or rhythm that, as they walk through their day, they can hum or dance or write or work or play with an enhanced feeling of light and love and sweetness.

Brad Goode
TRUMPETER, EDUCATOR, COMPOSER, ARRANGER

HOME BASE
www.bradgoode.com

GOT MUSIC?
Hypnotic Suggestion, Brad Goode,
Delmark, 2006

"I enjoy the challenge and thrill of working in many different jazz areas."

BACKGROUND AND SOUND
Brad Goode began at the age of four with the violin, which eventually led to the cornet at the age of ten. He earned his stripes in a very strong Chicago scene during the 1980s and 1990s. His main influences, including Von Freeman, Ira Sullivan, and Eddie Harris, have raised him to the level of a roaring fire behind the horn. Transfusing his lineage with a new standard of spunk, his diverse experiences and genres bring a bounty of worth to the jazz table. He holds a master's degree in string bass, works locally as a drummer, and plays with symphony orchestras on the trumpet, in addition to his usual gig as a jazz trumpeter. But there is a part of him that needs no definition—it is just in his blood. An incredible musician wearing all hats, he deserves a place in a new lineage of artists.

HIS STORY
I'm not particularly interested in focusing on any one style. I enjoy the challenge and thrill of working in many different jazz areas. My original music is forward looking, perhaps even experimental. I'd like to think

I have my own approach to phrasing, melody, et cetera that's not necessarily always bound by jazz tradition. The individualism in the playing of Von Freeman, Ira Sullivan, and Eddie Harris has inspired me. These artists reached for mastery in their respective approaches. Their sounds were the primary impressions going into my ears during my formative years. They were the ones setting the expectations that I had to reach through my own playing. At first, being on the stand with them was intimidating as hell, then later, inspiring. As I got older I realized I had become a person who could "hang" and carry on musical dialogues with them. They're still my favorite musicians, and the ways in which I learned from them are models for my own teaching.

I like to think of myself as a player first, teacher second. I teach and talk with students from a performer's perspective, hoping to prepare them for the varied challenges of a music career. I worry though, about the opportunities in their future. Many musicians have become too self-indulgent, and their audience is going to get smaller because of this. Tomorrow's musicians are going to have a difficult time finding venues. We can't blame anyone but ourselves as educators. We teach style and harmony, often overlooking the real substance of jazz: communication, development, groove, and creativity. Everyone's a little too concerned with sounding hip rather than reaching and moving the audience. Musicians forget that that's really important. As educators we must be wary not to kill the music we cherish. I try to present my students with a multitude of philosophies. Sometimes they may appear contradictory, but I want them to explore and understand the full spectrum. Jazz cannot be taught objectively, as if it was one clearly defined type of music. It appears in so many variations, so many different philosophies, that one can't really define or explain it simply to anybody. I value being well rounded and flexible. It's important to not get stuck in one version of jazz, whatever it may be.

I believe the hope for jazz lies in rebuilding regional scenes and in developing regional audiences. So many musicians feel that they have to leave for New York as soon as they can play. I understand the draw, the proving-ground idea, and the inspiration of being among so many great artists. There used to be more pride in one's own scene, and more excellent people staying home. If more great players would focus on revitalizing their own local scenes, I believe jazz could enjoy a grassroots revival of sorts.

Gordon Goodwin

COMPOSER, SAXOPHONIST

HOME BASE
www.gordongoodwin.com

GOT MUSIC?
Act Your Age, Gordon Goodwin's
Big Phat Band, Immergent, 2008

"It's more about the journey, one that takes a lifetime to finish."

BACKGROUND AND SOUND

Grammy and Emmy Award–winning Gordon Goodwin's signature style in big band compositions and commercial works has been embedded into modern jazz history for more than three decades. Prolific and in tune with the time, he has weathered trends because of his unique and clever approach. Students from around the world have studied his methods and his works in an attempt to hone their own craft. His big band, Gordon Goodwin's Big Phat Band, is based out of Los Angeles and has toured the world extensively. The top call LA studio professionals in this powerhouse group continue to tear down walls time and again. As one of the few remaining touring and successful bands in this country, he has created a heritage that will follow future generations with its own distinct, toe-tapping soundtrack.

HIS STORY

At one point in my career I woke up and realized there was a little more road behind me than there was ahead of me, which is why I decided to put the Big Phat Band together and document big band music as I heard it. That decision has brought balance to my life, and I am fortunate to be able to make this music with the great musicians in this band. My life is pretty jam-packed, and often I have to balance writing music for the Big Phat Band with writing music for money, or spending time with my wife and kids. So I learned to be disciplined when it comes to writing music. My inspiration comes less from nature, or things like that, but more from listening to other people's music. That usually primes the pump, and from there I just try to write music that sounds good to me, simple as that.

And whatever my accomplishments so far, I don't think I've really arrived anywhere—it's more about the journey, one that takes a lifetime to finish. Without discounting who I am, I think it's a good thing that jazz is a fluid music. At any moment the point of view can change. We're all still growing, playing the best music we can with the best of intentions. You learn to be accepting of the path that you choose.

I see how jazz is struggling in the marketplace now and it's upsetting and frustrating. But it is having difficulties from within as well. Petty fighting and jealousies take place, and there seems to be a feeling that if one given artist has some success, that means there is less chance for another artist to have success. We need to get over it already and work together to keep this music alive. Why waste energy fighting amongst ourselves? In the end, I have a great life. I'm one of the lucky ones that gets up everyday and does what he loves. And that has truly kept me young.

Wycliffe Gordon
TROMBONIST, VOCALIST, COMPOSER, ARRANGER

HOME BASE
www.wycliffegordon.com

GOT MUSIC?
Welcome to Georgia Town,
Wycliffe Gordon,
Bluesbag Records, 2010

"The most powerful thing about music is how it brings people together, and uplifting someone, especially those you love, goes beyond words and music."

BACKGROUND AND SOUND
Sprouting from the red clay of Georgia's soil, award-winning trombonist Wycliffe Gordon is a true master of his craft. His influences come from the greats, but his gospel and funk background heavily sways him in

his original works. Avenues such as a new soundtrack for the 1925 silent film *Body and Soul* and commissions from the Lincoln Center Jazz Orchestra and PBS have swept listeners off their feet around the world and through almost every avenue of media. He has toured extensively as a member of the Wynton Marsalis Septet and with his own group. Whether it is a solo with his group, a composition, or his full-bodied vocals, or changing the hearts and minds of the future generations through clinics and workshops, Wycliffe has found a voice that provides a powerful and divine contribution to the jazz history.

HIS STORY

I was raised in Waynesboro, Georgia. As we all know, it's not necessarily a mecca for live music. I heard music in church and on the radio. My father played classical piano. It wasn't until we moved to Augusta that I heard my first jazz recordings. I believe it was an anthology of jazz that went from the early slave chants all the way to Dizzy. But of all the music I listened to off of that recording, Louis Armstrong was the one that I was influenced by the most. I listened to him again and again. By the time I turned thirteen, I was listening to almost entirely acoustical music, and I picked up the riffs, breaks, and the call and response I had heard and could relate to from the music at the church I attended. I could hear my pastor calling out to the congregation and the riffs sung in the background in what these musicians were doing. At the time, I didn't know these were the same devices used in jazz, but I did know I liked it. I had no clue what would come of this.

Throughout my career I've remembered what my mom taught me. She always said that nothing in life worth having comes easy. But . . . through persistence and practice you can accomplish anything. I've been creative in music and creative in every thing I do, and even though I'm one to find out things the hard way, the experiences I've had and everything that's happened, happened the way it should happen.

Recently I worked on a project called *Welcome to Georgia Town*. Sometimes you go to a place where people say "welcome" and then show you around. I wanted to show people through this music the places I've been around and let them experience it and then say "welcome." Each song I wrote in this deals with a specific period of my life. But in the end it must be something good and entertaining for those involved. This piece began a long time ago, and I'm blessed to play with those on this recording. When I realize how long we've all been together and how many times we've played on each other's recordings, it's amazing. We have a kind of bond. It's not often that players get the chance to be leaders with great people like these guys, but when you do you feel as though what you make is something that sums up your life's work. The most powerful thing about music is how it brings people together, and uplifting someone, especially those you love, goes beyond words and music. That's what God has given me the gift for and the opportunity to do. Even lifting the person you're sharing the stand with to that next level is what I'm about. If I can convey the message that I want you to feel good, then I feel as though we're in this together, and that's the best feeling in the world.

Barry Greene

GUITARIST, COMPOSER, EDUCATOR

HOME BASE
www.barrygreene.com

GOT MUSIC?
Sojourner, Barry Greene,
Independent Label, 1998

"Jazz is the ultimate expression of freedom."

BACKGROUND AND SOUND

Barry Greene thrives in a space most would consider exhausting. A constant voice in education, composition, and performance, his work is prolific. He has produced numerous educational method books through Mel Bay, and he is an avid blogger and offers instructional videos as well. Barry is also the jazz guitar professor in the Jazz Studies Department at the University of North Florida. As a musician, he pretty much owns the scene in northern, central, and western Florida and plays regularly with Chuck Owen and the Jazz Surge as well as with saxophonist Jack Wilkins. As the leader of his own group, which features Kevin Bales and Danny Gottleib, he has produced four solo albums that have received critical acclaim through *Just Jazz Guitar* magazine and AllAboutJazz.com. Barry's command of the guitar and consistent, attentive teaching methods place him among the very best players in the southeastern United States.

HIS STORY

I grew up in the seventies and was a rock guy until I heard George Benson. He got me fired up about jazz guitar. This wasn't until I was halfway through high school. I knew way back that I wanted to be a musician, and it wasn't until my mother left me at Berklee and I was on my own for the first time, really feeling alone for the first time, that I remember an instant doubting of my decision. I had to ask myself, do I have the wherewithal determination to do this? But there was never a thought of going back. Branford was there, Steve Vai was there, almost the entire Tonight Show Band. I'd hear musicians do something I couldn't do, rock players would play at such a high level, and I couldn't do it. This is when I became determined to do it myself. It was a challenge at first, but the love for the music came soon enough. I was dedicated to a fault. I was so determined, I sacrificed a lot of social things. For someone like me, who enjoys the solitary and self-exploratory aspect, it was okay. The end result was something I'm very happy with.

All of us in the creative world are constantly working to improve and better ourselves. I think jazz musicians are often looked upon as being selfish, trying always to be cool. If you think we don't care what the audience thinks or that we're aloof, you're misinterpreting who we are. I'm very privileged to do what I do. It gives me joy when it's happening, and it's a way to deal with things when they're not so good; it gives a whole positive feeling about life in general. It's not an escape but something I'll always have and maintain. I fashion my life on this. Jazz is the ultimate expression of freedom, and I can't think of any other avenue where you can express yourself so freely and have a constant support and dialog among a group. This is the most wonderful thing on Earth, and it can leave you buzzing for days afterward to have that total freedom. I'm going to continue to ride this wave of good fortune, as my desire hasn't diminished at all. This is a gift.

John Gunther

SAXOPHONIST, WOODWINDIST, COMPOSER, EDUCATOR

HOME BASE
www.johngunthermusic.com

GOT MUSIC?
I Can Be There, Convergence,
Capri, 2008

"Music is a language and wavelength on which everyone can get together on a basic human level, and this is when wonderful, mysterious things happen."

BACKGROUND AND SOUND

Saxophonist and woodwind master John Gunther has handed over a diverse wealth of sound into the jazz community. As a composer, he pulls his works from a diverse and plentiful well of voices from around the world. His compositions have harvested commissions and grants from the National Endowment for the Arts and the Meet the Composer Foundation and have been featured regularly throughout all avenues of media, including animation features, film, and radio, and with his own group. His ability to regularly pull these influences together as a player yields a fiery energy behind each solo. He passes on this flame to his students at the University of Colorado, Boulder, where they can thrive upon his experience and knowledge. John is building a community of listeners, students, and peers who bring positive energy into the scene around him.

HIS STORY

I had the opportunity to improvise when I started playing in the third grade. A group of teachers started an afterschool program, and one of the things they did was teach us the blues scale. After giving us the notes, they told us to stand up and play. When you don't have the inhibitions and don't know any better, you just do it. You learn by ear, and that's a powerful way to learn. Getting an early start on improvisation changed me. There's so much crap in the airwaves now; kids miss out on this if it's not around them. Making music is a powerful thing. When I was younger I thought I needed fame and fortune, but as I grow older I see how teaching and the path I've chosen is a positive thing. I make my living through this.

Since I had exposure then, it just feels natural to me to be able to improvise. It's something everyone can do, and it doesn't have to be a big deal, nor does it have to have a lot of rules or preconceptions. It's perfectly healthy to just dive in and start without worrying about making mistakes.

There was a time I was living in New York and making my living as a musician. I wasn't having much fun at all. I got a call one day from a friend who had a preschool. They needed a music therapist for their kids. I started working there and suddenly I was singing and dancing, and it renewed my experience with music. I was making music again for music's sake. This inherent power and its ability to bring people together drew me back to it. I guess I still want the fame and to play with musicians around the world, but I realize it's now about being the best I can be.

The opportunity to perform is something I consider an obligation and responsibility to do my best at. I ask, how can I serve my community and those I teach? I don't just play the tenor sax. The spirit of music informs this hybrid music into what you want it to be. It's one of openness, creativity, and education that come down to one being mindful of relationships with people. Music is a language and wavelength on which everyone can get together on a basic human level, and this is when wonderful, mysterious things happen. I still find that mystery in it. Musicians have and are fathers, sons, mothers, daughters, et cetera. We're all those things that go on in lives that make us who we are. All aspects become a part of who you are and a part of your music, no matter what you do. Music is just a vehicle for exploring ins and outs and dealing with insecurities, fear, and egos. It's very deep and important, a place where people can bond and connect.

Janek Gwizdala
BASSIST, COMPOSER

HOME BASE
www.janekgwizdala.com

GOT MUSIC?
Live at the 55 Bar, Janek Gwizdala, Gwizmon Records, 2008

"If you truly believe where you're going, you'll have a staying power."

BACKGROUND AND SOUND

When electric bassist Janek Gwizdala took his leap over the pond from the UK to the US, the jazz community opened their arms and welcomed him into his new home. Janek has played, produced, and recorded with an entourage of greats, including Pat Metheny, Mike Stern, Danny Gottleib, Arturo Sandoval, and more. His secret? From keen observation, it seems to lie in his vigorous search for ways to become a better artist today than he was yesterday. Savvy in his dealings within the industry, Janek has surrounded himself with like-minded greats in order to get to the next best thing. As for the music he creates, it *is* the next best thing. He uses of some of the very best horn players and rhythm makers, and he is able to write original music that funks and rocks the fusion world into a modern jazz conglomerate. Janek has become a need within the industry instead of a want within all of his endeavors.

HIS STORY

Music is what led me to move to America. I felt I couldn't get as broad a musical or human experience through the music in the UK or London. When you move to the States as a musician you see things through a different light. Until someone sees what goes on behind the scene or what you do on tour, there's a certain myth of what a musician does. People perceive us as being and doing certain things. But until I began working in the States and started out on the road and experienced these things for myself, I thought these myths were true. I thought, "Wow! I'm going to be a musician and see all these things . . .", then I saw the back of a plane seat in front of me instead . . . this gave me a reality check. No matter what you do, whether you're a musician that has this perceived glamour or whether you write code as a computer programmer, you see a lot of very similar things all the time. There's definitely some sort of routine to every job. But the thing that keeps it interesting and fun with music is the storytelling—not just the musical stories that are told when you perform, but the camaraderie and friendship that's formed between people you spend your time with. It's an endless stream of stories, joke telling, and human contact and communication with a really close family.

The more time I spend promoting my music and working with this family and peer group around me who are of a similar mind-set, the more successful I am. When you're in this family you have to count on each other and create a scene everyone can work in. This helps us stay together and work better. But there are going to be problems. Sometimes you just have to stay the course and go through adversity to get to where you're going. If you truly believe where you're going, you'll have a staying power. History shows that everyone who's pushed through or been persistent has become successful. I just have to remember to give myself and those around me a lifetime schedule so that we can fill our calendars for the next thirty years with the things we aspire to do.

Tom Harrell

{LIVING LEGEND}

TRUMPETER, COMPOSER

HOME BASE
http://home.earthlink.net/~
tomharrell

GOT MUSIC?
Wise Children, Tom Harrell, BMG
Music, 2003

"[Music is] my focus . . . It becomes what I should be saying."

BACKGROUND AND SOUND

Countless articles and interviews in all forms of media have been done in an effort to find the secret to the absolute command behind Tom Harrell and his music. Despite this, the story is still untold, and he remains a revered soul throughout the past and present generations of jazz, everyone from Horace Silver to Phil Woods, Carlos Santana, Dizzy Gillespie, Cold Blood, Bill Evans, Vince Guaraldi and so on, along with the catalog of those who continue to envelop and perform his compositions. His reach stretches far beyond the jazz idiom. He has created a carpeted sound of his own that is rich to the touch and satiating to the senses. There is warmth there—whether it is your first or hundredth time listening, the aural landscape coming through his sound portraits is organic in its wholeness—a perfected core resonating pure nature.

HIS STORY

My main influence in composition would have to be Ellington. He, in a sense, created the idiom. When I started composing I had no idea about standard form, and the one thing I really gravitated toward was Ellington's use of texture. He related his textures to dance music, African rhythms, the blues, and European classical traditions, creating an entire tonal spectrum associated with physical movement. The beautiful thing is, there's still something that comes from Africa, Europe, Ireland, et cetera today in this music, and even more that's present from this in media music with this groove. There's swing and the phenomena of the hip-hop era, and Latin music, too. It's something that's always around.

Music that's soothing is where I try to create a feeling of peace for the listeners and within myself. There's a stream of melody that flows. This makes it seem as though everywhere is reachable through music. The expression and experience of music itself is mostly visual for me. It's my focus. The sound and absorption of sound is what I react to within myself. It becomes what I should be saying.

As a trumpet player my main influence was Louis Armstrong. His sound had this clarity I've always been attracted to. With Louis you could hear how he moved through his lineage and history with music. It's the same way with Miles and Dizzy, Clifford and Fats, Hubbard and Shaw. I'd like to think I retain this procession when I play and try to constantly project a glowing sound with added rhythmic aspects to the sound, using Dizzy as my influence. He encouraged my writing at a time when I was unsure about it; I was very lucky to have played with him. He was a rhythmic and harmonic genius and very kind to me. To this day, I still work on writing, piano, and playing endlessly, trying to think of something new I could contribute to music like Dizzy and Parker. Charlie Parker seems to be the most amazing musician I can listen to as the implications of what he did is very modern.

This place where the work and art leads you to is where a loneliness we all have to make do with exists. The boundary you have to go through with yourself and then your inner self is there too. Sometimes it's not as much fun, but there are rewards. I always say, to thine own self be true. When you do what you really want to do and believe in yourself, then you must be prepared to work and take criticism.

Ghandi, one of my role models, outlined the qualities of renunciation of worldly pleasure and desire. He says if you don't see the fruit of your action, you're then prepared to handle the criticism that comes with being passionate about your work. If you're not worried about the result, you'll always seek the right actions. I can respect people who are passionate about their beliefs. I am. Artists have a lot of power, and artists have to take responsibility and be faithful to their art. Do not harm anyone with it, and that's not always easy to do. I've spent so much time by myself because of my writing that I'm a little reticent and cognizant of my time. It becomes what I should be saying. Yet if I can find something I enjoy in my music, then hopefully other people do too. At the end of the concert it's nice to see smiling faces, and it gives me the feeling that they too found something positive and creative in what I've done.

Allan Harris

VOCALIST, GUITARIST, COMPOSER, EDUCATOR, ACTOR

HOME BASE
www.allanharris.com

GOT MUSIC?
Long Live the King, Allan Harris,
Love Productions Records, 2007

"Too many of us spend our time running away from ourselves rather than embracing who we are."

BACKGROUND AND SOUND

Award-winning vocalist Allan Harris is considered to be one of the most outstanding male vocalists alive today. Throughout his career he has shown the jazz world that it is possible to embody all of the original elements of jazz into a modern voice. Legends throughout the business, including Stevie Wonder, Vince Gill, and Wynton Marsalis, have sung his praises and invited him to share the stage. Chamber Music America bestowed one of their sought-after residency grants to Allan for the work he completed on his musical, *Cross That River*. Allan has also been featured on programming such as the Kennedy Center's Distance Learning Program, NPR's *All Things Considered*, and the Aspen Writers' Foundation Lyrically Speaking series. Throughout every aspect of the industry the one resonating theme that Allan consistently presents is a unfathomable respect love for life and his art.

HIS STORY

We shouldn't worry too much about pleasing the audience. They're not looking to be pleased . . . they're looking to be moved. Every night I make people smile. This is a wonderful job. I perform for audiences every night and they just want to feel loved like the rest of us. I'm glad that I'm able to unleash this feeling upon them. The reciprocated smiles and love is unbelievable when you do this. It's the last thing I see before I go to bed and one of the things I look forward to every day before I play. I just want them to enjoy what I'm trying to say and give them a picture of who I am as a human being long before I start to sing. When you interrupt their enjoyment by trying to be too animated or something you're not, it breaks their reverie. Hopefully this translates into my performance, as I don't feel that it's such a drastic change for me. But like everyone else, I'm still a work in progress. As time goes on, I'm discovering that who you are as a person is someone you can't run away from. Too many of us spend our time running away from ourselves rather than embracing who we are. I have fears and disappointments just like everyone else. I'm no different than you. I wake up every day and put my feet on the floor and at night I put my head on the bed. I was just lucky enough to find out at an early time during my formidable upbringing that this is what I truly believe in. It's great to be able to rely on myself. When you come to grips that this is the only thing carrying you through, you'll be successful. We're only here to express ourselves. Money, wealth, and adoration . . . it means nothing unless you feel it in your own psyche. There's really nothing else I'd rather do.

Stefon Harris
VIBRAPHONIST, COMPOSER, EDUCATOR

HOME BASE
www.stefonharris.com

GOT MUSIC?
Urbanus, Stefon Harris and
Blackout, Concord Records, 2009

"The real tradition of jazz is about innovation and authenticity."

BACKGROUND AND SOUND

Hailed as one of the most important young jazz musicians of our time by the *Los Angeles Times*, Grammy-nominated Stefon Harris has taken over the reins in the world of jazz vibes. His vibrations have accompanied notables Steve Coleman, Steve Turre, Wynton Marsalis, Cassandra Wilson, and Charlie Hunter. But it is Stefon's highly original group Blackout, which features the traditional notion of jazz turned upside down, that has earned him worldwide recognition. His group has been featured in many prestigious venues, such as the Kennedy Center and the North Sea Jazz Festival. This imaginative and in-with-the-times thinking has kept Stefon in demand as a performer and clinician. Each year he is featured in hundreds of clinics throughout the world. He has been awarded an artist-in-residence spot at the San Francisco Performances group and is an active member of the executive board for Chamber Music America. Reviews of his work have been featured in publications like *Rolling Stone*, the *Los Angeles Times*, and the *New York Times*. Stefon Harris verifies time and again that working hard and homing in on one's individual and creative voice can lead to success.

HIS STORY

The real tradition of jazz is about innovation and authenticity. Jazz is music of the people, and it is up to the artist to create music that is culturally relevant. The question is this . . . is jazz in direct correlation to our society right now?

Currently we're a very divided country, and if you look at jazz, it's a very segregated art in terms of mentality and generations. When you listen to music of the swing era, you can imagine the way that people danced and felt a sense of relief from the pressures of a country in war. Some have a set vision that jazz is from their childhood, and they don't want it to change even though it's seventy years later. How can I tell the story of the 1940s through my music when it wasn't my experience? It's already been told best by those who lived it.

For my generation, to echo our world and tell our own stories is a challenge. We're going to have to fight to have our voices heard. We love this music. We have integrity and conviction. You can hear desire. And just like the ones who came before us, you can hear an energy of ambition in our music. But if we insist on training musicians to learn and regurgitate music from the past and ignore our present, then we're going to miss out on the sound of an entire generation.

There are many cultures expressed in music. Authenticity depends on being honest about which culture you're a part of and how you experience the world. My mother is a preacher, and I grew up in the black church. I was also a classical music major, and the fact that this is my background should come through in my art. The sound of that experience is undeniable. I'm not convinced that people have to like jazz, but when you listen to John Coltrane I don't know how any human being can be exposed to that and not feel it. You have every right in the world to say you hate it, but you will feel it! I hope that when someone comes to my show they feel what I'm feeling. If I'm organizing sound into an emotion of fear, I hope you feel fear. It's my job to convey those emotions to the audience, and it's my fault if that doesn't work, no one else's. You have to have conviction and passion, and know that music is a reflection of who you are. When you're honest about who you are, then your music is going to be different, totally different, than the world was just moments ago.

Ken Hatfield

GUITARIST, COMPOSER, EDUCATOR

HOME BASE
www.kenhatfield.com

GOT MUSIC?
The Surrealist Table, Ken
Hatfield Trio, Arthur Circle
Music 2003

"Jazz musicians create to communicate, and communicate to create."

BACKGROUND AND SOUND

ASCAP Jazz Vanguard Award winner
Ken Hatfield is a one-of-a-kind musician.
Nylon string guitarists are rare among the
jazz community. Ken's virtuosic approach
to music, whether classical or jazz, has garnered the attention of students around the
world through his instructional and ètude
books published by Mel Bay and Arthur
Circle Music. He consistently proves his
skill as a performer and composer through
solo and sideman performances with some
of the best in the industry, including Pat
Benatar, Charlie Byrd, Chico Hamilton,
Marilyn McCoo, Lew Tabackin, and Kenny Werner. Original compositions
have been commissioned from him by the Washington Ballet Company
and the Maurice Béjart Ballet Company. He has done film scoring for television and film, including Eugene Richards's award-winning documentary,
But, the Day Came. With a flamenco flair and affinity for storytelling through
his music, his style is uplifting, refreshing, and a necessary tone to balance
out the modern jazz scene.

HIS STORY

Jazz musicians create to communicate, and communicate to create. Yet
America's greatest art form has a diminishing audience. In my opinion there

are reasons jazz artists don't have the audience we should. I don't blame critics nearly as much as I blame advertising and marketing approaches that pander to our lower instincts. The notion that you would challenge people intellectually or aesthetically is antithetic to the agenda of the mega-media businesses, which are solely focused on rapidly maximizing earnings by any means necessary.

In Immanuel Kant's *Critique of Judgement*, he talks about what's required for somebody to comprehend a work of art. First he says the work of art must fulfill its purpose to function as a conduit to a kind of spiritual experience we call an aesthetic experience. Achieving this requires the artist to create something that can actually fulfill that function, and do so as a means of self-expression. But the audience has a role to play as well. They need to approach such a work of art with a disinterested interest. For example, you can't understand a painting when your appreciation is limited to your interest in its investment potential or because it reminds you of the girl you lost your virginity with. Such distractions impede art's ability to speak to us. Both the artist and the audience must also bring to the encounter the capacity for a free play between understanding and imagination. This challenges them beyond their comfort zones. Our world cares little for the kind of imagination that can only develop throughout a lifetime of paying attention. To fathom Proust you must read attentively, as well as imagine what his characters look and sound like. This process involves the kind of imagination that channel surfing and video games actually inhibit.

The current lamentable state of jazz's dwindling audience is further exacerbated by the fact that so few people listen to instrumental music of any kind that most folks don't know how to appreciate it. The entertainment media encourages us to seek and expect little more than diversion or sensory titillation. Entertainment is intended as a diversion, while art gives you the opportunity to have a transcendent experience, because it stretches you beyond what you already know. Music as art can be daunting to people who don't want to be challenged, because it is music that's designed to be listened to with your full attention. I'm not playing atonal or free music, and I'm not playing smooth jazz. I'm playing music that is heartfelt and as deep as I can possibly make it. To comprehend it, all that is required is attentive listening.

Fred Hersch

COMPOSER, PIANIST

HOME BASE
www.fredhersch.com

GOT MUSIC?
Fred Hersch in Amsterdam: Live at the Bimhuis, Fred Hersch, Palmetto Records, 2006

"I'm lucky to have found an art form that's a good fit for me."

BACKGROUND AND SOUND

Not only is Fred Hersch an inexhaustible composer and pianist, but his body of work contains some of the most profound pieces of music to come out of this time in jazz history. Fred is continually challenged as commissioning funds and grants from organizations around the world push him with an endless demand for material. Awards and honors for Fred include the prestigious Guggenheim Fellowship in addition to grants from the National Endowment for the Arts, the Meet the Composer Foundation, and the Doris Duke Foundation. As a soloist and leader for his Pocket Orchestra and other groups, he has been invited to play around the world and for programming such as *CBS Sunday Morning* with Dr. Billy Taylor and various public radio programs, including *Fresh Air, Studio 360*, and *Prairie Home Companion*. Legendary musicians like Stan Getz, Art Farmer, Joe Henderson, and Jane Ira Bloom have requested his apt fingers and imaginative mind. Fred is also a known advocate, supporter, and fund-raiser for HIV/AIDS services and education. His collaborative efforts with much of the current jazz community have raised hundreds of thousands of dollars for this cause. Fred Hersch is one artist who has done more than leave a legacy; he has created an imprint in modern jazz history and a role model for all who have ever believed in a dream.

HIS STORY

It was the social aspect that drew me to this music: the culture, the clubs, the personalities. There's an energy in communicating with these musicians that's totally unique. Through this communication we're able to determine the content and shape of the music as we play. I'm lucky to have found an art form that's a good fit for me. Jazz is the hub of my wheel. Within that hub there's solo piano, trio, quintet, bands, my Pocket Orchestra, large projects, composing, teaching—it's all something I do on my own terms. I've had a very slow and steady career progression. My first album wasn't recorded until I was thirty. I've learned that when you play, in some ways you're playing for yourself. You have to explore, create something that's honest and appreciated. You don't want to play down to the audience, but you can't play over their heads all the time either. I was able to play with legends such as Joe Henderson, Art Farmer, Charlie Haden, and more. It was great to get into their world. They taught me to be strong without overpowering. Remaining flexible and open is a challenge. You have to learn to be in that moment while respecting all that's come before you while helping those that come after you.

Being honest and open in my playing also means I have to be honest with myself. I'm gay. I have AIDS. In the early nineties I recorded a benefit CD for Classical Action: Performing Arts Against AIDS. I got George Shearing, Mark Murphy, Phil Woods, et cetera. It was a stellar lineup, but no label. We put it out ourselves with a pro bono publicist, and I wound up on CNN, in *Newsweek*. That's when I came out to the world. The price of being in the closet is very high. You're constantly wondering who knows and who doesn't and what they think. It's sad. There are a number of musicians I know who are gay and who aren't out. Coming out enables you to put a face on it. If you know somebody that's gay you're less likely to stereotype and take away their rights. We're not all queens, and there's always a middle ground. It's had some impact. It's made me a better and more honest musician to not have to compartmentalize my life into a gay life and jazz life. It's *one* life, and I want people to know me as a person first and a musician second. Not someone who has HIV/AIDS and is gay. I realize I do what I do and that's fine. I don't worry about trying to keep up with the Joneses, and I stay true to my musical guidance. Jazz musicians do this because they love it. Anyone who knows jazz piano knows I have a place in it. I have nothing but love to offer this art, this community, and those around me.

Lisa Hilton
COMPOSER, PIANIST

HOME BASE
www.lisahiltonmusic.com

GOT MUSIC?
Twilight and Blues, Lisa Hilton,
Ruby Slippers Productions, 2009

"Jazz represents my life, and I absolutely believe in it and instrumental music."

BACKGROUND AND SOUND
Although Lisa Hilton has been compared to some of the best pianists in history, such as Bill Evans and Brad Mehldau, her sound and style are of her own. Prior to any formal training, Hilton taught herself how to play and compose. But by the time she entered college she was studying classical piano full time. Eventually she left that world because of a certain disenchantment with the music and went on to graduate with a degree in art. David Foster inspired her to return to music after a four-year hiatus, and since that time she has become not only a critically acclaimed pianist but also a prolific composer. Each album she has produced has featured heavyweights such as Lewis Nash and Jeremy Pelt. Her voice speaks of charm and aptitude for intense harmonic and rhythmic lines and solos.

HER STORY
With all of the new directions currently in jazz, I think that being an artist now is similar to being an artist when jazz was just beginning. There is this search now, as there was then, to find a way to express ourselves, respond to what is going on in the world, and to somehow broaden interest in this music. When jazz was strongest, around the time of the fifties and early sixties, the whole world was listening to our music—American blues and jazz artists were idolized by musicians like the Rolling Stones and Eric Clapton. As jazz branched into new directions though, it lost audience, and today we are still challenged to keep our fans—yet the music written by our jazz legends still remains popular. I think that we can find a way to create

music that is influenced by our past—by the icons of jazz—but speaks to the age that we now live and work in, so that we can inspire audiences with music of today.

Jazz represents my life, and I absolutely believe in it and instrumental music. I do think that it is changing form now, and we need to find a way, to connect again—we have to! For me it's about being completely, absolutely, nakedly honest and as real as possible musically. I have to share with the world. When you hear me you know these are my experiences and what is going on in my world. There are realism and human qualities that come through that I hope touch people. I think how you say something is even more important than what you say. But I think as a whole, the industry has gotten away from much emotional expression, too often getting caught up in studio effects or displays of virtuosity instead of universal feelings and emotions, and maybe that has been a detriment.

As artists, I'm not sure if we can put the world's definition of success into this need to communicate and create community. I ask myself day to day, week to week, year to year, am I moving forward? Am I exploring new things and communicating today better than yesterday? If the answer is yes, then I'm okay. I still have what I call "doubter days"; I call them "days" because they pass. It is a challenge to be a jazz artist, and we, each one of us, experience incredible obstacles. But I realize that I didn't really choose to be a composer or jazz musician; it really is what I was meant to do. This is the path I walk day to day, week to week, year to year. I left music once, and I will never, ever leave it again.

Laurence Hobgood
PIANIST, COMPOSER

HOME BASE
www.laurencehobgood.com

GOT MUSIC?
Left to My Own Devices,
Laurence Hobgood, Naim
Records, 2000

"It's never the tool; it's what you do with the tool."

BACKGROUND AND SOUND

Laurence Hobgood is a diamond among the rough. One of the truly hidden talents of today, his skill is virtually unprecedented. Laurence, other than standing as a solo performer in his own rite, has been the long-standing collaborator and accompanist for Kurt Elling. Laurence has received three fellowships through the Aspen Music Festival and has performed with other greats, such as Clark Terry, Charlie Haden, Bob Mintzer, and Claudio Roditi. What sets Laurence apart from the mass of pianists is his ability to pull slight-of-hand tricks throughout his solos. By allowing the unexpected melody to flow from the expected, he creates listeners out of the audience. His solos are at once relaxing yet unexpected in their content and leave his peers, listeners, and critics marveling at his skill.

HIS STORY

As a modern and civilized race, we don't have enough empirical respect for the pace of time. The way we live has been molded into being solely about answering our immediate needs. Everything is based on the moment. I think this puts us in danger of becoming a lot more mediocre in general than we should be. Music is definitely the bellwether of all of this. Instead, we should be realizing the importance of the incredible complexity of everything. It's increasingly difficult to find a single culprit or tag a certain group for this issue. Artists are endangered; the human expression is endangered.

I've always been an optimist, but it's hard to be this when you're art is hurting. I honestly believe that if we could sit down with most people and try to explain to them that ninety-nine percent of their music is made with a click track, they wouldn't care. The human art of counting and feeling time is something that's very important but is lost. There are people out there that are multimillionaires and they don't know how to count. It's not that they can't; they just don't, and they've never had to. Very few people are innately gifted in rhythm. The rest of us have to develop it and work on it. We have to work really, really, really hard on it, because in the world of grown-up jazz, musicianship and time and feel are the things that separate the masters from the wannabes. Everyone has to deal with this. But how can we, as musicians, deal with space and ultimately what gives your playing a true character without knowing or understanding time and feel? This is a very deep thing that extends back thousands of years. Human beings all have this organ in our chest that is all about time and rhythm and vibration. If it gets out of time you'll die. How much more information do we need to understand that this is really important? Yet it's being back shelved because of this industry and their big-quick-fix and make-a-hit production and advertising related approach to music. This is where music has evolved. All the music is done in studios for commercial purposes, and it's all clicked to a metronome. Of course this is removed from the track before people hear it. As cliché as it sounds, there really is a rhythm to life.

But we've come to a time where the group of people that embrace and support and are actively involved with the deeper esoteric aspects of expression has become alarmingly small. There are always rules, and I've always liked the analogy of humanity, in this sense, becoming this large amoeba. The artists are always out on the edges where the amoeba extends its little parts. But the truth of the matter is that the center and most of it never moves. Some of it will eventually be pulled along in some sort of new direction that's physically initiated by reaching out of one of the limbs . . . to a certain extent, you can argue that all is well as long as the mass of people aren't getting it, with an absence of humility and healthy curiosity that's overall detrimental to the mental and experiential expression and evolution of the whole species. I don't blame technology for this; I blame the humans. It's never the tool; it's what you do with the tool. As long as there's a governing MO of this attitude of "because we can and not because we should," everything else will be subservient to the lot of it.

Ari Hoenig
PERCUSSIONIST, COMPOSER, ARRANGER, KEYBOARDIST

HOME BASE
www.arihoenig.com

GOT MUSIC?
The Painter: Live at Fat Cat, Ari Hoenig, Smalls Records, 2004

"In the bigger picture, I think it's important to go for exactly what you want and what you believe in."

BACKGROUND AND SOUND

Ari Hoenig is one of the foremost rising stars in straight-ahead modern jazz drumming today. He has provided the beats behind Shirley Scott, Gerry Mulligan, Kenny Werner, Joshua Redman, Kurt Rosenwinkel, Wayne Krantz, Mike Stern, and Dave Liebman, to name a few, and also leads his own quartet, Punk Bop. This group includes heavy hitters such as Chris Potter and Jonathan Kreisberg. Ari's ability as a drummer is only part of the equation. His love for adventure and confidence is clear if you listen to his original music. This faith in his life and career has helped make him the innovator he is today. He is highly sought after as an artist around the world, and his musicianship and hard work has paid off.

HIS STORY

I was in high school, at one of those career days, when I realized what I wanted to do. I remember the reactions of people outside of school. They'd say, "that's great that you want to be a musician, but you should have a fallback." I have to say I made the right decision trusting that it was a possibility for me to be a professional musician, and I've geared my life according to that trust.

Now I'm spoiled. Playing with musicians that make my music into something that breathes is what keeps me going. In the bigger picture, I think it's important to go for exactly what you want and what you believe in. There will always be art, but sadly there may not always be arts education. Personally, arts education helped me out very much. I wouldn't be the same musician I am today without the boost of playing in the All-City Jazz Band or the All-City Orchestra in Philly. These were sponsored by the city and state, and they're the reason I got an early start. From that I learned that being a musician is an important part of society. I think music is a great way to break down barriers between people from different backgrounds, religions, and cultures. It creates a bond, a gift that happens unintentionally. It's more the feeling that we've created something that goes deeper than ourselves.

Lee Hogans
TRUMPETER, COMPOSER

HOME BASE
www.leehogans.com

GOT MUSIC?
The Vibe Orientation, Lee Hogans, Independent Label, 2005

"Everything comes at a certain time and place. With this patience you have to have confidence in yourself."

BACKGROUND AND SOUND

Trumpeter Lee Hogans has insisted on chasing down the shifting music scene throughout R&B, pop, hip-hop, fusion, and modern jazz. His own group, Pursuance, has performed in some of the hottest venues across this country, including the BET festival, Bluenote, and Groove. Lee has also stood behind headliners such as Prince, Jay-Z, Sean Combs, Missy Elliot, Jill Scott, and Busta Rhymes. Don't let these names fool you; there is a traditional foundation that composes the root embedded in the core of his sound. This is what has helped him transition from his roots in Georgia to the often unforgiving New York scene.

HIS STORY

The act of learning music takes patience and time, especially with jazz. It's an endless amount of work, and we can't force it. It's the same thing with life. Everything comes at a certain time and place. With this patience you have to have confidence in yourself. There were times I wished I had had more confidence in my ability when I was younger. I was too humble. Everything I did was more about just wanting to be at a certain level, and when I didn't get to that level fast enough, I'd tear myself down. I was never where I thought I should be. Even now I try to do that. But now I know that to do this, instead of rushing it you have to have a vision and faith that it will work out. It always does.

Charlie Hunter

GUITARIST, COMPOSER, PRODUCER

HOME BASE
www.charliehunter.com

GOT MUSIC?
Baboon Strength, Charlie Hunter,
Spire Artist Media, 2008

"My job is to be myself to the best of my ability and to be a prism for all the music I listen to and create."

BACKGROUND AND SOUND

Charlie Hunter was discovered and heavily influenced at the ripe and youthful age of eighteen by jazz organ greats such as Jimmy Smith and Larry Young. Prior to this he was just your average guitar student in Berkeley, California, who took weekly lessons from the at that time unknown guitarist Joe Satriani. Charlie has now skyrocketed into fame with a somewhat insane technique on his unique eight-string guitar (two bass strings and six guitar strings) and an expansively wild imagination, which adds vibrancy to original tunes and more traditional standards. Since their earliest beginnings in the Bay Area, Charlie Hunter's trio has turned the heads of major labels such as Blue Note, top national and international publications such as *Rolling Stone*, and venues such as the Elbo Room in San Francisco. Boundaries mean absolutely nothing to Charlie. His innate soul flips his funked- and sauced-up adaptation of yesterday's music for today.

HIS STORY

Since an early age, music is something I've always had an affinity for. It's the first thing in my life that I had a direct relationship with. I had a pretty rough upbringing, not as in people were beating on me, but a lot of hard psychological stuff. It's hard for kids to absorb those issues. But this is what made me into who I am. Whether or not I want to admit it, on a very deep level I communicate this to people just to feel like I'm heard. I grew up feeling like I was never heard or loved, so I have to do this. If I put myself out there in an honest way then people respond.

I've put a lot of work into it, and it's come back to me. Of course this music isn't without its issues and problems, but as I look back I feel incredibly lucky that I've been in this. You would think that I've been doing this for so many years, over twenty years now, that it's one of those things that would get old and tiring. But playing music never gets old. There's always going to be a certain element of soul and rhythm and blues that people just get. If someone gets hit by the art first and then start thinking about the artist after, they'll make a journey and find out about themselves. Unfortunately it seems that our culture gets caught up in the celebrity status of music. If you had a pie chart, music is only about five percent of the equation for someone like Beyoncé or whoever happens to be popular. It's really about how they look and what they wear, and it's all incredibly vapid and superficial. You have to ask yourself, what do you want to know about—the art or the artist? My job isn't to come and have people give a damn about who I am or what I did. My job is to be myself to the best of my ability and to be a prism for all the music I listen to and create. I want to project in some way that an audience can relate to me with nonverbal communication and understand that it's not necessary for me to have to say, "I'm this guy that did this or that," because ultimately who cares? As a musician I'm just a link in an enormous chain of musicians that date back to our ancestors. I have to find music I love and honestly be myself so I can translate that meaning within my greater community. I have to have the respect of my peers and know that I'm doing the right thing. I ask, do I have reverence for the people I play with, and do they have reverence for me? I want to be a contributor, a part of the solution, not a part of the problem.

Chie Imaizumi

COMPOSER, ARRANGER, CONDUCTOR, EDUCATOR

HOME BASE
www.thousandpictures.org

GOT MUSIC?
A Time of New Beginnings,
Chie Imaizumi,
Capri Records, 2010

"I want to make people smile through my music."

BACKGROUND AND SOUND

Chie's music lights up its listeners with every note played. Her unique tone carries light and brings that light into the world. This characteristic kindness in her music has won the hearts of countless fans and listeners around the world. As a young and budding pianist she left her native Japan to study at Berklee College of Music. Shortly after arriving in the States she suffered a repetitive stress injury and switched from performance to jazz composition. What emerged from this challenge was the exact opposite of negative. Her notes now have a triumphant and overtly positive ring to them. Soon to be a recognizable face among the composers in our time, Chie is but a North Star charting her course, with people everywhere following her guidance and unfailing kindness.

HER STORY

I moved from Japan to Boston in 2001 as a piano student, and it wasn't until I got tenosynovitis did I change my major to jazz composition. After I started composing, I felt hopeless at times. So many people said my music was cheesy, happy, too childish. They'd laugh at me, saying, "You want to make people happy? Awww, that's so cute!" et cetera. But my music wasn't cool enough. They'd ask me if they could change my lines during rehearsals. And even though they hated my music, I liked it. It made me smile, cry, and dance all at once. I didn't care and didn't try to even write cool songs for them in order to be nice to me. Talk about being self-conscious. But what they didn't realize is that when I create music, I want to inspire moods, emotions within my audience that range from tears of sadness to joy and laughter. Ultimately, my music has to represent people, places, ideas, and feelings tailored through my melodies, harmonies, and moods I've created. And not until I feel all of this myself do I truly know one of my compositions are finished.

My compositions aren't necessarily easy, but what I start out to do is very simple. I want to make people smile through my music. I'm still trying to figure out what jazz exactly is, but I think it is a form of freedom. Just as my personal and creative influences come from all over, such as riding my bike, traveling, walking around town, singing melodies, watching animals, anything I see, hear, touch, et cetera, I want my music to touch all walks of life. I have no boundaries to where I want my music to go. It is an energy we can all partake in.

After I met Greg Gisbert, a world-class trumpet player and inspiration, my life was changed. He encouraged me beyond belief. I've overcome quite a few obstacles throughout my life, although I know there will be more. But now, because of him, I've been encouraged. I have fans who cry, who laugh and dance, and some who say my music has changed his or her life. I still can't believe people actually love my music. If I could go back to my younger self, I would say that it's going to be okay and that I'm on the right path. People shouldn't listen too much to what others say to them. Instead, believe in yourself, your feelings, your guts. Keep doing what you're doing. I still have to tell this to myself, and it's hard when you can't see the end of your own tunnel, but never give up on something you really want to do. There is no regret if you at least try, and even if you try your best and fail, which has happened to me quite often, you only lose your pride, maybe your ego. This allows you to move on to the next stage without those awful regrets so you can once again feel good about yourself. After all, failing is easier than not trying, and this is the only way your dreams will come true, even if it's little by little.

Roger Ingram

TRUMPETER, EDUCATOR

HOME BASE
www.rogeringram.com

GOT MUSIC?
Blue Light, Red Light, Harry
Connick Jr., Sony, 1991

"Jazz defines my art."

BACKGROUND AND SOUND

When Roger Ingram came onto the scene early on in his career, he immediately began piercing through the ranks of musicians with his wicked and maddening range and ability to swing. It was one thing for a soloist to home in on this kind of commanding presence, but to lead groups with this was virtually unheard of. He has since gone on to grow by leaps and bounds as an artist. Roger continues to tour with Harry Connick Jr. and other entertaining and highly prestigious musicians like Woody Herman, Maynard Ferguson, Wynton Marsalis, and Arturo Sandoval. Roger is now the artist in residence at Chicago's Roosevelt University, and he continues to test the waters of teaching his craft trumpet players of all ages.

HIS STORY

Early on, I learned that the word "jazz" was first used in reference to the 1912 Portland Beavers pitcher Ben Henderson's new pitch. Ben said, in an interview in the April 2, 1912, *LA Times*, "I got a new curve this year . . . I call it the jazz ball because it wobbles and you simply can't do anything with it." Right away this tells you something about what jazz could be. Jazz wobbles; it can be loose and fun, and it has a purpose. What may seem to be an uncontrolled dynamic is confined within certain parameters of the artist's direction.

In the world of music, jazz defines a particular style. Jazz is the purest means of communication through music for expressing one's inner soul. Besides being a jazz musician, I also work in a commercial capacity. I embrace many styles of music, and this helps me earn a living. Even though I have to come to appreciate all music, jazz is the style that affects me the most on a spiritual level. It's important to stay open to change.

Experiencing new musical situations can remind you of the limitless nature of this art form. When this happens to me, I am inspired to continue learning and growing and filing away my past accomplishments. Like all art forms, music is constantly evolving. As I study further, I keep in mind that being a musician involves continually learning and adapting. Looking back, if I had the privilege to alter my life path, there are a few things I would change. For me, my ability to play lead trumpet and perform in the upper register has been a catch-22 of sorts. These skills have afforded me the luxury of being able to earn a living as a musician. However, it has stunted my growth in some respects as an artist. Had I the opportunity to do it all over again, I would have worked harder to develop my innate skills as an improviser.

In the last several years, I have conquered a number of personal challenges. As a result, one of the many things I do now is work toward artistic growth. When I'm not involved with performances incorporating the abilities I'm known for, I'm at home or playing with groups in an effort to hone my improvisational skills. It's interesting that improving in this regard has enhanced my ability to play lead trumpet in a jazz ensemble. I suppose this is the balance of life. Surviving as a jazz musician has taught me some of my most valuable lessons. In modern day society, jazz is not as highly regarded as it was decades ago. There are many reasons for this. Regardless of the what or why, this has forced me to learn how to survive in and represent what can be accurately described as a subculture. This can be difficult at times; however, I remain strong. Whether one is a jazz soloist or a jazz lead player, when it's said and done, it's all jazz. Since I'm a jazz lead trumpet player, jazz defines my art.

Aaron Irwin

SAXOPHONIST, WOODWINDIST, COMPOSER

HOME BASE
www.aaronirwin.com

GOT MUSIC?
Blood and Thunder, Aaron Irwin,
Fresh Sound/New Talent, 2008

"This music is where I find spirituality in my life."

BACKGROUND AND SOUND

Aaron Irwin is one of the younger voices and talents who display great potential in both performance and composition. After graduating from DePaul University, he honed his chops through playing on transatlantic cruises with legends like Joe Lovano and Louis Bellson. After attending the University of Miami for his graduate studies, Aaron made his way to New York, carrying his refined skills along with him. Once there, Aaron was able to quickly garner attention from intense heavyweights such as Ben Monder, Chris Cheek, and Rich Perry for his first recordings as a leader and composer. As a young talent in modern jazz, Aaron has set a pace that surely leads to a long and healthy career in the art of jazz.

HIS STORY

I'm not a religious person, but the work ethic that comes with giving yourself to something greater than yourself provides me with some kind of point to life. It's almost as if the point is being better than yourself. The work ethic associated with being an artist is something I value, and I find that the most rewarding times in music are often the quiet little victories in the practice room. When you really work at something you love, it's as if you're doing something divine. I'm just a person who's worked hard, and this music is where I find spirituality in my life. I feel that if one works hard at something for long enough it is inevitable that you will at some point have mastery over that craft. Imagine if a blacksmith worked hard for many, many years and then couldn't produce anything beautiful with his craft. That would be silly. I would like to think that anyone can; it's just a matter of those that choose to do it and get better.

When you play you bring your whole existence and being into your playing. Ideally a serious artist brings with his or her performance all the life experiences and deep feelings inside their person and shares that joy, pain, and love with the audience. The more one is tuned into that, the deeper the music is for the listener. When listening to the music of great jazz artists, the music that moves me the most is that in which the artists are true to themselves, and this is what I strive to capture when I play.

Vijay Iyer
PIANIST, COMPOSER, AUTHOR, PRODUCER, PHYSICIST

HOME BASE
www.vijay-iyer.com

GOT MUSIC?
Historicity, Vijay Iyer Trio, ACT
Records, 2009

"It's through this art that I've found a way to not only articulate but become who I am."

BACKGROUND AND SOUND

Voted the Number One Rising Star Artist, Composer, and Pianist in *DownBeat* magazine's International Critics Poll, Vijay Iyer has built his career on solidly beautiful ground. With one foot cemented deep into his Indian heritage and the other firmly placed against the traditional jazz roots of America, he has climbed up the ladder of greats in record time. Yet, Vijay's résumé does not end or begin with his music.

To add to an already noteworthy career as a performer and composer, Vijay boasts an equally as impressive BS in physics from Yale, a master's degree in physics, and an interdisciplinary PhD in technology and the arts from the University of California, Berkeley. The science publication *Seed* selected Vijay as one of today's most "revolutionary minds."

He has constructed an inspiring and expansive body of work as a composer and bandleader in the jazz world, and he has also composed for all avenues of media, including theater, television, film, radio, and full orchestra. A dozen albums are currently available under his name as a leader, and he appears on countless recordings as a sideman. His dramatic, poetic compositions have garnered him fellowships and grants from the Rockefeller Foundation MAP Fund, the New York State Council of the Arts, Chamber Music America, Meet the Composer, the New York Foundation for the Arts, and many, many more. Vijay is as prolific as they come in the arts, and his impact among the minds of this generation has yet to be seen. Set among the sonic boom of his art, his prowess as a soloist is virtually unmatched, with lines that seamlessly flow in and out of masterfully crafted organic music. Vijay is truly an inspiration to artists of any kind who dare to reach beyond their dreams and pull them down into their reality.

HIS STORY

Music is a fundamental part of who I am. You can't say that my music means this or that, because music always explodes with meaning. People's musical experiences are endlessly varied. I try to keep that reality in mind when I put music out there. I have my own specific reasons for every choice I make, but in the end I just hope that my work gives people something they can share—an experience or sensation that makes them think and opens them to new possibilities.

What I do feel is that my experiences as an American are reflected in my music. My parents are from India. They came here at a time when there hadn't really been many Indians. Due to the change in immigration law in the mid sixties, a major wave of Indian immigrants came to the US. My parents came at the front end of that wave. So I was part of the first American-born generation of South Asian descent. Prior to that, there were hardly any people like us here. We were literally a new kind of American. Over the last forty-five years in the United States, the population of South Asian Americans has exploded. Before 1965 it was in the thousands; now it's two and a half million.

I was born and raised in the United States, but that experience of growing up "different" in this country is also fundamental to who I am. Since we were on the early end of this explosion, learning how to *be a person* happened in the context of an experience of newness and difference. Improvisation is central to how we dealt with that reality. It's something I learned from my parents—their adaptive skills. They had to find or create a space for themselves in this culture. In a basic sense, it was all about improvisation.

None other than Charles Darwin said, "In the long history of humankind, those who learned to collaborate and improvise most effectively have always prevailed." That's basically a recipe for culture, as we know it: collective human responses to necessity. That's how we survive, build, and innovate. And of course it is exactly those two things—collaboration and improvisation—that breathe life into this music.

My relationship to Indian heritage is complex, but ultimately I cherish it, and it's an important part of me. I don't often wear my identity on my sleeve, but it informs the artistic choices and the creative alliances I make.

Through music I can engage and harmonize with this heritage. That's the transformative power of music. It's through this art that I've found a way to not only articulate but *become* who I am.

In general I'm trying to create music that responds to the world around me. I've been fortunate to participate in areas of inquiry in the arts, the humanities, and the sciences, and it all informs the music I make. My research examines the roles of bodily experience and cultural context in the perception of music. It draws from areas as disparate as music theory, psychology, African American studies, and robotics. Most rewardingly, the research has evolved symbiotically with my creative work.

As you can imagine, I believe that everyone should get exposed to a lot of different ways of thinking. When I meet people in undergraduate jazz studies programs, I am often concerned that they aren't receiving the kind of education that prepares them for twenty-first-century life. I'm talking about not just science and math, but also history, the social sciences, the political landscape, and just basic critical thinking. These music students are often not very politically aware, and their intellectual requirements are slender. This leaves them naïve and incurious, and ultimately scared and bitter, about their place in the world.

In order for jazz musicians to be true artists—vital voices reflecting our times, like Coltrane, Mingus, Max Roach, Duke Ellington, and Ornette Coleman did for theirs—I feel that in addition to innovating with the actual language of music, we need to be equipped to imagine how the music might make a difference in the world. That means we should read whatever we can get our hands on (as Coltrane did), align ourselves with causes for social justice (like Roach and Mingus did), place our work in dialogue with the world of ideas (as Ellington and Coleman did), and care about everyone and everything (as every elder musician I know does). When we are that deeply engaged, that's when we have a chance to make a *real* difference.

Jason Jackson
TROMBONIST, COMPOSER, EDUCATOR

HOME BASE
www.jasonjacksonmusic.com

GOT MUSIC?
Going Home, Jason Jackson,
Jacemus Records, 2002

"This is a living and continuously growing music."

BACKGROUND AND SOUND

Grammy Award–winning trombonist Jason Jackson has been a member of the Vanguard Jazz Orchestra for more than a decade, and he is the lead trombonist for the Dizzy Gillespie All Star Band and Roy Hargrove's Big Band. He is widely known throughout the Broadway circuit in New York for his work on the Tony Award–winning production *The Color Purple* and on *Wonderful Town*. Under the tutelage of J.J. Johnson he was able to grow and expand his repertoire as a soloist and composer. His original works contain flavors from within the tradition and are peppered with a hard-hitting rhythmic foundation.

HIS STORY

I loved music, even before I played the trombone. But jazz connected with me right away, and I didn't know why at first. I would listen to greats like J.J., Freddie Hubbard, and Woody Shaw, and then I'd try to emulate them. I didn't know what it was I was listening to, but it felt right. Later on, I understood that this music was about freedom; it was the music of African Americans and their tradition. That is what connected with me, my ancestry, and the democratic nature of the music. We work together to make the music, yet everyone shares his voice through improvisation. No other music does that. This is a living and continuously growing music, which is what I love most about it.

Life inspires you to play jazz. My music is loyal and an honest representation of my life as a developing musician. We musicians pour ourselves into the music and accept and love what we do for it to succeed. And the music rewards us in so many ways.

The impact this music has had isn't totally realized in America. I've played jazz on six different continents on this planet. I discovered that people who can't speak my language and have never set foot in America know what this music is. And, they love it! It's surely not dead. It's alive in so many forms; you just have to go out and see it live for yourself.

Nat Janoff
GUITARIST, COMPOSER, ARRANGER, EDUCATOR

HOME BASE
www.natjanoff.com

GOT MUSIC?
Looking Through, The Nat Janoff Group, Independent Label, 1999

"Jazz is meant to be an amazing creative outlet. It's an endless road that eventually takes on a life of its own."

BACKGROUND AND SOUND
Nat Janoff has recorded solo albums with some of the best, including bassist Matthew Garrison and drummer Gene Lake. Complementing styles of simplified and relatable rock, jazz, and fusion, Nat has placed stake in his voice. Streaming his zeal and excitement for the music through regular jazz hot spots in New York like the 55 Bar, Nat has solidly earned his place among the players of his time.

HIS STORY
In order to succeed, you have to be less afraid to play with people that get you into situations that will kick your butt. If you're working with people who have more experience at a higher level than you, you can't help but rise to their level. This may take a while, but you'll eventually realize there's no lightning bolt that's coming out of the sky to blow you away from the earth. There's nothing like experiencing these challenging situations. I just try to have fun with the music while learning with as much enthusiasm and joy as possible. If we're going to get more listeners we have to give it to them in

a different light. Taking a lot of people who come from a background where they know nothing about this music and making it an academic nightmare for them isn't going to get them to open up to it. It becomes just like a class you have to take. People need to discover this music as an incredible art form. Making this into a complicated and theoretical thing instead of telling them to just listen to it and get what they're going to get out of it just turns them off. This is working against everything this music stands for. Jazz is meant to be an amazing creative outlet. It's an endless road that eventually takes on a life of its own. For me, I have no choice. It's just what I love.

Ingrid Jensen

TRUMPETER, COMPOSER, ARRANGER, EDUCATOR

HOME BASE
www.ingridjensen.com

GOT MUSIC?
At Sea, Ingrid Jensen, ArtistShare, 2006

"It is my hope that listeners come to the table with clean palates and positive, peace-minded, groovy thoughts that will freely allow us all to go wherever the journey may take us."

BACKGROUND AND SOUND

Ingrid Jensen has built a name for herself throughout the years with her beautiful sound. Yet what she does now is more than tooting her own horn. A graduate of Berklee College of Music, Jensen is a powerful set of chops walking the New York scene in both large and small group settings. Her "it" factor is well versed and professional with a sublime sound. Ingrid has been a long-standing member of Maria Schneider's orchestra and has also shared gigs with Terence Blanchard, Clark Terry, Jeff "Tain" Watts, Badal Roy, Terri Lyne Carrington, and Geoffrey Keezer. It's clear that she has true command of her craft. As a leader of her own groups, she speaks out of a soulful and creative headspace that continues to mark her place among the top call musicians in New York City.

HER STORY

My mother was a classically trained pianist. She provided me with a highly creative environment, and music was the center of all we had. To her, music was something anybody could go to at anytime of the day. The piano kept her sane while raising three kids on her own without much support and holding down a teaching job. This was a very important lesson for me. Despite her initial image I didn't see any pictures of women playing jazz until I was in my teens. But it wasn't that big of a deal, thanks to the highly supportive artistic environment I grew up in.

Later on, I remember Diana Krall playing with Ray Brown in Nanaimo while I was in junior high. It was her strong command of both the music and her instrument that gave me the thought, "hey, I can do that," as well as her actual encouragement. She was a professional, not even singing at the time. Although playing trumpet was an odd choice for a career, my early roots in both improvising and speech arts equipped me with skills that, to this day, lead to new and exciting discoveries in music.

The connection between the lush West Coast scenery, the many books I read, and the endless hours of listening all seem to have set me up for where I am today by providing me with fabulous memories to draw from. In this respect, it's imperative for anyone that wants to improvise to have some historical base to tap into while creating a story in relation to a song. In other words . . . blowing over some changes.

Some of my tools came from playing with Mom's jazz records, learning the melodies of standards from the original lead sheets and falling asleep to the sounds of late night CBC jazz radio. All of this followed by years of study, practice, and playing with others has given me a fairly well-stocked toolbox to draw my ideas from. This toolbox is constantly morphing as I get older. It's the love of the language and communication that allows me to embrace my playing as the "high" and the "magic." It is my hope that listeners come to the table with clean palates and positive, peace-minded, groovy thoughts that will freely allow us all to go wherever the journey may take us.

Mike Jones
PIANIST, COMPOSER

HOME BASE
www.jonesjazz.com

GOT MUSIC?
Live at the Green Mill, Mike Jones
Trio, Chiaroscuro Records, 2003

"I'm lucky to play this music and it brings me great satisfaction to know I can bring this to those who would have never heard it otherwise."

BACKGROUND AND SOUND

Mike Jones has twisted the two-handed solo piano act into a career that has landed him on stage of many heavy performers in the industry. He has performed at sea and on land with Diane Schuur, Clark Terry, Oscar Peterson, Roy Hargrove, and many more. What he does now is somewhat off the grid and in the realm of a magical act. As the pianist accompanying the nightly Penn and Teller show, he has found a way to incorporate his style into a show and still bring quality jazz to the masses, who might not hear it otherwise. Jones is a fine musician with a kind and light-hearted soul accompanying his voice.

HIS STORY

Ninety-nine percent of kids get their first exposure to any kind of music through the classroom. This is how it certainly was for me. I was lucky enough to go to a school where in the third and fourth grade the teacher would bring in records and play them for us. Not to mention I had this crazy home life where music was all around me. But if you go to Europe you can see the kids learning about Duke and Stan Getz and Count Basie right alongside of Bach, Beethoven, and Brahms. It's not unusual to find a fifteen- or sixteen-year-old who loves Stan Getz in Sweden, yet it's almost impossible to find a kid that's even heard of Stan Getz here in the States. We cut the extracurricular activities first here . . . not the football team but the music classes. Then the sports teams get free equipment from neighborhood businesses or major corporations. Nobody really cares if you have a school band or not. It's just not treated with respect in the US as it is in other countries.

Jazz is an American classical music, and it's going away. This isn't because it's bad; it's simply because no one knows about it. Wynton has certainly done wonders with it by trying to move the patrons of classical music to jazz, and he has succeeded in about a twenty-block radius in Manhattan. But what about that kid in Wyoming who's never heard an Art Tatum record? How is he ever going to have the chance to like it or buy one if he's never heard it? Yet if he was in a classroom that taught music he might not only hear it, but also love it. This is the most important thing we can do to build our future. If the government can give billions of dollars away to corporations like GM, why can't they buy a couple of guitars for some classrooms in Oklahoma or Iowa? It's sad and strange, because jazz is as uniquely American as it gets. It's our national music and it's completely disregarded. I'm lucky to play this music, and it brings me great satisfaction to know I can bring this to those who would have never heard it otherwise, and unless there are more of us who do this, we'll lose our music forever.

Sean Jones

TRUMPETER, COMPOSER, EDUCATOR

HOME BASE
www.seanjonesmusic.com

GOT MUSIC?
Roots, Sean Jones, Mack Avenue Records, 2006

"[Jazz is] the perfect example of the best and worst of humanity in sound."

BACKGROUND AND SOUND

Expressing an entire spectrum of emotion in a single song is difficult at best. Yet, it is what Sean Jones does best. There's not a single word in the English language that accurately portrays his music's ability to stun one into listening. As a leader he has produced five albums that are a result of years of hard work in finding the source of his songs from within. His group's uncanny ability to speak to one another in a seamless harmonic conversation draws his music into an even tighter weave of sound. Sean has played with numerous notables, including sitting in the lead chair with the Jazz at Lincoln Center Orchestra. His place remains, sitting high atop the family tree of greats in jazz.

HIS STORY

No one influenced me to play trumpet at all. I was just always intrigued by it because I heard it while growing up in the church. People improvised and fed off of each other and followed the heightened emotions throughout the service. As a little boy I began to sing in the choir and would watch the director drop his hands and hear a person start singing. I thought his hands actually controlled the sound! One of my buddies, who was about a year and a half older than me, started to play sax in church, and everyone else thought he was cool and followed suit . . . I thought it was boring. I wanted something different. I picked trumpet and then discovered why no one ever picked that instrument . . . it was hard as hell. I wanted to defeat it front and back, and I began to practice constantly in order to do so. I guess I was a little bit of a nerd in this way. I wanted to be the best, and I've always had that tendency to run to the stuff everyone else run's away from.

It seems that as we get older we lose that desire and become more and more inhibited. People tell you things are hard now, but when you're young you don't care if anything is hard—you just do it or you don't. The key, I think, is to keep your imagination near and dear to you and dream big, constantly. You have to be able to see outside your circumstances. If you see only your circumstances, then there's no room for your evolution to take place.

My mother is smart and allowed that evolution to happen naturally with me. She never really bothered me, even though I would be upstairs all loud as hell playing. Never once did she tell me to stop or tell me this path would be difficult or that I would have a hard time. Instead, she said, "If you want to go into music, then find a way to do it." I wanted to play the impossible, and the harder the material got, the more I gravitated toward it. I wouldn't accept defeat, ever. I had to conquer it. This put me in a lonely and elite club. But there was something in the back of my mind that said this was right. We just have to make choices; everyone does. We can choose every day to stay among the bullshit choices we made in the past, or you can change it. You're the only one who can play the hand you've dealt.

I'm constantly evaluating my life in these terms. If I'm not happy and I choose to stay in the situation, then I know I made that choice.

Jazz represents these choices. It's the perfect example of the best and worst of humanity in sound . . . the human experience, cultures coming together, rhythm, sex, communism, freedom, and capitalism. It's an all-accepting sonic art that signifies basic humanity at its highest level. It's not just swing or blues. Don't get me wrong, the origin of jazz certainly has swing elements and blues in it, but that's our history, not a definition.

Throughout my career, I've spent less time defining it and more time thinking about where it's going. I guess I'm just a different kind of guy, or I should say, a different kind of black guy. When I go to a black church, I notice a lot of African Americans spend a great deal of their time identifying themselves. We should instead say, this is where we were and where we are now, and notice that there's a difference. We were slaves and emancipated. We dealt with it. We paid our dues, and things have most definitely evolved since. Yes, we're going to have assholes that are going to be racist, but that don't stop me from my job and having a house, et cetera. We have to open our eyes and look at all angles in every direction to be able to see every possibility. If you live your life seeing all possibilities of something, you'll be more open.

Everything I do and try to do and learn is in the spirit of love . . . everything. The people I meet, the ones I talk to, and even my mistakes and faults are in this spirit. Music is all about love; it's spiritual. It's not about a specific God; it's about my belief that God is love. It just happens that my love is a series of notes coming out of the trumpet. But our common denominator is showing and spreading love. If I were a visual artist or writer, I'd still be saying the same thing. I love playing music, but it's not the essence of whom I am, it's just the vehicle. When I get on stage nothing is emotionally confined; I'm throwing myself out there for you to see and hear.

Daniel Jordan

SAXOPHONIST, FLAUTIST, COMPOSER, EDUCATOR

HOME BASE
www.myspace.com/djorjazzmusic

GOT MUSIC?
Live at Birdland, Scott Whitfield
Jazz Orchestra, Independent
Label, 2004

"My primary purpose is to touch someone emotionally rather than musically."

BACKGROUND AND SOUND

Daniel Jordan has steadily worked his way into the jazz world since he was a kid. Now, he educates kids who were just like him on how to make it as a successful freelancing musician. The approach he uses is commonsense and relaxed, just like his soloing. He has carried this trait with him throughout everything he has done in his career, whether it be soloing and touring with Maynard Ferguson, performing locally with Chuck Owen and the Jazz Surge, or performing with larger acts such as Natalie Cole, Sammy Davis Jr., Elvin Jones, or Kenny Rogers, or simply catering to smaller audiences with his own group. Spiritual and moving is just one way to describe the Jordan connection that is apparent in everything he does, including his approach to life.

HIS STORY

I've never been a jazz musician; rather, I'm a person who likes to transmit energy and contact people on a conscious level and be more involved with communication. My primary purpose is to touch someone emotionally rather than musically. When I started to play, learning was a very slow and arduous process, the total opposite of natural talent. Music instead touched me on a profoundly deep level and has completely transcended a spirit that's deep outside the norm of the conventions other people do. It's forced me to set values that don't align with society. I realize I'm not going to make money. It's okay. Music forces you to value what you do, so no matter what amount of money you do or don't make your love for the music can't be shaken. I chose music and a lifestyle that allows me to be in a space where my life isn't out of control. I'm allowed opportunities to sit and practice and be a person instead of having a life that rushes around me. I work on a constant state of improvement.

Every new moment can bring this improvement and spirituality of how much you love and enjoy life into a basic building block of love and joy. Even if you don't get the love down, you can enjoy the next moment, and this completely changes every day. I see people always comparing their life force, but a comparison would be incongruous. Trying to make logic out of why others do this or that is just a perpetual negative energy machine. Once you crank it up, it taints everything you do. We should benefit from interconnectivity instead of comparison. I do. My talent is about making someone feel something, not sounding like someone else. When comparison isn't there, it's completely freeing and has the ability to restructure and reorganize what's immediately at hand. You just live and react. This is also the solution to the problem with jazz. We shouldn't call it a style or jazz. The word "jazz" is a corrupted word. When jazz started to mean everything, we consequently took an audience who knew what jazz they did like and pulled the rug out from under them. We should cultivate a grassroots model for what we want to play and create or recreate that relationship with what we want to play. Anyone who says there's not an audience for something that has confidence, value, and craftsmanship is self-perpetuating failure.

I'm always cognizant when I present music to make sure the talent is as creative as possible. I want to make sure people hear each person without the others playing and pay special attention to the program. The whole purpose of transferring energy and being open and honest with yourself and how you present the music is so you can provide people with something they'll want to hear. You don't have to be a showman or bow to who you're not. Just present yourself in original form. Make intuitive, bold choices, and present the audience with fun.

Matt Jorgensen

CO-OWNER OF ORIGIN RECORDS, DRUMMER, CONCERT PROMOTER

HOME BASE
www.origin-records.com,
www.mattjorgensen.com

GOT MUSIC?
Origin Records encompasses
the following: Origin Records,
OA2, Origin Classical, Ballard
Jazz Festival

BACKGROUND AND SOUND

When the record labels that were almost solely tuned into jazz artists turned away from being the product of a few conglomerate labels into a more independently promoted and financed industry, few people said a word about it. It was almost as if it was accepted as what was to come. Few people outside of the recording world realize what it takes to get a CD from the studio to the shelves in a store or online or even as MP3 offerings through a site like iTunes or Amazon.com. The recording and production of CDs, not to mention the distribution of those CDs, has now been left up to the artists. This can easily be a full-time job in and of itself and take away from creative time needed to write new material or even hustle gigs or rehearsal times with a group. Enter Origin Records. In the fall of 1997 a young and tenacious entrepreneur, John Bishop, created Origin Records out of the need for somewhere to produce, design, and distribute his own CDs and those of the various groups he worked with on a regular basis. Once his former student Matt Jorgensen climbed aboard as a webmaster and business partner, the business took off farther than either of them could have predicted. Their focus then shifted to acquiring larger distribution and performance experiences for prominent musicians of the Northwest. Today, with the addition of OA2 (the offshoot label that works on promoting farther-reaching artists and more experimental works) and their classical music label, Origin Classical, they're fast growing to become the leading label in jazz. They've won countless awards and praise from critics as doing "something right." Their artists are pleased with the results their getting and the new "model" of an industry has now moved on from being the unknown to the well-known.

Matt Jorgensen, who partners with John Bishop, is not only well known for his role with Origin, but like John, is a remarkable drummer and has worked with greats Corey Christiansen, Tom Marriott, and Hadley Caliman, among many others. Matt works tirelessly in his role as promoter of the Ballard Jazz Festival. This festival is one of Seattle's best and is produced solely by Origin Records. Matt is an industrialist, to say the least, and leader for the future of this music. His big-picture, grassroots thinking has not only created many opportunities for musicians but has lifted the spirits and hopes throughout the jazz community.

HIS STORY

The traditional model of being a musician just doesn't exist anymore. If we want jazz to survive we have to have a "ground-up" philosophy. Origin Records started because we wanted to get our music out. The same thing with starting the Ballard Jazz Festival; we just thought we could create a cool festival that people would enjoy. I think musicians are good at figuring out what needs to get done to be able to make music happen. Along the way, John Bishop and I figured out that we had some abilities to help get our music out that we could also use in helping other musicians as well, and now we have a fairly robust community involved with the label. What's exciting now is seeing more musicians stepping up and filling the voids that have been created in the industry over the last few years. So I think everyone is figuring out what they need to do to make it happen.

I think what is really important for the national jazz scene is the strengthening of our local jazz communities. This business is an ecosystem. You have jazz radio, musicians, record labels, presenters, festivals, local jazz clubs and the larger touring-act jazz clubs, record stores, and jazz fans. Any impact on one is going to affect the others, but at the absolute core are the local jazz clubs and local musicians. This is where you build an audience for the music, where young musicians are introduced to the scene, where jazz radio builds listenership, where jazz festivals get the word-of-mouth going, and where record labels have an opportunity to sell records. Fancy million-dollar jazz clubs are great, but what we need more of are joints with low overhead, great music, cheap beer, and a scene that a crowd can naturally gravitate to. I remember walking into the Cave in Portland, Oregon, for a gig, and it looked like they bought a bunch of orange paint on sale at Home Depot and threw down a couple of area rugs, but they had a grand piano, a sound system, a great staff, good food, and a crowd that came to hear music. As a musician, what more do you need?

I think it is the responsibility of all of us to go out and be evangelical about jazz. We need to be creating gigs, supporting our fellow musicians' gigs, convincing the local bar to have jazz on the weekends—anything and everything. In Seattle, we found a small local art-house theater that seemed like a great venue for concerts and was dark on Mondays. We talked to the owners, who agreed, giving us a set of keys and a couple years worth of Mondays for fifty dollars a week.

Sometimes thinking about all the things I do on a daily basis seems crazy when I look at my bank account, but I don't think anyone who really loves this music does it for anything other than the love of doing it. It is what I've known my entire adult life and it is just what I do to be able to play the drums and travel the world. I can't imagine my life being any different.

Geoffrey Keezer

PIANIST, COMPOSER

HOME BASE
www.geoffreykeezer.com

GOT MUSIC?
Àurea, Geoffrey Keezer,
ArtistShare, 2009

"Music is the one way I connect directly to that creative source and spirit that flows through everything."

BACKGROUND AND SOUND

Geoffrey Keezer has legends throughout the field and encompasses his own experiences into his sound. As the recipient of numerous awards and commissions from esteemed organizations such as Chamber Music America, the Carnegie Hall Jazz Band, and the Saint Joseph Ballet, he has earned his rank and keep among the young composers who are cutting their teeth on audiences around the world. Leading his own groups into the wildly unpredictable market of live music, he has ensured one thing: that what the listener will hear, each and every time, whether on recordings or live, will be original and far from a simple emulation of those who have come before. Thick, smothering doses of dense harmonics stride across all eighty-eight keys of his innovative and diverse style. Geoffrey reads like an open book the second he opens the lid to his piano, and an audience can't ask for much more from artists, other than to have them bare their souls.

HIS STORY

I didn't really have a choice but to do music. I was born into a musical family. My mother and father were both musicians, and I grew up thinking that's the way the world was. Music is just how I experience the world and relate to it. Everything I do is somehow connected to it, and it's the basis of everything I know. I've had experiences that seem like so-called esoteric, spiritual experiences or Zen moments. I guess they've been labeled a million different ways over thousands of years. They're the kind of thing prophets or enlightened masters talk about when they say one is directly related to a source. Music is the one way I connect directly to that creative source and spirit that flows through everything. I've experienced this firsthand. Now, it doesn't make me a spiritual master by any stretch of the imagination, but I believe the world works this way. Knowing I can get up on stage and be fed spiritually and validated creatively makes it possible for me to spend twenty-four hours traveling door to door, sitting in airports, eating very expensive bad food, and being away from my family for weeks at a time.

We hold up a big mirror when we're on stage. What's being reflected is our audience and their individual potential. There's certain beauty and perfection there, and we're being called to go within us to own our potential as human beings. As musicians we're telling our audiences that this is what's possible to do as a human being. Other great artists or musicians always blow me away. I once saw Mikhail Baryshnikov. He was absolute human perfection. I hope one day to achieve to greatness on that level. There are some moments when I'm channeling something that goes through and touches others. Allowing others to have that experience and feel that kind of joy or love is something I'm grateful to give them. This is also why we practice our asses off. Your chops have to be up so you can handle what's coming through you. Listeners are very discerning and intelligent. People are capable of understanding complex musical ideas and emotions. As musicians we tend to take for granted that we're lucky we get to make a living doing something creative that's also something we love. Not everyone gets this opportunity. As for me, I'm incredibly blessed to be doing what I'm doing. Knowing I can connect to that incredible flow of life-giving energy when I play is like nothing else that I've experienced in the world . . . yet.

Lisa Kelly-Scott
VOCALIST, EDUCATOR

HOME BASE
www.kellyscottmusic.com

GOT MUSIC?
By Request, Lisa Kelly,
Independent Label, 1997

"I remind myself that I'm making a living at what I love to do, I'm raising my family with music, I'm continually researching, growing, writing, exploring, and nurturing through this music."

BACKGROUND AND SOUND

Award-winning vocalist Lisa Kelly has torn through the hearts of audiences throughout the Southeast and various festivals around the world with her sophisticated and sultry voice. A graduate of the acclaimed Jazz Studies Department at the University of North Florida, she studied with jazz legends Bunky Green and Jack Peterson. During her time as a student she was the recipient of numerous *DownBeat* magazine student awards. Her music goes well beyond the notes on the page. She has created a mission statement out of jazz. Lisa has made tremendous strides and efforts toward creating a better future for women who wish to go into the music business by mentoring and by implementing and conducting programs, workshops, and clinics around the country. Her dedication to creating a future for women in the field is a dynamic that is not seen enough and one she will leave as her legacy long after her career is completed.

HER STORY

I think everybody questions themselves along the way, several times at least . . . some more than others. We all begin to ask if we're good enough, if we're doing the right thing, are we at the level we hope to be at, how does everyone else see me? A lot of this questioning is about perception—other people's perception of you and your perception of yourself and how you're fitting in the scene at that time. I remind myself that I'm making a living at what I love to do, I'm raising my family with music, I'm continually researching, growing, writing, exploring, and nurturing through this music. That I am a messenger giving to others and never sitting in the same place . . . I'm teaching and perpetuating the art form to the next generations, and all of this is my success.

There is no such thing as a nine-to-five in this business; this is a twenty-four/seven job. For me, there's always this feeling that you can never get off your guard; you're constantly hungry to "feed" your art. But I think you can find a happy medium in pursuing your career while enjoying all other facets of your life. There is a way to enjoy your passion and not let it be all consuming to the point that you've missed other blessings in your life. There will always be choices, sacrifices, and responsibilities to be considered, and an awareness that maybe sometimes things just happen when they're supposed to. I wanted to be here for my children, to love and raise them instead of letting someone else do it, performing and nurturing my music too, expanding my career as they have moved on more independently in their lives. Now the time is right as my career launches into a much higher level. But when all is said and done, go with what you love to do, be responsible for learning all the skills you need to be successful, be honest in assessing yourself, and remember you're also out there to be a blessing to those you touch. Be consistent and affirmed in whatever it is you do.

Frank Kimbrough
PIANIST, COMPOSER, EDUCATOR

HOME BASE
www.frankkimbrough.com

GOT MUSIC?
Play, Frank Kimbrough, Palmetto, 2006

"Jazz is a democracy at work."

BACKGROUND AND SOUND

Frank Kimbrough's music is progressive and diverse. Whether as a leader or as a sideman, he is considered to be one of the very best pianists among key players throughout the world. His style has been influenced by legends such as Shirley Horn, Paul Bley, and Andrew Hill, but these influences in no way discount the years he has worked to become who he is today—a voice standing out from the crowd, with a warm and welcoming tone that draws listeners to him time and again.

HIS STORY

I got started in music when I was very young, maybe three years old, living in a small town in North Carolina. My mother and grandmother were both piano teachers who taught at home, so as far as I knew everybody played piano. They'd take me to church on Sunday morning, and when we got home I'd pick out the hymns and songs and improvise on them. At the age of seven I began piano lessons, but I always continued to improvise.

As I entered my twenties I began to look for my own path and turned to people like Shirley Horn, Andrew Hill, and Paul Bley for confirmation. I never formally studied with any of them, but they were all very kind and shared a lot of time with me. When we hung out, they imparted their knowledge through conversation, but that very rarely led to talk about the mechanics of music. Our conversations were usually more conceptual in nature, confirming what I had learned from listening and observing them as musicians.

I admired these musicians from afar as a youth in North Carolina, and came to see them almost as deities. But they don't want to be treated that way when you meet them in the kitchen at the Village Vanguard. They're people who live their lives as anyone else does. There's a lesson here: where adoration creates distance, respect and understanding bring you closer.

All of the longstanding associations I have with musicians started out with just one gig, and one of the most beautiful things I've experienced in music is having one gig blossom into a relationship that lasts for decades. Therein lies the life of my music. It comes through common experience, and lives on the edge—you're not just reading music on the bandstand, you're keeping a ball in the air, creating a support system for each other through the music. Jazz is democracy at work, with every person listening, responding, and contributing to the music no matter the circumstances.

I'm not a nationalistic person, but jazz is America's music. It sprang from the melting pot that is America, and by its nature is inclusive of many ideas and feelings. It's different every time we play, a living thing.

Michael League
BASSIST, COMPOSER, PRODUCER

HOME BASE
www.snarkypuppy.com

GOT MUSIC?
Bring Us the Bright, Snarky Puppy, Snarky Puppy, 2008

"People are attracted to common ground."

BACKGROUND AND SOUND

Some in this industry have bestowed upon Michael League the nickname Energizer Bunny. They are entirely correct in this observation. Not only does this ceaseless energy come through his music and original works, it comes through in his drive to become one of the great bandleaders of his time. Comparisons are in order. His group Snarky Puppy is one of the most inventive in sound and funk since Maynard Ferguson's fusion years. His jafunkadansion (self-termed genre of music, and quite aptly so) band, Snarky Puppy, is composed of eighteen family members and has garnered a cultish following throughout the country. The mastermind behind all things Snarky specializes in acoustic, electric, and key bass. As a sideman he has played his way through gospel, blues, and jazz venues throughout the country with Dave Brubeck, Ari Hoenig, Myron Butler and Levi, Bobby Sparks, and Wayne Krantz, for starters. With this pace and a little more sweaty hard work, Mike's career will lead straight to the core of the influential in jazz.

HIS STORY

I feel that seeing "jazz-educated" people playing jazz is more of a deterrent than an encouragement for me. I owe so much to my college, and I'm grateful for jazz education, but I feel like the heart, soul, and spirit of jazz is more in the playing of church musicians and people that have a more natural relationship to the culture that birthed this music. Having lived most of my musical life in the Dallas area, most of my closest friends were guys that grew up in Southern black churches. I saw the spirit of John Coltrane, Miles Davis, and Louis Armstrong in them. When they're playing gospel, funk, R&B, pop . . . I see the spirit of jazz in it because their relationship to music wasn't developed in an academic environment. This spirit is in the food, the family, the church. When I got out of college and moved to Dallas, almost every person I played with was black. And not just in their skin color but their cultural upbringing. They all grew up in a black church, and every one of their first musical experiences was in church.

The more I thought about it and researched it, I found that the pioneers of jazz—the ones jazz professors teach about and the ones we regard as heroes and icons—their first experiences with music was through the church, too. The more I became immersed in Dallas's black music scene, the more I saw the undeniable link between the church and jazz. So it seems to me ironic. . . . maybe not ironic but a least a little disconnected, that so many people who are thought of as a part of the jazz tradition today have never set foot in a black church. How does one start to understand a culture without being immersed in it? And isn't this culture the one that gave America jazz? After I fell (accidentally) into the Dallas music scene, almost every in-town gig I played for three years was in those churches. The experience changed the way I thought about everything. I began to see how the organist plays behind the pastor when he preaches and then how the church calls out to the pastor while he's preaching or the way the congregation encourages a singer during a solo. I began to hear the Basie band, Ellington, and Mingus more clearly.

Most folks say New York, my new home, is where the spirit of jazz is alive and well. To me, it's alive and well in its original form in the spirit of those that don't even consider themselves to be jazz musicians. Some of them don't even know the names of chords they're playing . . . they grew up in a certain environment, ate certain kinds of food, heard a certain dialect, and lived according to a certain set of cultural principles. All of it comes out in their playing. It makes sense that this was the environment that birthed jazz. Even though the aesthetics have changed, this is where the spirit of jazz really is. It's soul . . . raw soul and the necessity, not just the hope, of connecting with something higher.

Today, there seems to be a quiet racial divide in jazz. I think it's unintentional, and it makes a lot of sense that certain clubs have largely white audiences and musicians and others black. People are attracted to common ground. You see it in school cafeterias across the country—the Asian table, the white table, the black table, et cetera. I lived in the Dallas area for eight years. Five of those years I was in or around college, surrounded completely by white musicians. Three of those years I was surrounded completely by black musicians. The race thing was very visible to me and something I'm incredibly comfortable with. Speaking about the differences I've observed between white and black relating to music is a touchy thing with some people, but with me, it isn't at all—our cultures and experiences make us play differently. Jazz as a form of popular music has submerged significantly since the forties and fifties. Now the academic realm has been the thing that's kept it afloat because that's where the funding comes from. If the people holding on to this life buoy are largely white college students and professors, it only makes sense that the scene would show signs of this segregation.

Ultimately, people will make beautiful music regardless of how they came up or what they've been exposed to. You don't have to grow up in India to play Indian music. You don't have to grow up in the black community to play jazz. But when we speak of the jazz tradition it's important to at least recognize its roots. In terms of that tradition, I'm not exactly sure whether to consider myself a part of it or not. The people I idolize— Louis Armstrong, Miles Davis, Weather Report, and Wayne Krantz—are considered jazz musicians but aren't famous for doing what people before them did. They're famous for doing something new, inspiring, and fresh that roughly fit into the idiom. They had something different inside of them that needed to get out, and this is how I've always felt as a person. I don't think I'm alone in it either. I understand the mentality of being immersed in several musical traditions and using them to articulate what you specifically have to say about life. This is the spirit that has defined me.

Tim Lefebvre
BASSIST, COMPOSER, PRODUCER

HOME BASE
www.ruddermusic.com

GOT MUSIC?
Matorning, Rudder, Nineteen-
Eight Records, 2009

"Music has been a mirror or reflection of everything that's going on in my life."

BACKGROUND AND SOUND

Electric bassist Tim Lefebvre is one of the most skilled and sought-after bass players in the country. Tim is regularly spotted with the greats such as Patti Austin, Jamie Cullum, and Chris Botti. In the underground he is more likely to be seen standing on stage with groups that combine rock, fusion, and funk into one mad genre of goodness, such as Rudder and Wayne Krantz. Various other appearances include *Saturday Night Live*, the soundtracks from *Ocean's 12* and *Ocean's 13*, and television themes such as *The Sopranos, Late Show with David Letterman, 30 Rock*, and *The Knights of Prosperity.*

HIS STORY

Music has been a mirror or reflection of everything that's going on in my life. I've been through a lot of profound changes over the last few years, and the one thing that's been a constant is my music career. Actually it's been like this since I was a little kid. It's an anchor that gets better and better in my career. I'm changing every day as a person, and I'm just trying to do better and be myself when I play. But when I play, I hope people feel whatever I'm feeling. For the most part how people play is how their personality is. This is what reaches people. It's personal, almost like a common ground for everyone. This common ground depends also on communication. Musicians are just like everybody else. Some of them do have trouble communicating on a personal level with their words, so they often do it with their music. I'm one of them. At first, when I started playing, I was flattered that people wanted me to play with them. At the same time, I definitely got taken advantage of. I should have exploited these opportunities better and put a cap on what I thought I could do versus what I should be doing. I just figured out what I wanted to do by default. But it all came back to me not communicating what I wanted, what my goals were.

As of today, I still play, and it's the thing I'm most comfortable with. I'm still managing to do everything I want to do creatively. It just seems that our generation doesn't have the same hunger to work and make something of themselves. It seems that everything comes so easy. People get paid to tell others what's great and what's not. We should, instead, form our own opinion. There's no accounting for individual taste. I may not personally be the best player in the world, but I've played with people that blow my mind, and this is more important than what someone else thinks of me. I try to just be wallpaper. I don't really care about the few things people have said along the way. I hope whatever anyone likes about me is nice. I just want to take you, with whatever is happening in the music, on some kind of journey. Hopefully, we'll all land together on the other side.

Sara Leib
VOCALIST

HOME BASE
www.saraleib.com

GOT MUSIC?
It's Not the Moon, Sara Leib, Panfer Records, 2003

"When I try to interpret songs, no matter how I try to do this, I want that arrangement to serve the song and convey the song in a new way."

BACKGROUND AND SOUND
There's mature warmth not usually found among the youth in jazz today that's deeply woven into the vocals of Sara Leib. Having studied at Hamilton Music Academy Arts Magnet in Los Angeles, Berklee College of Music, and the New England Conservatory with the likes of Esperanza Spalding and Hiromi Uehara, Sara is a loud and kind voice emerging among the very best throughout the LA scene.

HER STORY

I started piano lessons as a kid. Eventually I moved onto other things, but it wasn't until high school and jazz choir that I became interested in jazz vocals. I'd listen to the New York Voices and Coltrane, Miles, and that's how I got into my music. Yet, reading Billie Holiday's bio, about the terrible life she had, made me stand up and listen more closely to the music. I think a lot of people graduate music school with the idea that they'll be discovered and no longer have to worry about finances. This is just the American ideal of entitlement a lot of young people have. They have to realize that their version of being a star doesn't happen right away. Even being somewhat of a star in jazz doesn't pay the bills. When I was reading about Holiday and her personal struggles, I decided not to take that romantic notion of being a musician. If you have a grounded sense of history, then there's knowledge from the outset that you're not becoming a jazz musician for the money. I'm a jazz musician because I have no other choice. It's just in me. If I can affect people emotionally with my music, I can sing to one person in the audience or five hundred, it doesn't matter. If my music moves them, I've met my goal. Because jazz is an improvised art, there's no point in playing to an audience if you're improvising for yourself. If you don't get feedback and no one is enjoying it, then who, if anyone, do you sing for? You might as well make it a hobby. When I try to interpret songs, no matter how I try to do this, I want that arrangement to serve the song and convey the song in a new way. If I can do that, then hopefully people will always enjoy what I put out for them, which will always be the best of me.

Ramsey Lewis
PIANIST, COMPOSER, EDUCATOR, NEA JAZZ MASTER

HOME BASE
www.ramseylewis.com

GOT MUSIC?
Songs from the Heart: Ramsey Plays Ramsey, Ramsey Lewis, Concord Records, 2009

"Success begins with your ability to perform at the highest level possible in your career at any particular moment."

BACKGROUND AND SOUND

Grammy Award–winning NEA Jazz Master Ramsey Lewis is one of the most successful pianists in the history of jazz. Over the past four decades Ramsey has earned seven gold records, three Grammy Awards, and innumerable other grants, awards, and accolades from around the world. His style reaches beyond the creators of jazz and dips into the pools of the gospel and blues traditions. Even his larger ensemble works echo this subtle touch of influences. He was a mainstay throughout the nation's airwaves from 1997 to 2009 with his show, *The Ramsey Lewis Morning Show*, and although that program has been discontinued, his voice and insight into the music can still be heard in more than seventy-five cities within the United States as he regularly hosts *Legends of Jazz with Ramsey Lewis*. He has touched thousands of listeners and musicians with his insight and indelible enthusiasm for music. His foundation (2005–2008) helped see kids through their high school years and into college, and he is one of the chief organizers of the Ravinia Festival's Jazz Mentor Program. The jazz community has most certainly been strengthened by his generous contributions to the music and his ceaseless efforts to educate the public and bring a wider, more appreciative audience to the art.

HIS STORY

Success can be looked at in two ways. Many people define success in monetary terms. But I think if you're honest and sincere and work hard at your art, that monetary support will come. To me, success begins with your ability to perform at the highest level possible in your career at any particular moment. The other side of this is that you must be able to express yourself in the way that you feel in that moment and be sure that this is what you're trying to say in your music. It's never going to be perfect. There's always going to be a Monday morning where you wish you had done it differently. Ultimately, success is seeking the most simple and honest way to express an idea while being able to support yourself and still do the things you love to do the most.

David Liebman

SAXOPHONIST, COMPOSER, EDUCATOR

HOME BASE
www.daveliebman.com

GOT MUSIC?
The Loneliness of a Long Distance Runner, David Liebman, CMP (Germany), 1985

"In spite of what may happen in the real world, there is another world where beauty and truth reign supreme."

BACKGROUND AND SOUND

Legendary saxophonist David Liebman is probably one of the most pragmatic and industrious musicians that has ever lived. Since the sixties, David has had listeners and musicians eating out of his hand with his out-of-the-box group and ever challenging music. His career began under the tutelage of Elvin Jones and Miles Davis. Around 1970 David took the initiative to form the musician's cooperative known as Free Life Communication. Funded by the New York State Council of the Arts, this co-op involved several dozen musicians and was a central component to the scene at the time. Other groups he has formed throughout his career include Quest (Billy Hart, George Mraz, Al Foster) and the David Liebman Quintet. Members of his quintet have changed throughout the years, as all bands do, but since 1991 Liebman's group has had the same personnel (Vic Juris, Marko Marcinko, and Tony Marino), although the music is anything but stagnant. Liebman's work in composition and improvisation in small and large ensemble settings has earned him two grants from the National Endowment for the Arts, two Grammy nominations (including one for best solo), an honorary doctorate from the Sibelius Academy of Music in Helsinki, Finland, and an induction into the International Association of Jazz Educators Hall of Fame. David Liebman has single-handedly dipped his thoughts and ideas in the way we hear and experience modern jazz today.

HIS STORY

I don't think I'd be the same person if it weren't for music. I certainly didn't think I was going this way in the beginning. Music was just the thing in the family you did. You played piano, and in those days the piano was the center of the living room. Of course there was a television, but it wasn't like it is now. Taking piano lessons was required of us, especially in a middle-class Jewish family in Brooklyn. But right away, when I heard music, I liked the sax. The tenor sax was very prominent in early rock and roll, and Elvis was one of my first heroes after Mickey Mantle and Willie Mays. But my mother was hip enough to know the best advice of all time, which was that I had to have at least two years of classical piano before I could choose my instrument. So it wasn't long until I got to the sax. I was first exposed to jazz hearing someone play in front of me at the neighborhood school where I took lessons. It was very fascinating to see someone moving their fingers so fast with no music in front of them and their eyes closed. When you're a kid that's all you see. But the real epiphany for me was the night I saw Coltrane live at Birdland in the city. I was fifteen years old. Whatever that was, I couldn't believe it was the same instrument I had back in Brooklyn and that *this* is what could be done with it. Of course I followed him till the end. I saw him as much as I could and from then on pursued his music. If it wasn't for 'Trane, I would have played and enjoyed music, but I would have probably become a music teacher or something else. I wouldn't have seen that there's something behind the veil.

With the arts in general, you have to get turned on to it like I did. You don't just come out of the shell appreciating Picasso. You have to be taught, and in those days there was no instruction like there is now. What I do in one hour with my students is more instruction than I got in my early years—exaggerating of course. We just did things our way, the street way, and I was exposed to it at the right age. It formed my life, my vocation, and my worldview. In spite of what may happen in the real world, there is another reality where beauty and truth reign supreme, serving the better side of humanity.

Jazz is about being a part of a group and at the same time being assertive and an individual on your own. I like this combination. This is exactly what we all deal with in life everyday. We do it every minute. I consider jazz as a light, a kind of shining beacon, and those that do it are great folks. I don't know anybody hipper and nicer than jazz musicians. We're not in it for the money; you just can't be. We just try to keep our integrity in spite of the forces around us that are usually way stacked against honesty, forces that are for profit and all that stuff, not for love and beauty. You have to have an inner strength, as there's a certain amount of wear and tear in playing this music. I'm not comparing it with labor in the fields or anything, but you got to be strong, sensitive, and focused, with your eyes on the ball, not what's necessarily around it. You can't be alive now and not see the degradation of culture staring us in the face. These days the world's so much more complicated, with little time for art. You have to pick and choose where and why and who and be very specific about what you want to do. There will always be a segment of any population that not only wants the magic that comes from great art but also needs it. These are the people we play for. And I think that as long as you keep your sights reasonable, you're okay. I don't want to be a saint; I just want to play the music I believe in.

Joe Lovano {LIVING LEGEND}

SAXOPHONIST, COMPOSER, EDUCATOR

HOME BASE
www.joelovano.com

GOT MUSIC?
Folk Art, Joe Lovano Us Five, Blue Note/EMI, 2007

"Every day there's a new light that shines on the music."

BACKGROUND AND SOUND

Grammy Award–winning Joe Lovano is a fearless leader in jazz. His compositions and soloing abilities have reset standards time and again for instrumentalists of all types. Continually challenging the notion that jazz has to be a structured within a certain feel and time, he has pushed the music world over and above this all too imitated pocket. He has been awarded and recognized for this very school of thought in many ways, including numerous Jazz Journalists Association awards, *DownBeat* magazine poll awards, an honorary doctorate from Berklee College of Music, and more. He is signed to Blue Note records and has more than twenty-five recordings as a leader of his own group and hundreds of recordings as a sideman. It is legends like Joe who will not only push but also sign, seal, and deliver that envelope of greatness each and every time he steps to the mic.

HIS STORY

I'm inspired by the whole aspect of creating music. Every day there's a new light that shines on the music. It's inspiring to live and create in this way. I can develop a free and organic approach to the music even within my own voice. If you try to tell someone else's story through your music, it can become an ongoing struggle for you, and it's easy to then become trapped by the music. This is why you have to tell your own story. The ones that have left us talked about this, too. People like Gillespie, Parker, Coltrane, and Monk taught us that we had to stand on our own two feet out here while we're being creative. But everyone has a different story and level of experience in their own personal history that they bring to the stand.

When I listen to music today, I'm touched when someone does this through their personality and sound. They have this warmth in their feelings and expressions. When I play I like to explore with a sense of celebration in the feelings in my music. This doesn't have to be complex; it's just a matter of that joyous feeling the musicians create on stage in the moment. That aspect of being alive and celebrating life everlasting is something artists have to be passionate about. Too many people live in their own world and refuse to let anything in. This is why, as musicians, we have to be open. You have to be yourself, and it's only you who chooses to take critics, even your inner critic, along with you. This is always going to be a heavy struggle for artists, so the best thing we can do is be honest and share ideas and talk about how to develop the ideas in order to create a continuum. We should never criticize anyone for being expressive about who they are, even if you can't embrace who they are. If someone puts themselves out there with a lot of passion, then they're doing the best they can. The more you realize the passion others have had before you and have around you, the more confidence you'll have to be yourself. This music is about who you are, and it's best to hold that love for the music and yourself in your heart at all times.

Dante Luciani
TROMBONIST, COMPOSER, EDUCATOR

HOME BASE
www.danteluciani.com

GOT MUSIC?
Dan zon, Arturo Sandoval,
Grp Records, 1994

"It's the exploration of this art form that will make you a better person."

BACKGROUND AND SOUND

Maynard Ferguson discovered trombonist Dante Luciani early on in Dante's career. Following Maynard's lead, Woody Herman, Paul Anka, and Frank Sinatra brought him onto their stages, too. His crisp and engaging sound burns through his horn, leaving a trail of resonant tone behind him. Leaving the impressions of standard bop to the rest, he insists on leaving his legacy as one that is but a stolen moment, a treasure rarely seen. He passes this heritage on to the students pooling around his stories at the University of Miami. Dante is truly a rare gem.

HIS STORY

Jazz is a form of communication, just like any language, but it's very deep and advanced communication between musicians. It can be very intimate at times. Personally, I'm not a traditionally religious person, so music has become the closest thing for me, if there is some kind of God, that's as powerful and does as much spiritually for a person. It inspires the most awe and wonder in me, continually causing me to ask if there's something more than a common existence. How else can you explain how music crosses cultural boundaries and musicians can regularly play in places where there are government warnings telling you not to enter there? When I was with Maynard in India we had no language in common to bond with them. The music transcended the language barrier and politics and bickering, and went beyond the government.

When musicians share their passions it goes way beyond any set boundaries. What I try to do is to get others—my students, listeners, et cetera—to preserve the love and freshness they feel when they first played or heard this music. Our educational system is turning out a lot of culturally uneducated kids. There are those who have no idea about art, sculptures, music, and this is a sign of a society on its last leg. So I have to talk with my students and ask them why they're doing this. It's not going to be easy. But I know that it's the exploration of this art form that will make you a better person overall. They have to keep that mind-set and perspective in check while striving to have as much fun as you can have. But this entails a lot of work. It's a labor of love, and even when you get dark you have to realize that your ability as a musician is a gift and a privilege and your job to pass the torch to the next generation.

Russell Malone

{LIVING LEGEND}

GUITARIST, COMPOSER, EDUCATOR

HOME BASE

GOT MUSIC?
Sweet Georgia Peach, Russell Malone, Verve/Impulse, 1998

"So many people have come before me who have given their lives for this music, and the best way to pay tribute to them is to not let the standard drop."

BACKGROUND AND SOUND

Rising out of the steamy South, Russell Malone is one of the best jazz guitarists on the scene today. Having spent time in bands led by Ray Brown, Jimmy Smith, Freddie Cole, and Ron Carter, he has learned his trade the old-fashioned way by coming up through the ranks. He buttered his strings on countless solo albums and has performed with heavy hitters such as Aretha Franklin and Diana Krall. But as a mentor to many in the field, he is a rare breed. He uses a sly ability to convey both the present and the past through each note. This is a skill many attempt to bring to the table, and he pulls it off with ease, grace, and subtle charm.

HIS STORY

When I was young, in my teens and twenties, and trying to learn how to play the music, it was only about guitar and getting the notes in. As I got older I started to think about other things. I hear a lot of good players now, and I know they practice, practice, practice all the time. This is good. You have to stay on top of your game. But then they get on the bandstand and that's what it sounds like: practicing. There's a fine line between not spending enough time on your instrument and spending too much time. Music for me is about life. Life is not about music. Charlie Parker said, "Music is your life, your thoughts. If you don't live it, then it won't come out of your instrument." It's very important to develop as a human being first. As musicians, when we play, we're as naked as we can be. We're exposed, vulnerable.

I try to play good every night, and hopefully I'm reaching someone. That's what we should do as artists. So many people have come before me who have given their lives for this music, and the best way to pay tribute to them is to not let the standard drop. Acknowledge history, but don't be a slave to it. You have to arrive at your own conclusion on how to approach this music. Each generation brings something different to it, and everybody has a voice, an identity. But what everybody doesn't have, especially when they're young, is the confidence to speak with their voice. They seek validation instead. As much as I love the people who have come before me, when it comes to being Russell Malone, I'm the best there is. No one will ever be able to outdo me at that. Once I realized this, I was able to make honest music. I want people to feel good when they hear me. I may not change the world through my guitar, but when I play I'm very sincere.

Marko Marcinko

PERCUSSIONIST, EDUCATOR, COMPOSER, FOUNDER
OF THE PENNSYLVANIA JAZZ ALLIANCE

HOME BASE
www.markomarcinko.com,
www.scrantonjazzfestival.org

GOT MUSIC?
Blues All Ways, David Liebman
Group, Omnitone Records, 2007

"I'm an advocate of the arts being a part of anyone's life."

BACKGROUND AND SOUND

Marko Marcinko is the founder of the
Pennsylvania Jazz Alliance, a leader of
his own quartet, and a long-standing
drummer of the David Liebman Group. His
ability to sing and use auxiliary equipment
in conjunction with the many timbres of
a set lends a personable yet expert touch
to the music he expresses himself through.
Marko is doggedly driven to build a world
centered on this music. Waiting around for
others to help complete his dream is not
something he is too fond of. Instead, through
hard work and tenacity he has turned this
dream of his into a well-oiled machine that functions and thrives on the
path toward a better community surrounded by jazz.

HIS STORY

I'm an advocate of the arts being a part of anyone's life. The arts can
help you become kinder, more compassionate, and well rounded in your
approach to things that happen in this world. It's definitely had quite
the impact on me. If I didn't have music in my life, I would have had to
go to some sort of art, because I'm not sure how I could even function
without it.

But I would like to see our arts become more of an universal language.

This way it could bring more people together, and we could begin to appreciate different cultures, styles, and art forms across the board. I've always been an idealist, but when I begin to think about where we are today I become completely pessimistic. There's a certain reality in what we do. You can show up at a club and know that there is only a limited amount of people that are there that are going to get it. The rest of them are home, either watching TV or trying to deal with the kids. Or maybe they'd rather go see something other than jazz that's more mainstream and popular. But jazz to me is the ultimate of all musical art forms. You get to create a side of music that takes you to another level. When the pistons are firing in the jazz engine inside of you, you're really doing something that's truly unique and beyond the call of duty as a general practitioner of music. It delivers the most of the musical language to me and into my soul.

Eric Marienthal
SAXOPHONIST, COMPOSER, EDUCATOR

HOME BASE
www.ericmarienthal.com

GOT MUSIC?
Got You Covered, Eric Marienthal, Peak Records, 2005

"Every day we get that chance to wake up, as creative musicians, and reinvent ourselves."

BACKGROUND AND SOUND
Grammy Award–winning saxophonist Eric Marienthal's career began with a one-year stint with trumpeter Al Hurt in New Orleans. This fateful gig marked the beginnings of a fantastic life and career. He has held long-standing gigs with Chick Corea's Elektric Band and is currently in the lead alto spot with Gordon Goodwin's Big Phat Band. He has performed with artists such as Elton John, Barbra Streisand, Dave Grusin, Lee Ritenour, the Yellowjackets, and many more. He has also recorded eleven solo CDs, which have consistently risen to the top of *Billboard* charts. In his "spare" time, Eric is also the musical director for the nonprofit organization High

Hopes. Based in Los Angeles, this charity works with traumatic head injury patients. His efforts have raised more than half a million dollars for this worthy cause. An extraordinary musician and philanthropist, Eric's glistening tone and all-too-human song sings directly from his heart.

HIS STORY

There is such a strong parallel between what a musician plays like and what their life is like. Playing in the different groups I've played in, especially in the world of jazz, where music is improvisational and conversational, I can especially see the parallel. A band is very much like a family, and the way we communicate in our solos is comparable to how we communicate in our speech. Often, in jazz, one person will state the melody, and this is like stating the subject the group is talking about. Then something the drummer plays inspires the keyboard player, which, in turn, inspires the horn player who is soloing, who in turn inspires another musician. But we have to do this without playing on top of each other, because what each of us is saying is important. This is a lot like a family sitting around the dinner table . . . if everyone starts talking at the same time, or arguing, nothing good comes of it. There are so many comparisons that it's almost an identical situation, and the more successful we are as creative musicians, the more successful we are as contributing members to our family and friends as well.

But every day we get that chance to wake up, as creative musicians, and reinvent ourselves by coming up with new and creative ways of—if it's from an artistic standpoint—writing, recording, or practicing. A lot of what's important as a player is to be as proficient as possible on our instruments. Even at the age of fifty-one I'm still looking at ways to improve myself. You have to do things differently so people will continue to be interested in you. This thinking keeps it fresh. As a leader, sideman, and writer, I have to also create something people will want to continue to work with. My music has to speak for itself, and my playing has to be as enthusiastic as I can make it while at the same time still be something I believe in.

Thomas Marriott

TRUMPETER, COMPOSER, EDUCATOR

HOME BASE
www.thomasmarriott.net

GOT MUSIC?
Flexicon, Thomas Marriott, Origin
Records, 2009

"Being an artist is a crummy way of making a living, but to me, it's the only way to live."

BACKGROUND AND SOUND

Award-winning Seattle-based trumpeter Thomas Marriott is considered to be one of the brightest trumpet players on the scene today. His work covers a broad scope of influences and tastes from the outright traditional to covering Willie Nelson in such an original way that he has even the most die-hard jazz fans reeling. He is signed to the Origin Record label and is a regular player throughout the national touring circuit with his own group and with legends like Hadley Caliman. Combining the best of both worlds in the West Coast cool tradition and the East Coast hard-driving bop of yesteryear with the fresh, raw sound of today, Tom is a great representative of the shape of things to come.

HIS STORY

When you do this for a living and you're not a superstar, your commitment to the art is constantly being challenged. Having this commitment tested is a healthy dose of reality. Ninety percent of the jazz musicians I know are not superstars.

When you're a working jazz musician you don't aspire to stardom or being on the cover of *DownBeat*; that's just ridiculous. I, just like most, work toward the goal of just being a jazz musician, to just keep working. I've done this for more than half of my life.

What does this mean? It means I'll never be satisfied with who I am or where I am at. In this music there's always new ground to break. It's like a supreme challenge. To be an effective artist you have to work on you. The scary thing is that an artist experiences life and translates its meaning, even with all its impossibilities, into their art. Unfortunately, we're in a society that constantly sends messages that are opposed to this experience. When this is what we see and hear, it's difficult to be ourselves. As musicians we have to be ourselves to make our own music, or to make the music our own. At all times we have to think about our particular beliefs and how we feel. This is accompanied by self-examination away from the music and the instrument. We have to try to answer questions for ourselves over and over again by articulating through our art. We ask constantly, why am I doing this? Hopefully we can come up with answers that will satisfy you when you listen. Musicians will always be realists but also we'll bullshit ourselves to the bitter end by saying this will one day pay off. Yet the truth is that we will never know how to actually pay it off. Being an artist is a crummy way of making a living, but to me, it's the only way to live. My mission and goal is to propagate the art form in terms of modern improvised instrumental music, or "jazz." We're all trying to be artists of our own time. The ones who don't have competency in their music and don't have a sense of the human experience or a sense of romance or intimacy in the way they play won't change the perspective of a listener. Lots of people have decided for themselves that they don't like jazz, but often they have yet to have a positive experience with it. People respond to the "realness" that lies in seasoned professionalism. This competency has to come from your personality and expression of the human experience. It's hard for us to be dedicated to a craft no one cares about anymore. Some place a stigma on the word "jazz." But to those of us who play the music or aspire to play it, this word has meaning. It's our life.

Delfeayo Marsalis
PRODUCER, TROMBONIST, EDUCATOR, COMPOSER

HOME BASE
www.dmarsalis.com

GOT MUSIC?
Minions Dominion, Delfeayo
Marsalis, Troubadour Jazz, 2006

"Jazz is a lifestyle, a way of thinking, an abstract impression of reality."

BACKGROUND AND SOUND

Grammy Award–winning producer and trombonist Delfeayo Marsalis has more avenues of talent streaming down his lines of creativity than most of the jazz world knows about. His true passion lies not in the performance position of the business, but the production aspect. While attending Berklee College of Music he majored in equal parts trombone performance and audio production. As a producer he has worked with and produced more than seventy-five major label recordings. Quite a few of these have gone on to win Grammy Awards or various other peer and critic awards. The artists who worked under Delfeayo's carefully skilled guidance include Harry Connick Jr., Marcus Roberts, Spike Lee, and of course his brothers Wynton and Branford. His keen ear and attention to detail on the chopping blocks in the studio have earned him a 3M Visionary Award. Artists like Elvin Jones, Art Blakey, and Max Roach strengthened his chops on the horn by taking him on numerous international tours. Delfeayo's investigative foray into his own artistry, combined with the pliability in the production insight he has, has kept him disciplined in maintaining his superb reputation as a jack-of-all-trades.

HIS STORY

Perhaps the perfect anecdote for a family of musicians is represented by a mythology spawned from the loins of Austria's Leopold Mozart and furthered in the histrionics of the Jackson 5. Ah, yes, the proverbial domineering, self-serving father who undoubtedly locks his offspring in a basement or closet to practice until the desired results are achieved is indeed a universal theme. For us Marsali, life was far more practical and didn't center on music—rather, purpose. As children we were Boy Scouts, played on all the sports teams, participated in school functions, and had a general sense of community involvement. Born in pairs, Branford and Wynton were running partners, Ellis III and myself were the same, and, alas, Mboya and Jason became two peas in a pod though separated by seven years. Our mother, Dolores, insisted that we take advantage of every available opportunity as she prepared us to become responsible, respectful young men. It was pretty wild and noisy in the house when we were younger. She spoiled all of us by preparing hot meals every morning and keeping up with our whimsical idiosyncrasies. Hard-boiled eggs for Branford, scrambled for Wynton, egg whites for Ellis, only the yolk for me. . . . Who would imagine a mother catering to her sons in such a fashion, while insisting that they accept the responsibilities of education and the burden of integration? We are talking about the late sixties after all, when equal rights in the South was still a new ideal.

Many parallels might be made between the dynamics of family interaction and the performance of jazz music, from the extraordinary to the mundane. In fact, some of the great relationships in jazz have been the result of one person providing a type of support that was not prevalent in another's childhood. That contrast is found as early as King Oliver playing the role of guardian to the fatherless Louis Armstrong. Another classic example was drummer Elvin Jones's undying love for saxophonist John Coltrane. "You have to be ready to die for a motherfucker to play like that," Jones exclaimed. The youngest of ten children born to honest and hard-working, yet financially poor parents, Jones mastered the art of compromise. Coltrane on the other hand, was reared as an only child and grew accustomed to the inherent solitude, undergirded with unabashed selfishness. Had Jones been an only child, it is less conceivable that he would have supported Coltrane's endeavors with such an obsession. He clearly understood his role in one of history's seminal musical ensembles.

Understanding how each instrument functions in the jazz band is an integral part to New Orleans musicians' ability to create spontaneous polyphonic arrangements that are cohesive and precise. It sounds simple, but for the most part the trumpet plays the melody, the sax or clarinet plays a harmonious counterpart, and the trombone complements the two while serving as the bridge between the horns and rhythm section. The tuba and drums must support the other musicians on every beat, and the piano oversees the ensemble, being careful not to intrude while filling in the necessary riffs. In the Marsalis clan, the chosen instruments have suited the corresponding personalities with remarkable accuracy.

That my father plays piano makes perfect sense, as it is central to jazz composition both written and in real time. My dad loves music! As boys, my brother Ellis and I watched impatiently as his jazz sextet played passionately to a quintet of patrons. Much to our chagrin, he refused to quit his gigs prematurely, choosing instead to carry us to the car one at a time after it was over and we were fast asleep. Though the differences between us brothers are quite profound, everyone in the family is an old school traditionalist. An old school teacher (much like an older relative) is personally offended by a youngster's inability to comprehend the lesson at hand. The delivery of said information might include quotes from the Bible, generational anecdotes, old wives' tales, or pure unadulterated profanity. A traditionalist thanks his elders for enduring the pain for the future generations' sake—in song, in prayer, in spirit, or in person, man-to-man. What other idiom or vocation has created as much artistic profundity by brothers and families as jazz? It embodies the hustle and bustle of American life through the past 120 years through its elegant groove, spirit, and, of course, swing.

How I love the sound of swing and the act of swinging. Instrumental technique must be respected, but that commitment to the sound of joy is not what we hear so often today. The greatest musical aspect of the late 1950s—the most profound period in jazz history—is that there were about twenty different styles being played on a high level at the same time. The younger musicians were checking out the older ones and vice versa, each group keeping the other honest. Now the older folks don't necessarily have to be kept honest like the adolescents, but they always embrace an opportunity to lay down the law. My time with the village elders has been extremely important in my development as a musician and a man. Elvin Jones, Art Blakey, Max Roach, Abdullah Ibrahim, Ray Charles, Ron Carter, Slide Hampton . . . and the list goes on of individuals who loved European opera, symphonic concert music, Eastern (Asian/Egyptian) tonalities, African rhythm, and any folk song. All music is related, anyway. Is not music one big happy family?

In that family, the older generation provides example and encouragement for the youngsters, distilling those facets that are most valuable for artistic sustenance. Their message, as I have heard it, is first and foremost, love music. Through love most things are possible. Dedicate yourself to that which you love and the rest will resolve itself. Jazz is a lifestyle, a way of thinking, an abstract impression of reality. . . . It represents individuality and teamwork, personal growth and development, commitment and sharing. It is an indication of where you are from, who you are, and who you aspire to be. The older recordings sound human, beautiful, and alive with spirit. That's the beauty of the thing. The black and white, north and south, east and west, old and young, long and short of it. The most important aspect in the interpretation and presentation of music has nothing to do with music at all!

Joe Martin
BASSIST, COMPOSER, EDUCATOR

HOME BASE
www.joemartinbass.com

GOT MUSIC?
Not by Chance, Joe Martin, Anzic
Records, 2009

"Being a musician is just something I've always done."

BACKGROUND AND SOUND

Growing up in an overtly musical family, Joe Martin has had a wealth of inspiration surrounding him throughout all of his years as a musician. He has risen to the top of the call lists throughout New York. Joe is truly an indispensable bassist within the many different subgenres in jazz. Musicians of the highest caliber call on him regularly, including Jane Monheit, Kurt Rosenwinkel, Chris Potter, Maria Schneider, Mark Turner, Mingus Big Band, Aaron Goldberg, Ari Hoenig, Grady Tate, and Michael Weiss. His thick influences from early on in his career, like Stanley Clark and Jaco Pastorius, still haunt his booming voice. But Joe has not let these voices taint his own. With an understated warmth, he knows how to balance on the tightrope of solo performances–versus–sideman positioning. This search and hunt for the balance in his craft has rendered him a crucial cat in modern jazz.

HIS STORY

Being a musician is just something I've always done. It wasn't something I did consciously when I was younger; in fact, I don't think it was until I was in college that I even thought about doing this professionally, to make it the my main focus in life. In the bigger sense, I'm happy I chose to pursue music. It's very important that we spend our lives doing what we really love to do. I'm just grateful I can make what I love into a career. When you do something you love, you're often rewarded in ways you'd have never dreamed. Being a jazz musician does this for me. It gives back to me in a very deep way ... It's like falling in love. As a matter of fact, most musicians I know go through this. At some point we really do fall in love with the music, and it becomes a big part of our lives. We almost have to fall in love with it, as it's the only way to get better at it. The music demands it. As musicians our rewards are great but not when it comes to the financial aspects of the music. If someone was to look at jazz from a purely capital standpoint, they would ask, why do you do this? It's insane . . . but as musicians our lives are full of absurdities like this. We're known to travel around the world just for one concert and then spend days in airports and hotels trying to get back home. Yet most musicians I know do this purely because they love it or feel the absolute need to do it.

Of course I've been challenged in having to deal with these absurdities, too. I didn't move to New York and have a regular gig or get "picked up." I've had to instead learn how to have faith and be patient with the way gigs just seem to come and go. In order to do this, I had to believe that what I was working on would help carve my place in the scene. I had to know that the path I was on would help me find my voice within the language of music. I've learned to be diligent about working on what I want to work on and that it doesn't matter what gigs I'm doing or not doing as those are just outside things. And these outside things are not going to determine who I am. Instead I have to take what I can from my experiences, positive or negative, so I can learn to have more faith and vision and confidence in what I'm doing.

Brad Mason
TRUMPETER, FLÜGELHORNIST, EVI PLAYER, COMPOSER, EDUCATOR

HOME BASE
www.masonbrothersband.com

GOT MUSIC?
Two Sides, One Story, Mason Brothers Band, Independent Label, 2010

"When listening to music I crave emotion, so when I play it, I have to try to give that emotion back."

BACKGROUND AND SOUND
Since the age of nine, award-winning trumpeter Brad Mason has slowly unleashed his inner power into the jazz, pop, and R&B communities.

His sixth sense for timing, rhythm, and harmonic structure creates a balance in his playing many musicians would envy. His roster of stage mates includes John Mayer, Alicia Keys, David Liebman, Eric Clapton, Mike Stern, Willie Nelson, Natalie Cole, Joe Zawinul, Jessica Simpson, Gary Husband, and many more. In addition to his boundless energy as a player, he has adapted the use of the EVI (electronic valve instrument) into his repertoire. Along with his brother Elliot, Brad coleads the Mason Brothers Band. Together, Elliot and Brad have painted the walls in many venues throughout New York with their highly infectious groove. By walking their continuous uphill walk to greatness, they're certain to be one of the most original and bold groups to ever enter jazz history.

HIS STORY

In the beginning, I had no choice. Jazz chose me. I was on stage surrounded by this music while in my mother's tummy. She was a professional singer, and my father was a professional trumpet and trombone player in the UK. Jazz was always playing in our house while I was growing up. My parents were huge fans of this art form, and both my brother Elliot and myself were saturated with it from a very early age. It just seemed the norm to me. Everything was jazz influenced, my T-shirts, mugs, posters, going to gigs and concerts on the weekends. Even our dogs name was Tacet, and he listened to jazz. But it wasn't until I was twelve years old that I chose jazz. When I got my first Aebersold Play-A-Long record I realized the excitement it gave me to solo and improvise; creating my own music on the spot just like I heard my idols do growing up was incredible.

Years later I see how this music has shaped and influenced many things in my life. Since I grew up in England, my playing and my music have been touched and influenced by much of the classic UK pop and rock music that was injected into our modern culture. This, mixed with my heavy American jazz saturation while growing up, has shaped and molded me into who I am, musically, today. Jazz has demanded throughout that I be very honest with myself when it comes to practicing and self-improvement.

This helps me grow and expand intellectually and has taught me how to have discipline, patience, and respect. I'm a very passionate and emotional person. I need to be in order to connect emotionally with the music I'm playing so that I can project this to the listener. I love creating and discovering new things, musically or not. Although I agree that personal expression is the key to jazz, I try not to let this interfere with the overall musical picture or the positive experience I want my audience to have. Musicians can sometimes get a little selfish on the bandstand and get too wrapped up in themselves. The audience is such an intricate part of the jazz performance, and it can often influence the path of the music. A single reaction can send you to embellish or expand on an idea. Sometimes it even takes things in a completely new direction. This is one of the reasons jazz needs an audience. On stage, as musicians, we're very lucky to get to enjoy special moments that happen spontaneously around us. These are usually due to the people and the setting we are performing in. I try in each performance to act on and incorporate the emotions I'm feeling into each solo so the listener can hear and feel something different every time. When listening to music I crave emotion, so when I play it I have to try to give that emotion back. Jazz has forced me to play in that moment, which in turn has helped me live more in the moment.

Elliot Mason

VALVE TROMBONIST, TROMBONIST, BASS
TRUMPETER, COMPOSER, EDUCATOR

HOME BASE
www.masonbrothersband.com

GOT MUSIC?
Two Sides, One Story, Mason Brothers Band, Independent Label, 2010

"It's about how you tell the story rather than the story itself."

BACKGROUND AND SOUND
Originally from London, England, Elliot Mason is one of the most powerful voices in the brass family today. Emerging through the channels of genius both Stateside and worldwide, his virtuosic technique and hardy yet booming style stand out as an accented beat away from the path most traveled. Elliot is also a Berklee graduate, an adjunct professor at Northwestern University, and a member of the Lincoln Center Jazz Orchestra, not to mention a top-call voice throughout the New York and Chicago scenes. This comes

as no surprise. Elliot and his brother Brad have recently formed the Mason Brothers Band. Aware of the need to clean the streets of any dull music, they've brought in their own wave of cool. Elliot's accomplishments on multiple brass instruments and compositions drive his individual groove to a centered place in his soul.

HIS STORY

My mom was a jazz vocalist and my father played bass trumpet. I looked to my father as a mentor. I started out like him on bass trumpet, but he thought my embouchure would be better for a trombone. Eventually I went back to the valves, and by the time I got to Berklee, at the age of sixteen, I was playing both instruments fluently. Now I represent only who I am when I solo and can't get away from that. When I pick up either horn it comes out. Everybody, I believe, to a certain degree, has this distinctive sound of his or her own. I'm maturing and trying to concentrate more on the bigger picture of who I am and the moods I create when I play. It's about how you tell the story rather than the story itself.

As a musician you can get to the bottom of a lot of things about your personality and what you want to say and why you say certain things and where and how and why you're going with it. There's something to be said for creating your own scene rather than striving to play with others. Musicians you went to school with and those from your era will be the musicians of your day, and creating something within that realm is what you want to be a part of. That's how I'm being true to myself. Jazz is such a big part of me. I'm speaking a language that can touch people when done right; this passion is what fuels me. It's my hope that the audiences and those not in the audience will explore more of what's out there. You have to find the artists by looking into it for yourself, and when you find them, listen to them with an open mind. It's disturbing, though, to think that younger people, namely of my generation and younger, don't even know what instrumental music is. How is it possible to go through life not knowing this? The thing about jazz is—and people need to realize this—that you don't always need lyrics. It's the musician who has the intent behind it and has something to say. This is when it will hit you, and you'll understand what they're saying to you. You might not like it the first time, but you might the second or tenth time you hear it, but someday these people will be the jazz greats of our day.

Maysa
VOCALIST, SONGWRITER, COMPOSER

HOME BASE
www.maysa.com

GOT MUSIC?
Metamorphosis, Maysa, Shanachie
Records, 2008

"I do the best I can by staying true to myself no matter what anyone else says."

BACKGROUND AND SOUND

Maysa has remained at the top of the *Billboard* sales charts throughout most of her career. As a young talent, Maysa was picked up by Stevie Wonder to perform in his production *Wonderlove*. In addition to that she has performed on movie soundtracks, such as *Jungle Fever*, and on TV shows such as *The Oprah Winfrey Show* and *The Tonight Show*. Her velveteen timbre has earned her membership among the jazz/funk group Incognito, and she has collaborated with great artists such as Rick Braun, Will Downing, and Jason Miles. She also spends her time as a spokesperson for respiratory synctial virus (RSV), which can be fatal for premature babies, and regularly makes appearances for the March of Dimes. Her luscious yet naturally dense vocals and emotional side reach far beyond the mic stand and demonstrate adoration for all life.

HER STORY

My mom took me to see *Purlie* when I was six. Melba Moore opened her mouth and sounded like an instrument, a part of the band. It moved me all at once. I heard my first bit of jazz when I was twelve years old. I mostly listened to pop music at the time, and my Uncle Caleb thought I should be listening to jazz. He turned on the TV to PBS; Al Jarreau was on and scatting. I knew from that moment on that's that what I wanted to do. Now that I sing, I would think you hear my influences as well as every bit of happiness and pain I've felt and have been through. I'm not here nor there; my sound is indicative of how my body feels. This music has everything to do with my mental, emotional, physical, and spiritual state. It's very personal.

I don't think I've been defeated yet, but my image per the industry hasn't been the right image. I'm a beautiful, big woman. It's played a part in the fact that I haven't had some recognition others have. I'm overcoming this, as there are people who love my music and me just the way I am. They don't care. Regardless, I hate that I've allowed myself to get depressed by this. I'm nothing but love. Everything I touch and think about and do when I walk through life, love is the foremost thing in my mind. It's how I deal with other people and how I react. Since I was a baby, per my mother, I was always in love with everyone. But this doesn't mean I've compromised my morals to sing a single note. I do the best I can by staying true to myself no matter what anyone says. This industry can be all smoke and mirrors, but don't let anyone tell you that you have to do anything you don't want to do. You can't have too much pride and be afraid to ask for help. I want to personally be better at it, and I'm still learning. It's a part of me. God put me here so I can be a servant to people through my music, and sometimes this is hard to explain in words. This love is as deep as my heart is beating every day, and I wouldn't be the same person without it. Jazz is probably the only art form in America that was born out of America from the very beginning, and it means a lot to me to be able to carry it on and place my signature on it. We all need for jazz to be the best it can be, as it's truly loved by so many people in the world. It's ours, and we need to keep it as beautiful as it has been and will be.

Christian McBride

BASSIST, COMPOSER, EDUCATOR

HOME BASE
www.christianmcbride.com

GOT MUSIC?
Kind of Brown, Christian McBride
and Inside Straight, Mack Avenue
Records, 2009

"Jazz starts with a dream."

BACKGROUND AND SOUND

Grammy Award–winning bassist Christian McBride is one of the finest musicians both in skill and in personality to have ever graced the genre of jazz. Within weeks of entering Julliard as a freshman he was scooped up by some of the heaviest names in the business, including Bobby Watson and Roy Hargrove. Since then, he has gained international attention and recorded hundreds of albums with some of the more preeminent musicians of our time, including Kathleen Battle, Sting, David Sanborn, George Benson, Natalie Cole, Carly Simon, and Pat Martino, to name a few. Other serious merits include a commission by Lincoln Center, the Portland Arts Society, and the National Endowment for the Arts. As an ambassador to the public for this art form, he has been named the codirector for the Jazz Museum in Harlem, artistic director at the Jazz Aspen Snowmass program, and the creative chair for the Los Angeles Philharmonic. These accolades are merely side dishes on his already full plate. He has become a beacon of hope for the jazz community and has dutifully and tirelessly worked this calling to lead jazz back into the public eye.

HIS STORY

With each passing year, I'm more and more amazed at my mother. Being raised by a single mom who worked and went to college at the same time, I wish I had just a small bit of her work ethic. If I had her work ethic, I'd already be Duke Ellington! My great uncle is also a bass player, a huge jazz historian and aficionado. He knew names and names. He gave me the first record I truly enjoyed in jazz: the Massey Hall concert with Charlie Parker. What I remember the most was the energy from that record. I'd grown up listening to a lot of pop music on the radio, and I couldn't believe how something that had been made in 1953 could sound so fresh. It sounded like they were having fun. You could hear them shouting and hollering. Dizzy was such a great entertainer. I could hear what the bass did, and it changed everything for me. But it was Ray Brown whose style I connected with so intensely. The first time I heard Ray play live I thought, "That's the way the bass is supposed to be played!" When it comes to swinging hard and sitting in the pocket, not only did it inspire me and put me on a certain track as a musician, but when I got to know him and be around him it was a true blessing.

Jazz represents the highest level of creativity. Being a bass player, on the other hand, is like being an offensive lineman in football. They're both very dirty and unglamorous jobs, but they're two of the most necessary and important jobs in their fields. Most musicians on the scene nowadays were able to study jazz in school. It's not a bad thing. It's just how you use it. One of the reasons jazz has been taught in the colleges in the first place was this fight to legitimize jazz. As an American tradition, European classical music was taught as the standard to be judged by. Allegedly, only the most talented could play it. The jazz world has been challenging this for years. It's fine music, but not quite as fine as jazz. There's an element of street in jazz, and all of the best musicians in jazz have a certain level of grit in their playing. You can make the argument that jazz is entirely too clean and sterile and has gotten away from its roots, but I think there are a lot of musicians who are keeping it real.

Jazz starts with a dream. You have to be able to paint a picture on your own, and you can't let anyone else paint that picture for you. I worry how young kids are going to somehow sidestep all of the bull they get fed twenty-four hours a day. The entertainment, food, and concepts of what love means . . . how do they get around that and still understand what is real?

This music also starts with the family. I've been fortunate to have a mother who thought out of the box and a whole bunch of family members who were appreciative of the arts. They took me out to experience all kinds of things as a kid, even though they may not have liked it. But they said you have to understand what this is, and I always appreciated that. Like most black kids from any inner-city neighborhood, we saw winos, drug dealers, and I was told that if I wanted to do that stuff then fine, but that's who you're going to end up like. I was allowed to make my dream come true. I fell in love with the music and thought to myself, "it's obvious these great jazz musicians are on a higher level than your average musician." I wanted to be around them because I felt that I could really learn something. I saw these jazz musicians who were very influential to musicians from they had a sense of dignity and a real proudness to them. How they felt inside and accepted themselves as a person is something you evaluate.

This is what's different. James Brown, who was my ultimate musical hero, was someone who became successful and understood that if you got to the level of money and success, you turn that around and do something for the community. You don't run to hide in Hollywood Hills. It's time that we all gave back to the community.

Pete McCann
GUITARIST, COMPOSER, EDUCATOR

HOME BASE
www.petemccann.com

GOT MUSIC?
Extra Mile, Pete McCann,
Nineteen-Eight Records, 2009

"We have a choice to make: we can either do it exactly as the ones before us did, or we can go to the right or left of their footprints and make our own path."

BACKGROUND AND SOUND
For more than two decades Pete McCann has been driving his fast-moving, no-nonsense career into the ears and sound of the New York scene. Combining the best of both worlds, his music is seasoned with the zest of rock and the wildly mixed pepper of traditional jazz. The combination of the two strikes an almost perfect balance that attracts appetites of all kinds. He has toured and performed with legends Patti Austin, David Liebman, Kenny Garrett, and Maria Schneider and lesser-known but remarkable forces like Chris Tarry and Alison Wedding. He has been heard on more than fifty CDs, including four as a leader of his own in-demand group. Pete is also fashioning young minds to believe in their dreams by teaching at New School and City College of New York as well as summer camps like the Maine Jazz Camp.

HIS STORY
I don't think it's ever going to be possible to turn off Christina Aguilera or Britney Spears or the pop music icons. But what I would like to see—and

maybe this will happen soon—is for live music to happen in front of kids again. I think this is important . . . Whether it's classical or jazz doesn't matter, but they need to see something other than what's on television. When I was in the seventh grade, I listened to these guys play at a jazz camp. This greatly affected me and turned me on to jazz for the rest of my life. But today, when I look out into the audience, now that I'm on the other side, there aren't many kids who are listening. It would be my guess that we're reaching maybe only five percent of the kids out there, and those are the kids that go to places like jazz camps. So many of them or even the adults don't know this music or even care to. Most people at this point would rather look at their computers. I'm not sure if there's anything I can say to get them to appreciate this, as it's not really something you can force on people. It's a dying art form. I hate to say it this way, but I'm sure I'm not the only one who thinks this. We have to remember that it's just as important to keep our legacy going and keep the interest in what we're doing to a high level. Any time I get to play and perform for a school is very important to me for this reason. I just hope they're receptive to what I'm doing.

When you get up to play your first gig in New York or wherever you're going to call home, everything you've ever learned goes out the window. It's frightening to open up your heart and soul and let everyone know that this is a personal thing for you. And if they're not receptive to even listening to you, then how are we supposed to get comfortable doing this? It's like being nude in front of people. When I got out of school I thought I was the shit. I thought anything was possible, but I didn't necessarily count on it straight out of the gate. I had to take a step back. The hardest thing and the most important thing I learned was that I had to be myself, especially in jazz. There are so many great people who have done it better than me. We have a choice to make: we can either do it exactly as the ones before us did, or we can go to the right or left of their footprints and make our own path. I think, for the most part, I've gone to the left of those footprints and made my own trail in the sand.

Donny McCaslin
SAXOPHONIST, COMPOSER, EDUCATOR

HOME BASE
www.donnymccaslin.com

GOT MUSIC?
Declaration, Donny McCaslin,
Sunnyside Records, 2009

"This music is vital to my self-preservation."

BACKGROUND AND SOUND

Grammy-nominated saxophonist Donny McCaslin has been investigating his artistic roots since early childhood. By the time he got to Berklee College of Music, he was a full-fledged member of the current pack of young lions. He has performed with his own group on half a dozen recordings and throughout the country, and as a sideman he has swapped creative thoughts with a bevy of talent, including Maria Schneider, Dave Douglas, David Binney, Luciana Souza, Tom Harrell, and Pat Metheny. His eclectic tastes in music skip beats between every subgenre of classical, jazz, and world. The Doris Duke Foundation and Chamber Music America teamed together to have him compose more of his outstanding compositions and guaranteed him the recognition he so utterly deserves as a soloist and composer.

HIS STORY

My father is a jazz musician, and on the weekend when I stayed with him he would take me out to the Pacific Garden Mall from noon to five so I could listen to him play. My stay with my father pretty much revolved around this gig. I was exposed to jazz so much at an early age I wasn't even aware of any other options. When I started playing around the age of twelve I immediately began with jazz. It was my natural environment and gave me an outlet to express myself.

This music is vital to my self-preservation and has taught me patience and the value of diligence. This doesn't mean my goals were realized right away. Whose are? I've had to work consistently to improve and grow as an artist. And goals aren't going to happen when your twenty; they'll only happen for you over time and through honest self-reflection. I've grown to be able to realize those dreams and goals. I was recently on tour in Europe with a group of mine, and I had to tell the booking agent that this was a dream come true for me but on a completely different level. There was excitement for the band and music, shows were sold out, and I knew this was one of the things I'd worked for all my life. Who cares if I'm forty-two?

When I came to New York it was like I'd stepped in a boxing ring. I got a little roughed up at some point, but I knew my key to survival was to hang in there even when I had more body blows than I could handle. There were many experiences, though, in my career where I feel like I failed miserably. I thought I played so terrible my career would end right then. But I shook off the disappointment of that moment and moved forward. Time and again things worked out. Often it's the perception of a situation that ends up being a lot different than the reality. You can't get pulled back and forth on your emotional strings; you have to stay even keeled and persevere.

I read a book about John Coltrane when I was a teenager. I think someone asked him about his music. I don't have the book anymore, but he said it was like he was spreading this feeling of warmth, love, and community throughout the room. For a long time this was all I thought about. To exude this feeling of love and community in some ways is how someone can experience the love of God through a stained glass window. It reflects into your life, and hopefully you can reflect your music through other people. I would hope that the grace and beauty that come to me come from God and that they reflect through my music and touch other people. This is all I want.

When I'm feeling most creative and in the zone, it feels effortless. It's like I'm close to the creator somehow. I just want my ego to get out of the way so love can flow through me and touch others in a positive way. This is cathartic so much so that sometimes I have a difficult time playing. I don't think I'm the most gifted artist by a long shot, but this is what I feel called to do with my life. This is a serious undertaking. I haven't thought about whether I've been successful or not as I do feel I've reached a certain measure. It's a long haul. I've just got to hang in through the self-doubt and bad gigs and stay focused on always growing.

Jim McNeely

COMPOSER, PIANIST, EDUCATOR

HOME BASE
www.jim-mcneely.com

GOT MUSIC?
Up from the Skies, Music of Jim McNeely, The Vanguard Jazz Orchestra, Planet Arts, 2007

"If I start to define what it is I do, then I've started to damage it."

BACKGROUND AND SOUND

Jim McNeely's swift fingers on the piano have accompanied legends both present and past, including Chet Baker, Stan Getz, David Liebman, Art Farmer, the Thad Jones–Mel Lewis Orchestra, and his latest and greatest own tentet, which is recording his new installations of creative music. Even more challenging than his small-group works are his original large-ensemble compositions. These range from twisted and upside-down arrangements of standards to wholly original and extreme compositions, and they are fun to listen to, especially when poured out of the bells of masters like those of the famed Vanguard Jazz Orchestra, the Carnegie Hall Jazz Band, the Metropole Jazz Orchestra, and the Danish Radio Jazz Orchestra. Despite his unconventional way, Jim has kept within the tradition by reaching dedicated fans and new listeners through innovation.

HIS STORY

My motivation can vary from project to project. Sometimes it's sheer panic. I imagine myself premiering a piece or going to a first rehearsal and telling them that they gotta understand, it's not finished, there was a baseball game I had to watch . . . then I imagine their reaction . . . so a lot of times I work myself into this big snit and I mull over it and mull over it before I even get started. I guess working this way makes a lot of people nervous, including me. If you look at what I've got on paper, as time goes on, it's very little, but my mind is a seething wreck. I wake up in cold sweats at four a.m. and that's when I run to my room and start writing. Sometimes it's just a feeling or atmosphere or emotion. A very basic thing. I'll think of elation or exhaustion, absolute sadness, et cetera. I wrote a piece called "Absolution." I later realized it was about a young Catholic boy that was racked with guilt and begging for forgiveness. On one hand it was autobiographical; on the other hand, it was just a very mechanical process. I can throw three notes on a piece of paper and start manipulating them. It's a right side of the brain thing, then a left side. When one side isn't working, you've still got the other. Sometimes I get gripped with an idea that seems like a movie. Sometimes it's a basic color or temperature or a flavor in food that's overwhelming. Sometimes that overwhelming thing is a certain person that's inspired me. But for all the times I'm inspired, I'm also a professional. There are deadlines to be met.

Life, like jazz, gives you a frame to work with. Just don't sabotage yourself in the beginning by judging your ideas as good or bad; don't compare them to anyone else's. Your ideas are worth pursuing *because they're yours.* I have never consciously set out to develop my own style or design this ahead of time. Everything was just a combination of hearing things that really spoke to me. And just like life, you have to learn to move on and grow and search and don't stay satisfied with the same things. Keep in mind a glimpse of your goals not only in music, but also in everything. If I start to define what it is I do, then I've started to damage it. I just have to feed these ideas and look for different kinds of music and challenges and see what develops. In one sense, I'm someone who gets paid to make things up. When I'm composing, in a way, I'm a storyteller, just nonverbal. I can tell people that I'm a musician, but sometimes they'll respond by asking what I do for a living. I've learned to accept that they look at music differently than I do. In this culture what you are and who you are tend to be defined by how you make your living. Why is this the only criteria by which you're judged? I'm someone who's alive, enjoys life, and loves the work I do. I have ups and downs, but on the basic level this is who and what I am.

John McNeil

TRUMPETER, COMPOSER

HOME BASE
www.mcneiljazz.com

GOT MUSIC?
Rediscovery, John McNeil and Bill McHenry, Sunnyside, 2008

"Jazz is something we need in this life."

BACKGROUND AND SOUND

John McNeil has augmented the face of conventional jazz for more than three decades. Growing up while nipping at the heels of legends Horace Silver and Gerry Mulligan, he was able to hone his craft on the traditional chopping block. But once he broke off into his own abyss of style, his versatility grew wings and flew into places yet to be defined. Today his compositions are best known as harmonically expansive lyrical messages. He can be heard throughout New York's scene. His own compositions and arrangements are regularly documented with a revolving door of talent, including Jeff Jenkins, Matt Wilson, Joe Martin, and Bill McHenry.

HIS STORY

Jazz is something that was born out of real despair. It's not happy music. At least it didn't start out that way. The people who created it had profound despair and in many ways were deprived of everything they had except for their ability to make music. And in slavery, they were encouraged to make music because the slave owners wanted them to appear to be happy. When you have very little, that which you do have you value a great deal. These slaves, in turn, put everything into this music: their frustrations, their despair, and their sadness. Jazz isn't and never has been a chamber music that's supposed to be played quietly. There's an edge to it. And if you ignore this edge . . . you become separate from the experience of this music.

Often times, I think people don't realize the possibilities of this music. But then again you're not really free to make choices if you don't know things. If you don't know something, are you free to choose it? If you don't know it, are you free not to choose it? The more you know, the freer you are. Jazz is a continuum, a force in and of itself that's independent of you and me. Jazz is something we need in this life. As a player the only thing I can do is take advantage of the opportunities that scare me. But if you wait to see how it fits for you, whether you're a player or listener, you'll miss the moment we have right now. It'll already be moving on to something else. If you don't move with it, you'll miss an opportunity that will take you away . . . all you have to really do is listen.

Scott McQuade
PIANIST, COMPOSER, EDUCATOR

HOME BASE
www.playitagainscott.com

GOT MUSIC?
Life Just Couldn't Be Better, Scott McQuade, Independent Label, 2005

"I don't think there are many people who take the leap to do what they love for a living."

BACKGROUND AND SOUND
Scott McQuade has delighted listeners with his throwback to the slightly frayed yet still strong moral fibers found within the traditional roots of jazz for almost twenty years. He has had the pleasure of playing with Randy Brecker, Curtis Fuller, Delfeayo Marsalis, Jason Marsalis, Arturo Sandoval, and various faculty groups throughout the university system in Florida, including the esteemed faculty of the University of North Florida Jazz Studies Department. Now he teaches privately and performs throughout the Tulsa, Oklahoma, area.

HIS STORY
I've always had a lot of support. My whole family prepared me for this. I think this is very important. A lot of kids have parents tell them they're crazy or nuts. They become the black sheep of the family for doing what

they love. This is about seventy to eighty percent of the battle. If you don't have people, whether family or peers, digging what you're doing, you'll be lost. It is possible to make a living in the arts, and it shouldn't be such a shock to people that others do this. I'm always being asked what I do for a day job. Why is it so hard to understand that what I do is in the arts? I don't think there are many people who take the leap to do what they love for a living. I really love what I do, and even in slow times I make money at it in some capacity. I just have to keep in mind that every year could be different. I'm not ever going to be rich, but happiness is rich enough for me.

Gabriel Mervine

TRUMPETER

"Jazz is the culmination of what a musician can learn."

BACKGROUND AND SOUND

Gabriel Mervine is one of the Denver jazz scene's best-kept secrets. Gabe is a regular member of and soloist with the Chie Imaizumi Jazz Orchestra and the modern jazz group Convergence. Stomping grounds like these are as good as any when it comes to building chops. As a soloist his lines weave in and out of the harmonic structures within tunes with a mature weight. Showing great potential and continuous growth as a musician, Gabe is clearly establishing himself as an up-and-coming contributor and voice among the jazz world.

HIS STORY

My first band director was my inspiration. Once he saw I was going beyond what the program was offering, he provided me with more. It wasn't that I was the teacher's pet; we just got along great. I got thrown into improvisation and playing more through him, and after a couple of years of bullshitting I started learning jazz. It's the one way I can express myself, and I honestly love working at it. I try to get better day by day, as I believe jazz is the culmination of what a musician can learn. In this day and age though, it's difficult to play and live. I have a huge disagreement with society now because of this. I've had nine-to-five jobs and worked in different fields but was never satisfied. After some tough times I worked as a bank teller. Six months later I quit. They only wanted to listen to the same twenty songs daily and didn't get into anything culturally. Most were only into TV or computers. I believe this is what's going to keep people from accepting what we do as artists.

With cell phones and the Internet, it seems our history is being quickly forgotten. But with jazz or art there's a direct link to history. I wish more people were inspired despite their nine-to-five job. Instead of learning anything new, people run in the other direction out of fear. I understand where people come from in these jobs; I guess I'm just lucky to make music and hang out with musicians, artists, and poets and make a living at it. I love learning; as a matter of fact . . . this is how I stay afloat. I learn about why this music is the way it is and how it fits together, and playing with the other cats makes me realize what jazz is supposed to be. I want to learn because I want to be the best person I can be. Music and art require you to go deeper in yourself, and maybe this is why people don't get into it. It takes years to internalize it. But if you go into it by judging it, your mind will definitely block what you can get out of it.

Anthony Molinaro

PIANIST, COMPOSER, FOUNDER AND OWNER
Of NINETEEN-EIGHT RECORDS

HOME BASE
www.nineteeneight.com,
www.anthonymolinaro.com

GOT MUSIC?
The Molinaro-Levy Project: Live,
Anthony Molinaro and Howard Levy, Nineteen-Eight Records, 2003

"If you work hard at something and continue to search and experiment, you'll always find something new."

BACKGROUND AND SOUND

Anthony Molinaro's eighty-eight keys have been slammed, twisted, and transformed from the traditional concert pianist's repertoire to that of modern jazz. Stereotypes need not apply. It was no surprise when Anthony, who was the winner of the 1997 Naumberg International Piano Competition, turned to the church of hard-core jazz. For years he had been improvising cadenzas on major orchestral works and symphonic stages. Ingenious compositions and arrangements have been featured with esteemed groups such as the Chicago Jazz Orchestra, and his record label, Nineteen-Eight, is producing some of the hottest jazz talents in our country. Anthony's highly accomplished and auspicious beginning has pushed him into the wealth of young artists that bring light to our cultural future.

HIS STORY

One of the reasons I took the university position [Loyola University Chicago] was to get students to listen at a slightly higher level. If each day people listened to Coltrane, Bach, and Miles, they would all begin to think at a higher level. Learning how to listen is not easy. If I go to the Chicago Symphony and they're playing a piece I've never heard, it can be overwhelming. To someone who's never had music lessons, it has to be like watching a foreign film without subtitles. This stems from how people study music as kids. They don't really study music. Instead, they are studying instruments. When they quit, they may know how to read music, but they don't generally know anything about the music. It would be great if you could hip people to Coltrane and Mahler, but I'm happy just to get students listening to Stevie Wonder. It's great if you appreciate good music, but if you don't understand it, then it's hard for me to imagine you're going to truly dig it. For me, composing often starts with one simple concept or vision. From there, it's simply a matter of working with the concept until the bigger picture reveals itself. The answer is there, and I just have to find it. If you work hard at something and continue to search and experiment, you'll always find something new.

Ben Monder

GUITARIST, COMPOSER

HOME BASE
www.benmonder.com

GOT MUSIC?
Oceana, Ben Monder, Sunnyside, 2005

"From an early age I've identified myself through music."

BACKGROUND AND SOUND

As one of the more exclusive guitarists on the international jazz scene, Ben Monder has been widely recognized by greats and his peers alike. Having been on the scene for more than twenty-five years now, he has had the opportunity to perform with greats such as Lee Konitz, Kenny Wheeler, and Jack McDuff. Monder is also a regular member of the Maria Schneider Jazz Orchestra and the Paul Motian Octet. He has served on the faculty at the prestigious New England Conservatory and remains in demand as a clinician around the world. Monder's talent reaches beyond the strings as he creates copious amounts of inventive music. He allows a bright and striking sense of melody to pour out of the body of the guitar, and he is one musician who has defied the margins of his instrument and stepped over to the true essence of jazz.

HIS STORY

From an early age I've identified myself through music. As a child I remember devouring all the records we had in the house, classical and pop mostly, and remember spending hours a day improvising little songs on a piano my parents had rented for a short time. I've had very transformative and spiritual experiences as a listener to both live and recorded music. These have shown me the potential power of music to affect the minds and souls of others, and I feel like the highest thing I can achieve is to create such experiences and share them with others. To begin to effect this, I think an artist has to go deep within himself and strip away the superficial and facile to get to the essence of what makes him resonate. Only then can he hope to find resonance with others. It's the idea of going through the personal to reach the universal. I'm attracted to the idea of creating worlds within myself and then inviting the listener to join in on the journey, and I believe the loop is completed only when you share what you have.

Jane Monheit
VOCALIST

HOME BASE
www.janemonheitonline.com

GOT MUSIC?
Taking a Chance on Love, Jane Monheit, Sony, 2004

"Jazz is such an intrinsic part of who I am, I can't imagine my life without it."

BACKGROUND AND SOUND

Jane Monheit's vocals, even from the earliest point in her career, have been compared with the very best in history: Judy Garland, Ella Fitzgerald, and so on. Storming the scene with her stunning voice, Monheit is one of the most accomplished vocalists of today. Under the tutelage of Peter Eldridge of the New York Voices, she placed runner up in the Thelonious Monk International Jazz Vocals Competition in the beginning of her senior year at Manhattan School of Music. She was the youngest musician to have placed in this competition to date. But the resonance from within her is far from youthful. An illustration of silken sound, Jane is constantly moving with the moment, and it's this aspect of her artistry that makes her one of the most recognized vocalists of any genre.

HER STORY

Jazz is such an intrinsic part of who I am, I can't imagine my life without it. It's in my blood and just who I have been forever. As for my style, I think it changes all the time. There's always a favorite thing of the moment. But what I love about singing is the interpretation of the music. This is why I go after different genres and projects and try to work with a lot of different musicians. It's my hope that people realize that I'm a musician and not just a vocalist. I see a lot of singers who try to get away with not being the best musician they can be. In order to be successful they will have to know the science behind what's going on and actually take time to learn the music just as well as an instrumentalist. Peter Eldridge, my teacher at Manhattan School of Music, the one who changed my life and was and still is my idol, ingrained this point in me. He was the one who got me to pay more attention to the lyrics and not be so worried about proving my musical knowledge. I hope this comes through when others listen to me. I want others to see that I'm being sincere; otherwise, what's the point? As musicians we just have to keep at it and not give up. There's always room for jazz in the world. Even if the glamour isn't there, we should just be happy playing the music.

James Moody
SAXOPHONIST, WOODWINDIST, VOCALIST,
COMPOSER, NEA JAZZ MASTER

HOME BASE
www.jamesmoody.com

GOT MUSIC?
Moody 4A, The James Moody Quartet with special guest Kenny Barron, IPO, 2009

"I'm just trying to play better today than I did yesterday."

BACKGROUND AND SOUND
For more than six decades James Moody has brought his lyrical soloing and spunky style to audiences around the world. As one of the original members of the Dizzy Gillespie Big Band in 1946, he established himself as one of the heavy hitters in jazz. This reputation has certainly held up since that time. The energy and generosity Moody demonstrates toward other musicians, jazz supporters, and all who meet him speak of an overwhelming love for life and music. Throughout his career Moody has won many awards for his contributions to the history of jazz. The most notable of these was being named as a National Endowment for the Arts Jazz Master in 1998. Moody's distinguished and marked career is a testament to what can be achieved in

this life when one has a positive attitude and zealous dedication to their craft.

HIS STORY

I guess I've got a different attitude about a lot of things. Maybe it's because I'm eighty-four years old and came up with nothing but racism around me. Back when I was coming up on the scene I could do one night with someone like Ella Fitzgerald or Dizzy Gillespie down South, and they would put a rope down the middle of the ballroom when we started playing. On one side would be colored and the other would be Caucasian. People just need to be truthful with themselves and stop thinking they're better than someone else just because of their skin color. My mother always told me to take people as individuals. Maybe if the whole country would just tell the truth and do this for a change, things would start rubbing off on people and we'd be better off. But the challenge remains. I always say, blessed are those that run in circles for they shall be called Big Wheels . . . and just because twenty-five million people call an automobile a television set doesn't make it one. Too many people believe in what's not there, and that's why America has become the land of mediocrity. If it's dumb, they want more . . . people shy away from anything that has intelligence to it. But, anything that's intelligent survives. Consequently jazz will be here forever. Our solution is to play decent music. I've been around intelligent people all my life; jazz musicians are pretty smooth and slick when it comes to the world. And I'm just a loving person who's trying to do the best I can. I've always said that I'd like people to be happy, joyful, and also be able to cry when they hear my music. Different people get different things out of music no matter what you do. When you do something other than what you want you're not being honest. So, if I'm honest to myself and giving you the best I can, then I'm fulfilling my goal. I'm just trying to play better today than I did yesterday.

Jason Moran

PIANIST, COMPOSER, EDUCATOR, AUTHOR

HOME BASE
www.jasonmoran.com

GOT MUSIC?
Modernistic, Jason Moran, Blue
Note, 2002

"This music is my therapy."

BACKGROUND AND SOUND

Award-winning Blue Note artist Jason Moran is one of the most prolific and multifaceted composers and pianists alive today. His compositional chops are refined and displayed regularly in on the stand. Folks such as Chris Potter, Dave Holland, and Nasheet Waits regularly dine on his harmonic delight. This exceptional ability to group together individuals who sing off of each other's phrases with a streamlined voice has caught the industry by surprise and won over critics and listeners alike. Composing for short films like *All We Know of Heaven* and *Five Deep Breaths* has introduced him on the independent film circuit at festivals like Cannes and Sundance. His extensive and well-deserved list of accolades will only continue to build as his already refined talent takes on new forms to move with the times.

HIS STORY

My parents listened to jazz in the car ninety percent of the time. This was the eighties, when children, myself included, wanted to only listen to Run DMC instead of jazz. But it was my parents' intro to jazz that got me into it. My father was playing a Thelonious Monk record one day, and I walked into the room when "Round Midnight" was on. At this point it was clear to me that that was what I wanted to do.

I stopped defining music a long time ago. It's just a part of life. This music is my therapy and allows me to put every bit of me into it. Whether it's my twins, my mother's passion, a recent trip to Istanbul, it's the model from which I follow through. It's born out of simple relationships with human beings. But the good thing about this art is that it doesn't come with an expiration date. It's always going to be an expression of that moment you're in. You can do it until you die if you believe and do what you do because you're into it. It's that ability to have others connect to their own life through the music I play that keeps me going. With my trio, our dialog is over eleven years old. There's a deep connection with the notes I've played and will play. Jazz is fun that way. The thought that you have to be poor, play late at night, and get paid nothing is just bullshit. This music is at it's best when it's a great big ball of fun that has emerged from anguish and manifested itself as pure joy on the bandstand.

Matt Moran

VIBRAPHONIST, PERCUSSIONIST, COMPOSER

HOME BASE
www.mattmoran.com

GOT MUSIC?
Taketron, Slavic Soul Party, Barbés Records, 2009

"Art is not supposed to be with us or for us; it is us."

BACKGROUND AND SOUND

Matt Moran and his vibe antics have completely distorted all recognizable features of genre margins within music. Matt's extreme range of imaginative gifts and tools as a composer has placed him in a category that has yet to be named. He is the leader of the group Slavic Soul Party and heavily involved in the Balkan folk music scene in New York, and it seems that he has found the perfect outlet to combine his compositionally oriented pyrotechnics and highly entertaining qualities as a leader and performer. John Hollenbeck's Claudio Quintet and the Mat Maneri Quintet have engaged his talent as well. Regardless of the day or avenue he is cruising through, Matt delivers, on cue, an amusing and mostly unexpected thrill.

HIS STORY

People that play music never really wrestle with the "why music" question. I don't think it ever feels like a choice; it's something you feel drawn to or compelled to do. Most of us start at a young age, and it's just what we do.

It's just a part of the spiritual realm, and the mystery of that is important. For me, music is also a way of understanding the world and communicating in ways I can't do verbally. It's the fabric of my life and what I walk on. Music feels like the one continuous thread in my life. I even knew I was going to be a musician before I made music. There was something that I moved alongside, touching, that felt very much like who I am. This is what keeps me moving along and is an important part of being human. I think it exists solely to get us through our lives. One of the problems artists have in this society is dealing with the ever increasing demand for quantification. Basically we're dividing the mind. We have to separate by type and divide and categorize and analyze like crazy. If I had to separate music from me, I wouldn't feel very whole. We all go through hard times in life, and most of us experience a lot of great times, too. It helps people if you give them an experience they'll cherish, and that's what's been entrusted to us as musicians. Somehow we have to help bring them up on their way up or ease them on their way down . . . to get through life really. Art is not supposed to be *with* us or *for* us; it *is* us.

Mike Moreno
GUITARIST, COMPOSER

HOME BASE
www.mikemoreno.com

GOT MUSIC?
Between the Lines, Mike Moreno, World Culture Music, 2007

"Jazz lends itself to be changed."

BACKGROUND AND SOUND
Guitarist Mike Moreno is one of the most important young figures in jazz today. His career began early and quickly moved him to this position. Performing and recording with artists like Nicholas Payton, Q-Tip, Joshua Redman, Jeremy Pelt, and Gretchen Parlato gave him solid experience and ground to stand upon. His sophisticated and narrative music is accessible to any ear and contradicts all stereotypes that might be placed upon his youthful shoulders.

HIS STORY

Communities are important. These are the people who inspire you to reach new heights and show you the world and keep you grounded all at the same time. In my early years, these people were very specific about taking time to find a sound and to always play with feeling and not just technique. That was the most important advice I received. I'm still working on this now, and it never ends.

Jazz is a little different than other types of music. I would think that this same idea of community varies. Playing classical music, for instance, in a lot of ways is a much lonelier lifestyle. A lot of times you're playing what you've prepared by yourself at home or with one teacher. And even if you're in a group setting, it's a different kind of thing. You are playing music right off the page exactly how it was written. And many times you have a specific reference recording on what it "should" sound like, or you're just playing it as the conductor hears it and you just have to express that. In jazz though, there's no way to learn how to play it sitting in your bedroom or from one teacher, or one bandleader. You have to get out and play live with many players in many different situations. It's about communication and playing off of what others have to say. Even in rock music, if you're in a band, you're basically playing with the same four guys and working on the same songs constantly. Which is great too. But most are never really called to step up to that world where you play lots of different original and standard music in different ways all the time.

Jazz has an ever changing element to it. Even if you've been playing on tour with one band, the music is going to be different from night to night, even if it's the same songs. It doesn't always necessarily work, but it doesn't keep anyone from trying to keep it evolving. I don't really want to be able to explain what jazz is, that's the beauty of it. And I don't really know sometimes—it's different for everyone. Some people can't deal with this uncertainty in the music. There are also so many types of jazz listeners and jazz critics. And each one of them likes something different. I don't really care so much for all of that. I've just always tried to play and listen to music that moves me, not just interests me theoretically.

If my music can put someone in a mood, whether it's uplifting, meditative, or thoughtful, then I'm doing what I set out to do. But in order to bring more of an audience back to jazz again, I think some jazz musicians have to get people more emotionally involved. There are some people who already do this, of course. But the audience has to be able to say the music sounds nice as well as interesting, and this is a hard thing to pull off. So many players are out to just beat jazz into their audiences' ear with no apology, playing very selfishly. I don't want to do that anymore. For the future, jazz lends itself to be changed, and I think people can accept this change. It's always adding new ideas, and the sound will always evolve … it's impossible to be bored with it.

The music I write is a part of me. I'm not playing the guitar just to show you how much I learned in music school, instead I'm writing from an emotional place where a lot of the things I don't portray in my personal life come out in the music. As long as I can survive and always create music, then I'm happy with what I'm doing.

Carli Muñoz

PIANIST, COMPOSER, ARRANGER, EDUCATOR

HOME BASE
www.carlimunoz.com

GOT MUSIC?
Maverick, Carli Muñoz, Pelosenel Q Lo Records, 2006

"Music is a very powerful healing source, especially if it comes from one's deepest yearning to make a difference."

BACKGROUND AND SOUND

Carli Muñoz has ridden the wave from Puerto Rico's jazz scene to the mainland as both a sideman and a leader. Established among Puerto Rico's famed and honored musicians, he is finally delivering his gift to the rest of the world. His companions in this journey have included legendary musicians such as Eddie Gomez, Charles Lloyd, George Benson, and Jack DeJohnette. Outlining the scene no matter where he is found, Munoz demonstrates his pulsating voice through an enriched and strong dialect. His voice is one many have missed, but he will soon be heard.

HIS STORY

I was born a musician with no one musical in my family. I don't believe it was really a choice, at least on a conscious level; I guess everyone has a calling and I'm just fortunate enough to be on the continuum of what I was meant to do. Music is in my spirit, reaching to something beyond my DNA or any other physical explanation, considering that I am completely self-taught. One can argue that, given sufficient diligence and intelligence, one can excel in whatever one focuses on, but music was all too familiar and easy to know for me to neglect.

So my life became music and music became my life. I loved music so much—and this may sound contradictory to some—that I chose not to study music formally. Instead I went to college to study cinematography, which I did enjoy and practiced for some time, but without departing from always keeping music front stage. To me, not taking on music studies formally was a way to keep it real, since I had already developed my own learning method and was developing my own style. Of course, I was nurtured tremendously from listening to many of the masters in jazz piano and other instruments. Between listening to the masters and playing frequently with great musicians, I evolved and set out to master the art of playing, improvising, and composing.

The other thing that became significant and important in my life was life itself. What I mean by that is that it has been hard ignore all the suffering that goes on in the world. It is all around—be it self inflicted or inflicted by another, I believe that ignorance, hence spiritual blindness, is the culprit. Music is a very powerful healing source, especially if it comes from one's deepest yearning to make a difference. I have been often bugged by the idea that I "don't do enough," that maybe I should be a missionary of sorts, that I should join this or that charity group, et cetera. But it is in those moments when someone viscerally reminds me that my music has made a difference in his or her well-being that I feel that something is really working by just doing what I do—music.

Lewis Nash

PERCUSSIONIST, EDUCATOR

HOME BASE
www.lewisnash.com

GOT MUSIC?
The Highest Mountain, Lewis Nash,
Happy Beat Music, 2009

"The skillful manipulation of melody, rhythm, and harmony communicates through sound things that simply can't be expressed in words."

BACKGROUND AND SOUND

World-renowned jazz drummer Lewis Nash has been a heavy hitter on the scene since his early twenties. Throughout his career he has performed and recorded with notable legends such as Betty Carter, Dizzy Gillespie, Milt Jackson, Oscar Peterson, J.J. Johnson, Tommy Flanagan, McCoy Tyner, Sonny Rollins, Ray Brown, and many others. As the leader of his own groups, he has brought his music to thousands of listeners worldwide. Adding to this already impressive list of accomplishments is the fact that Lewis can be heard on more than four hundred recordings in all genres. In demand as a clinician around the world, Lewis is quite literally shaping the future of the rhythm section. Yet his legacy reaches well beyond technical methods. Standing strong with the spirit of jazz by his side, Lewis is a positive force impacting the future of this art.

HIS STORY

I consider myself a latecomer to jazz in terms of my knowledge of the music's history and great players. There wasn't much jazz around my house while I was growing up, but I heard lots of great R&B, blues, and gospel. My introduction to jazz was more gradual, and I was already in college when

I became familiar with the work of many of the icons of the music like Bird and Dizzy, Louis Armstrong and Duke Ellington.

My high school band director liked jazz and was very encouraging to me early on. During that time of my life I enjoyed playing music, but I wasn't considering it as a career choice. My first gigs were in bands playing the music of groups like Earth, Wind and Fire or the Commodores, mostly for dances and parties. After high school, once I began listening to jazz, I learned to appreciate the artistry of great drummers like Max Roach, Philly Joe Jones, and Art Blakey. A college professor suggested I consider a career in music instead of my major at the time, which was broadcast journalism. By the time I was twenty-two years old, I'd moved to New York to join the trio of jazz vocalist Betty Carter. Thus began my presence on the international jazz scene. I'm involved with jazz education, and there are many great players today teaching at universities and conservatories. I'm sure they remind their students that you don't become a jazz musician expecting to get rich. Only do it if you really love it, not just because you do it well or somebody says you're good at it.

When I'm playing, I try to express my deepest feelings and emotions through the instrument. I find myself in a very concentrating, almost meditative state . . . physically there but drawing from somewhere else . . . another plane. You learn to let go and trust the music to go its own direction. The skillful manipulation of melody, rhythm, and harmony communicates through sound things that simply can't be expressed in words.

Ted Nash

SAXOPHONIST, WOODWINDIST, COMPOSER,
EDUCATOR, ARRANGER, CONDUCTOR

HOME BASE
www.tednash.com

GOT MUSIC?
Rhyme and Reason, Ted Nash,
Arabesque Recordings, 1999

"Music has taught me humility. It's encompassing, open, and amazing. Almost like the universe itself."

BACKGROUND AND SOUND

Ted Nash is more than a player or composer. He is light sifted through sound. His compositions have been heard around the world. Nash, a veteran of the world of jazz, plays every woodwind on the scene and is the go-to man in the Jazz at Lincoln Center Orchestra. But this isn't his only gig. As a leader for his own group and a composer, his brilliance cuts through the stage lights as a multifaceted and valuable diamond in the business. Dancing and waltzing, a rumba of sound on whatever instrument he chooses to charm his audience with, his technical ability is only half of his show. Nash's charismatic sound and unyielding tonal beauty streams into the ears of his listeners with each performance, turning them into loyal followers and fans time after time.

HIS STORY

During my junior high and high school years my main instrument was clarinet. I wanted to be a classical clarinetist, and it wasn't until I heard Charlie Parker's expressive, swinging sound that I realized jazz saxophone is what I wanted to play.

I began studying improvisation with vibraphonist Charlie Shoemake, and in a couple of very dedicated years I was able to fully assimilate the bebop language. Although by the age of sixteen I could play quite convincingly well, my initial strength as a player was more technical than emotional. It took several more years to understand what it was to express at a deeper level. As I matured I discovered jazz could be a strong way of getting to know yourself, and that in speaking this rich language you also give others an opportunity to get to know you as well.

My early influences were firmly rooted in the bebop tradition. I was exposed to music and encouraged by my father, Dick Nash, and uncle Ted Nash, both well-known studio and jazz musicians. They had both come out of the big band era and were great improvisers. Becoming fairly well versed in the more mainstream language, I moved toward exploring a more avant-garde approach to playing. Realizing there was something missing, I went way back to the twenties and thirties to explore early jazz, and in particular the swing style of Coleman Hawkins and Lester Young. I think some of my greatest training, however, came from sitting between Dick Oates and Joe Lovano for ten years in the Mel Lewis band. I've also spent a lot of time enjoying Sonny Rollins, Wayne Shorter, Stan Getz, Joe Henderson, and

John Coltrane. I have mentioned all saxophone players here, but I think the musician that moved me the most, the artist that truly encapsulated what I think jazz is all about, would have to be Miles Davis. He wasn't afraid to be himself. He didn't try to please anyone—he was one hundred percent Miles Davis.

It's a challenge to be a jazz musician—we have to be performer, attorney, graphic designer, booking agent, and publicist. That's a lot of hats to wear. And I don't even like hats. I think the biggest test for an artist of any kind is to continue to grow, continue to be creative, and to embrace this creativity inside us. When you are truly connected to this, it can generate such an overwhelming feeling that at times I believe people shy away from it, instead of going toward it. We can find many excuses to keep us away from addressing this feeling.

Composition has really become an important part of my identity. For years, like many musicians, I felt satisfied to just play standards as vehicles for improvisation. There's certainly a lot you can do with a standard, but when you realize that writing your own music exposes more about who you are—what you think and feel—you can now take the music to a deeper level and create an environment in which you can really be yourself. I love to compose, and enjoy the process itself. Sometimes the journey is just as interesting as the destination.

Music has taught me humility. It's encompassing, open, and amazing. Almost like the universe itself. I feel like a speck amidst the possibilities. It's incredible to be among all of the great musicians with whom I share this passion, and all those that have come before me. I was blessed to have discovered jazz music at an early age. I didn't have to go search for it—it was all around me, in me. The older I get, the more I realize how much music allows me to express something from within. I am no longer interested in impressing people with technique or knowledge of harmony. My aspiration is to move someone emotionally, to have an affect on how they feel. The one thing I can possibly hope for is to change someone's life in some way through music. I think that is what jazz can be.

Seeing somebody achieve their potential, especially when you get to watch somebody who has talent figure out how to really develop it and make something artistic, and make a career out of it, really inspires me. Like Wynton—I watch him work twenty hours a day and he doesn't sleep. He achieves so much. That dedication and diligence is inspiring.

Despite being called a young lion at times and a veteran at others I don't really know which of the two is the more accurate description. But I do believe I have a very young spirit, like a child. And like a child, I want to keep learning and discovering new things.

Ken Navarro
GUITARIST, COMPOSER, OWNER OF POSITIVE MUSIC RECORDS

HOME BASE
www.kennavarro.com

GOT MUSIC?
The Grace of Summer Light,
Positive Music Records, 2008

"Creating isn't about sitting in the studio for six months; it's about walking, reading, and building a bank account of inspirations both musical and non."

BACKGROUND AND SOUND

Award-winning contemporary jazz recording artist Ken Navarro has topped charts with his solo CDs for more than twenty years. His latest albums have received critical acclaim from smooth jazz radio and *Jazziz,* and he has recorded or performed with legends such as Eric Marienthal, Nell Carter, John Patitucci, and more. Soon to be a legend himself, he has raised the bar considerably throughout the contemporary and traditional jazz scenes with his ability on his ax and compositions that brilliantly set a mood and tone for any occasion. With an open and honest approach to everything he does, Ken Navarro allows the listener glimpses into his loves and his life as they hear his story unfold through his music.

HIS STORY

I grew up listening to Eric Clapton and Jimi Hendrix. A friend then lent me John Coltrane's *A Love Supreme*, and although I had no idea what I was listening to, I loved it. It molded me just as much as Hendrix did, but I understood Hendrix better because that's what I'd been doing up until that point. Yet Coltrane was as electric as any distortion guitar had ever been.

He created a buzz and magic, and that's what it's all about. I try to live my life that way and recreate that same feeling in my music.

Sometimes adult responsibilities make it difficult to always be spur-of-the-moment and stay true to it. This is why I play jazz. Playing becomes a rediscovery of something creative you haven't thought about in a long while. Writing's the same way. The process of pulling out the work becomes one long inhale for six months on end. Everything that's been going on in my life in the interim begins to come out. Creating isn't about sitting in the studio for six months; it's about walking, reading, and building a bank account of inspirations both musical and non. The upside of living this way is that it always frees me and brings with it a new set of challenges. You can spend and filter your life account however you want, just filter it so it becomes you and not an imitation or interpretation of influences. It has to be organic. This is when smoothing the rougher transitions will happen. Even though I have gone through periods of time where I didn't want to go on with music, everyone goes down their road the way they go down it.

There indeed has to be a certain artistic integrity. Part of our individual worth is to be able to support ourselves. Musicians want to play. I hold them in high regard no matter what style they call their music. It's those that reach and obtain their dreams that put their personality, body, and soul on the line. We're all different. I'm in a genre that has a certain vocabulary that allows me to express what I have to share. My music is complicated, but I want the net result to be that I'm still reaching out and meeting the listener halfway. Moving in that direction is a realization that I have to make as a musician, and any one way you expose others to jazz is good.

Sammy Nestico
COMPOSER, ARRANGER, PRODUCER, EDUCATOR

HOME BASE
www.sammynesticomusic.com

GOT MUSIC?
A Portrait of Sammy, Sammy Nestico, Fenwood Records, 2005

"It's hard to be simple and good, but it always works."

BACKGROUND AND SOUND

Composer and arranger Sammy Nestico has had his name and style associated with more than six hundred compositions and arrangements throughout his lifetime. From 1970 to 1984 he was the Count Basie Orchestra's chief arranger and composer, and he has more than ten albums of original music credited to his name. He has been credited with more than sixty-three albums through Capitol Records and has arranged and composed theme music for dozens of television programs. The United States Air Force Band has an annual award called the Sammy Nestico Arranging Award. His textbook, *The Complete Arranger*, has been translated into four languages and is marketed throughout the world. Sammy exudes an utterly contagious positive force field of energy in everything he does. The jazz world would never have been what it is now without him. Sammy Nestico is an irrefutable asset in jazz that's helped turn it into what it is today as an art, a community, and a footnote in history.

HIS STORY

In high school, I was so eager to write that I would spread manuscript paper on the kitchen table, pouring notes down, just for the sake of seeing them on paper. Being a trombonist when writing my first arrangement, I proceeded to write all the parts in bass clef. Upon returning a week later, I neglected to transpose the saxophones' parts. A belching cow would have been a distinct improvement over the sound I wrote for that orchestra. By the time I was seventeen I joined the ABC Staff Orchestra as second trombonist. Since then I've worked with Count Basie, Phil Collins, Julie Andrews, Barbra Streisand, and scores of great talents. My greatest love and impetus for this music came from Count Basie. He was like a father to me, and his wife, Katy, made us all feel like family. He was my benefactor, and I know Basie alumni Quincy Jones, Frank Foster, and Johnny Mandel all feel the same way. It was fun scoring for the Basie band, and in all the years that I worked with him, I was never told what to write. Many times during our relationship, which culminated in the recording of ten albums, Bill Basie would quietly caution me to "relax, and let good things happen." He always remained true to the spirit and essence of big band jazz, a man who was very sensitive, and who played music for the sheer pleasure and happiness that it induced. When in his presence I had always hoped that some of those qualities would rub off on me. For the most part, I write uplifting music and joyful tunes. It's in my soul and just comes out. Although I've learned a lot from my "hits," I've definitely learned more from my "misses." When your name appears at the top of the score, so does your integrity.

I think it is very important to be pleasant with the people with whom you work. I try to pay back for all of the help I've received in the past, and have never regarded money as the prime criterion for my services. Writing music that touches the heart is something that I regard as important. I wake up to a new world every morning and am glad I've lived so long, because the last ten years have been the greatest . . . I've met many honest, good people through my music. And as my mentor Count Basie taught me, I've learned that it's hard to be simple and good, but it always works.

Ed Neumeister {LIVING LEGEND}

COMPOSER, CONDUCTOR, TROMBONIST, EDUCATOR, PRODUCER

HOME BASE
www.edneumeister.com

GOT MUSIC?
Reflection, Ed Neumeister,
ArtistShare, 2006

"Music in general is an organic, living entity."

BACKGROUND AND SOUND

Grammy-nominated composer, trombonist, and producer Ed Neumeister has been leading his own groups throughout New York and San Francisco since 1978. His original and often thematic works have been commissioned and performed by groups all over the world and awarded grants through the National Endowment for the Arts and the American Society of Composers, Authors and Publishers (ASCAP). Performers who have featured his works include the Vanguard Jazz Orchestra and the Metropol Orkest in the Netherlands. As a performer he has intensely serious chops in both jazz and classical trombone arenas. Performance credits include everything from the Duke Ellington Orchestra (under the direction of Mercer Ellington) to the New York Philharmonic. His dynamic voice and spirited work equals that of a significant body of work any artist or patron of the arts can appreciate.

HIS STORY

When I was twenty-one years old, I quit school. This was around the time of the Vietnam War and Richard Nixon's election, and I was fed up with politics, especially with Nixon. I knew he was lying; it just seemed clear to me. I had to leave, so I bought a one-way ticket to Paris and lived in Europe for two to three years. I was in Amsterdam working and studying as a jazz musician, living rent-free. I lived there for a couple of years and toured a bit, but mostly I became a serious student of jazz at the University of the Streets. I've studied music on my own by reading record liner notes, books, or whatever else I could find. I would talk to people and practice. I never really had a formal lesson. Not until later did I end up in an old abandoned building where some musicians were staying. I got a room, cleaned it out. Every now and then the police would come crashing through the door and ask for my passport and money. There was no electricity, and we only had propane gas for heating and cooking. But when they cut off the water, I left. This was the beginning of my jazz experience. I lived it.

Jazz means this kind of freedom and experience as a concept. It's not experience in the past tense, but the present. It's your experience in life. I've always been an explorer, a chance and risk taker. It's a hunger for what's next. My life experience has been more or less one hundred percent music and artistic expression. The improvisational aspect of it is experiencing the moment and getting deep into the musical space. I'm not sure if jazz taught me this concept or if it was just life. Music in general is an organic, living entity. Jazz is vibrant and alive now. It's a style of music I enjoy and play. People often think of me as a jazz musician more than I think of myself as one. I don't usually put the "jazz" in front of the word "musician" unless someone needs to pigeonhole me. Some people have a very narrow view of what jazz is. Mine happens to be very wide open. "Jazz" wasn't a term coined by the musicians; it was coined by someone on the outside. Do I think of myself as a musician? Yes, I'm just a musician who plays a hybrid of styles and loves what he does.

Adam Nitti
BASSIST, COMPOSER, PRODUCER, WRITER

HOME BASE
www.adamnitti.com

GOT MUSIC?
Liminal, Adam Nitti, Renaissance
Man Records, 2009

"If you continue to base your progress on the success of others, you'll never attain any true success of your own."

BACKGROUND AND SOUND

Nashville bassist Adam Nitti has recorded and performed with a varied group of artists, including CCM greats Steven Curtis Chapman and Casting Crowns, as well as the Dave Weckl Band, Jeff Coffin, Keith Carlock, Mike Stern, and blues artist Susan Tedeschi. Working the studios in Nashville, his reputation has grown to fit his abilities. He is changing the way our next generations learn music through the project he co-founded called MusicDojo, the first-ever interactive online music school. *Bass Player* magazine and *Bass Musician Magazine* also include his columns on technique and the industry on a regular basis. The work and magnetic energy he has displayed throughout his career only complement his brood of talent and ambition to make it to the top of his field.

HIS STORY

Jazz has helped me to learn more of who I really am. The reasons why I play and the reasons why I do what I do now are so different from when I started out many years ago. I discovered early on in my musical development that music could win me the attention, praise, and approval of my peers. But those were the wrong reasons for my pursuit. Later in life, after I decided to embark on a serious career in music, there came a time when I realized that my growth wasn't meeting my expectations. I would compare my progress to the progress of my musical colleagues and would feel frustrated and dissatisfied. Ultimately, I would emerge from that season with a positive new perspective, but it wasn't until I first had to go through some very hard times in my emotional and spiritual growth. There's a little mantra

I coined after learning these lessons, and that is this: If you continue to base your progress on the success of others, you'll never attain any true success of your own.

There are times when being in the instrumental world is a challenging and thankless musical existence. We all aspire for excellence in our music, but hard work, dedication, and talent aren't always recognized or rewarded. I connected to this music on a fundamental level and believed that I had the talent and potential to find my voice in it. As my career evolved, I began to think about how hard I worked to be the very best I could be. When I began to evaluate where I came from and the work I'd put in, I began to compare myself with everyone else. I felt like I had fallen short. I was looking at other players and seeing their success financially or otherwise and began to question why I didn't have what they had . . . why I wasn't as far along as they were. This was the beginning of a dark time for me as a musician. I grew frustrated and depressed. The symptoms and the cause were much deeper than what I realized. It brought me to a dark place. I had had enough, and I wanted to walk away from music. I was also angry with myself for heading down this path in the first place.

The truth was, I had already accomplished many great things musically and should have been grateful. I was experiencing a significant level of success of my own, but it didn't matter. When you're in the dark like that, you can't see outside the cave and pit you're in. I finally got to a point where I threw my hands up at God and shouted, "I'm not doing this anymore. I want to do something else." Dealing with the disappointments and letdowns was too painful. I felt so defeated that I finally just surrendered. It wasn't until I reached this point of surrender that I was finally able to emerge from the darkness and see the beginning of a new "season." In my mind, I was ready to go on that next path. It was the beginning of a musical healing for me.

When I finally gave up and let everything go, I finally learned what music was supposed to be, what it was for, and how it applied to my life and calling. Prior to that, it was like I was misusing the gift that had been given to me in order to just acquire a false sense of confidence. I relied on music to fill a huge void in my life by using it to draw approval from others, and I was more concerned with what other people thought than how to truly be myself. After I was able to see this with clearer vision, I made a decision to change my reason for playing music altogether. From that point forward, I was not going to play just for myself, but instead for the benefit of others. I believe music has to be something you give away and not take from as a musician. This realization changed my life. It hasn't always been easy and having a career as a musician can be a tremendous roller-coaster ride with extreme highs and lows. However, I suppose this was just the place I had to go before I could finally find out who I was. I'd like to believe that my music carries now a more intangible and spiritual aspect that is able to communicate on a deeper level with the listener. This is a very real thing, and it taps into the core of what my vision is. I wish to communicate and convey emotion beyond words. That is one of the reasons that I have really enjoyed finding an identity in instrumental music. I know there's a force at work beyond our understanding that ties all of this together, so all I can really do is open myself up to be that channel or medium that the message is translated through. I have to be as honest as I can and do my best to respect this.

Adam Nussbaum
DRUMMER, EDUCATOR

HOME BASE
www.adamnussbaum.com

GOT MUSIC?
Standards, The Nuttree Quartet, Kind of Blue Records (KOB), 2008

"[Jazz has] helped me see the humanity in everyone."

BACKGROUND AND SOUND
Grammy Award–winning drummer Adam Nussbaum strides right along with past and present heavyweights. His driving beats have been a part of the Gil Evans Orchestra, the Michael Brecker Quintet, the David Liebman Quintet, the Carla Bley Big Band, and the John Abercrombie Organ Trio. He has also played with James Moody and Sonny Rollins, and present and past collaborative efforts have resulted in the groups Nuttree and BANN. His personable approach to educating young drummers has carried him around the world as an in-demand clinician. Adam Nussbaum's amiable

sound and personality have made him one of the most accessible players in jazz.

HIS STORY

Jazz was just music I heard and loved. It combines discipline, a chance for expression and freedom that allows elements of an individual to be viewed through their voice. When I was twelve I heard Jimi Hendrix. It freaked me out. It opened up the door for me because it was so new and exciting. It really resonated with me. I got into his drummer—Mitch Mitchell, who was inspired by Elvin Jones,  who was John Coltrane's drummer, and this opened another door. Later on I got to see Dizzy and many other incredible musicians play, too. Growing up near New York, where my heroes were living, was an incredible thing. They burned deep into my whole sense of being. I was so taken by it. These experiences greatly affected me and shaped how I view things. I went for years after this trying to do something predictable, but the pull of the music was so strong I had to come back to it . . . this music picks you.

Jazz encompasses so many different feelings and styles. It's helped me to see the humanity in everyone. With everything going on in this world I have to try to maintain my positive attitude through it. It really is fascinating to travel around the world and see how universal this language is. It truly cuts through the BS of politics, race, and bureaucracy. I did a gig in the former Soviet Union where people showed up to play at our jam sessions where the saxophone was once considered illegal. They had horns that were held together with rubber bands and gum. You could tell these were the crusaders, the ones playing in their basements . . . these were the freedom fighters. They were truly underground with their instruments.

When you're dealing with music and people from all over the world it can affect how you reflect on what you're doing and what the real definition of jazz is and where it's shifting and going to be. You have to be aware of the scope of things in this world to live this life and have something to say, and jazz has helped me with this. Yet it seems that a lot of people don't appreciate it. I think that maybe it's because they don't get exposed to it.

If we had someone like Beyoncé talking about Billie Holiday or Usher talking about Louis Armstrong, we'd have a connection. If people were exposed to it through MTV or VH1, and those channels gave just five percent of their schedule to what this music is about, it would be enough to whet people's appetites. If every hour they played a clip of Basie or one of the music's forefathers, it would bring an awareness of jazz into what's going on today and have an invaluable effect. People will feel the energy when this music is played. It's not in the mechanics of what we do, it's in the feeling. It's my job as a musician to give them the right thing that they're looking for. Every night it's a new adventure, and I'm going to be in a different experience every day. I just try to bring this experience into the real world. I'm still working on this and striving to improve in the process.

Miles Okazaki
GUITARIST, COMPOSER, VISUAL ARTIST

HOME BASE
www.milesokazaki.com

GOT MUSIC?
Generations, Miles Okazaki, Sunnyside, 2009

"Music is an end in itself."

BACKGROUND AND SOUND
Miles Okazaki is more than a composer. His works are tributes to modern creative jazz. His body of compositions is thoughtful and profound, reflective of today's most progressive movements. Leading musicians such as Miguel Zenón, David Binney, Jen Shyu, Chris Potter, and Dan Weiss are regularly appearing members of his group. To claim that Miles is a visionary is an underestimation of his sheer talents. He is instead a voice that has the potential to change how audiences hear and view jazz as an art.

HIS STORY
I'm interested in a lot of things besides music, like arts—visual and literary and more. I guess it's really the human expression and technical aspect of

it that interests me, how people practice and perfect their type of craft and discipline. Music requires a type of sacrifice. Even when I was a kid, others would play outside and I would practice alone. I just liked the feeling of being able to see progress, and with music you can see physical progress. It's a way of measuring your own ability as a sort of self-affirmation. There are all these ways it trains your mind and body the same way athletes train.

Improvisational music requires quite a bit of physical work. It's not like you're strumming the guitar and writing a song about a girlfriend ... there's a lot of tedious work that has to be done before one can enjoy it. You have to imagine your goal and set forth to do it and accomplish it. You have to know the history and find your place in it. Maybe the reason I set out to do music is because personally I'm addicted to learning and inputting more information. It's just one of those things that will never end. The more you learn, the more you realize you don't know. This has taught me humility. I imagine it's the same thing with those who study religion or who are religious. There's a wonder, humility, a faith in something that is intangible. Exposing yourself to more and more things out there is the only way to progress.

In this way, music is a metaphor for what you're doing in life. Hopefully you're developing and transferring the process of how you developed in music into how you develop as a person. This is the part that continues to make me get up and practice every day. Music is in the rhythm of the heart and body, and we're all trying to access this, to connect to our own nature. My goal, in a lot of ways, is to present this template to people in the form of sound. I believe that if the intent of the performer is honest, and they know their instrument, then the sound produced will contain all kinds of information that directly communicates directly to the brain and body. A listener can analyze this information if they want, but they don't have to, as music is an end in itself.

Greg Osby

SAXOPHONIST, COMPOSER, PRODUCER, EDUCATOR

HOME BASE
www.gregosby.com

GOT MUSIC?
9 Levels, Greg Osby, Inner Circle
Music, 2009

"We have to be proactive and take music to the people."

BACKGROUND AND SOUND

For more than two decades award-winning saxophonist Greg Osby has been shaping the world around him with his provocative work as an educator, composer, and soloist. He has performed, toured, and recorded with jazz legends Dizzy Gillespie, Herbie Hancock, Jim Hall, and Muhal Richard Abrams. He has steadily gained the attention of the international scene as a clinician and workshop leader with his free-thinking approach to creative music. Greg has more than twenty recordings to his name as a leader and recently formed the label Inner Circle Music, which now offers a world stage for many who are deemed up-and-coming talents on the scene today. Greg's impressive art and his pure, sincere nature provide guidance that readily meets the wants and needs of artists and listeners.

HIS STORY

It's quite possible that we wouldn't still be talking about Charlie Parker and John Coltrane if what they did was considered safe. When you craft an art, sometimes you have to see things through and take the lumps and stick to it. To have that kind of fortitude is rare. I don't get the overwhelming sense that people that people understand that. Many want comfort and settle into complacency without rocking any boats. The same goes for musicians, who worry that if they change they may not get booked again, and that fear, historically, has killed what this music has come to represent. The way this music is presented and portrayed requires a tremendous facelift.

As artists, we have to be proactive and take music to the people. When I do concerts in Europe, kids come in with their family in tow. This is very normal. Children just sit there in wide-eyed wonderment. This is because their parents instilled in them that they're listening to real Americans playing our very own music. These people recognize the value of a culture and its contributions.

Over here, good music is used as space filler for the emptiness in people's lives. This music, when you realize somebody is doing something great, provides a lot of possibilities for people. It stimulates and encourages achievement. I'll never be the same because of this music. I'm deeply moved by it. It's something you don't take for granted, and it makes you realize the level of influence music and art have and makes me respect it more deeply. I'm trying to share this. But it lights my fire when musicians themselves are disrespectful and have a cavalier attitude about it. They need to realize that it's a tremendous gift to have people pay to come see what you have to say as an artist. Every time I go out I try to give a little more, working harder than before. This gives audiences something to look forward to, not just the same offerings in different gift wrapping. We wouldn't be at this point now if our predecessors thought this way. Instead they pushed the envelope. They lived for tomorrow and refused to ride the wave of yesterday.

Unfortunately, today, we don't really have a thriving music scene like they did. A faction of artists who have similar goals and a united front helps to define a scene. There are fewer places for people to play and fewer people working on the constructs of building a scene. But I think we're on the threshold of a new breakthrough. I personally know legions of young musicians who are working on new concepts. We have people who are choosing to take the unpaved road, the hard route. We're cultivating a whole new league of leaders. I'm optimistic because as a teacher I'm hearing this league everyday. They've got immediate access to everything and are only limited by their bandwidth. They're becoming much more proficient at an earlier age. All they need is someone to take them on the road for a bit and show them the ropes or to go to jam sessions.

When I think about presenting my music, I'm just hopeful that people will get the same charge from listening to it that I got when I was first inspired to compose it. I use my experiences as I would use a spice or ingredient in food. I'm curious to find out what happens if I incorporate certain ingredients into my music. Will it be substantial? What if I change the values and proportions of the internal components? Would it be rendered invalid or would it leave a hole that would artfully be filled that is just as effective? This curiosity is what keeps me going and is my fuel.

Keith Oshiro

TROMBONIST, COMPOSER

HOME BASE
www.myspace.com/keithoshiro

GOT MUSIC?
Live from London, Maynard
Ferguson, Avenue Jazz, 1994

"This music is therapeutic for me."

BACKGROUND AND SOUND

Trombonist Keith Oshiro is one of the most skilled and in-demand brass players for large ensembles today. He was a member of the illustrious One O'Clock Lab Band in the Jazz Studies Department at the University of North Texas and later went on to join the Maynard Ferguson Big Bop Nouveau Band, the Harry Connick Jr. Big Band, and the Woody Herman Orchestra. Now he regularly appears with Chuck Owen and the Jazz Surge and other groups including professional groups throughout Disney World in central Florida. His zinging sound and soul appeal as a player are highly sought-after qualities, and Keith releases this fire in each and every performance he gives.

HIS STORY

My parents are Japanese American. My father, Edward, was born and raised in Hawaii to a very poor family. As a child, he didn't even have shoes. He witnessed the bombing of Pearl Harbor. My mother, Lily, was born and raised in San Jose, California, and during World War II, her family was sent to Heart Mountain, one of the Japanese internment camps. Later, during the Korean War, my father came to the mainland and worked as a mechanic in the US Army. The military basically gave him the choice of dying in Korea or living in San Francisco. He chose life.

In addition to his trade, dad played both cornet and saxophone. My earliest memories come from going to his Wednesday night band practice. I am not sure what it was. Perhaps it was Japanese folk music, but definitely not pop. He played more than twenty-seven years, and arranged maybe four hundred tunes for the band. It was very influential just being around that band. During the forty-minute drive home from rehearsal, I would lie with my head in his lap and listen to him practice his singing. I was about five years old, and I would tell him the correct key was higher or lower, and when we got home he would go to the piano or his ukulele and see that I was right. I never forgot that. Dad was dedicated to music throughout his life.

With jazz, I believe this same dedication is a must if you are going to do this art form. There is a complexity to this music that I never grow tired of. It is just like an artist getting ready to paint on an unbound canvas. The possibilities are endless. You have to know the theory, feel and understand its sophistication to perform this music. Jazz also takes a particular audience. I sometimes wonder how someone who is not a jazz musician can fully appreciate what the performer is doing. This is one reason why I think jazz is not more popular. We are one of the only societies that do not embrace its own art form. Every major city has a symphony; why not a jazz ensemble?

Awareness can help. How are students and future generations going to get excited about something they do not know? Teachers are also motivators, and they must get students excited. Students are so impressionable at this age, and at the very least this would help develop their personalities.

One of the greatest desires in life is acceptance, while at the same time our greatest fear is rejection. This applies to anything you are involved in. As artists, we want to be accepted in our own culture and with our audiences. I am truly blessed that I can be creative and that my vocation and avocation are the same. Jazz and music in general have been such a big part of my life. In many ways, this music is therapeutic for me. Having looked upon it in times of sorrow, joy, and uncertainty, it is my source of counsel, my source of inspiration. The very thought of what I have contributed to jazz makes me laugh. Rather, I think what *hasn't* Jazz done for me?

I think it is important for people to be open and to try and understand the sincerity most musicians have. I try to be kind and respectful, both musically and personally, and to keep my eyes and ears open, and my mouth shut, walking with my head bowed, humble, like my father. As long as I do that, never stop dreaming, have fun, and be honest with myself, I will have no complaints, no regrets.

Ulysses Owens
DRUMMER, COMPOSER

HOME BASE
www.usojazzy.com

GOT MUSIC?
Dedicated to You, Kurt Elling,
Concord/Universal, 2009

"I play music because there's nothing else in the world I'd rather do."

BACKGROUND AND SOUND

Creating fire between his sticks, Ulysses Owens is combing the halls of greats with an energetic panache. Mulgrew Miller, Kurt Elling, and the Basie Band have embraced him and placed him at the helm of the masters. Always searching for that something new, he has arrived at the styles of his forefathers such as Philly Joe Jones, Buddy Rich, and Lewis Nash. But as a licensed minister and graduate of Julliard, he has surrounded himself with the music of life, a flame that holds the beat of hearts and rhythm around him. Ulysses is an assurance that the future of jazz is in good hands.

HIS STORY

I started playing at the age of two while growing up in a church where my mother was the choir director. She would take me to rehearsals and sit me right next to the drummer, where she could keep her eyes on me. When the drummer got frustrated with his position, I took over. That was when I was about six or seven years old. I've been playing ever since. The first drummer I fell in love with was Buddy Rich—and just for his virtuosity. People laugh at him but he was one of the first people to do great things on the drums. Lewis Nash, too. For me, he was one of the reasons I went into the program at Julliard. There was something about his sound I fell in love with . . . a precision. He embraced me. Sometimes when you're young and up-and-coming, people don't embrace you as much as they should. It's almost as if they're afraid of the young lions, but the future of jazz is in very good hands.

At this point though, I consider myself blessed. I play music because there's nothing else in the world I'd rather do. When I'm sitting on stage and all the crap you go through, like leaving your family and practicing for hours, paving your own way, when I climb upon the stage there's nothing like the feeling that you're connecting with those musicians. Jazz specifically is great this way; it's so expressive and something you can always create. Even when I'm struggling to barely make the bills I still wouldn't change my life. You can feel when your audience is connected to you. Those are the ones I think of the most. It's very life changing, and you can feel they get it and communicate with them. But as a musician and a licensed minister I just live my life with love and integrity, and my inspiration extends beyond music and more to the one who my gift came from.

Mark Patterson
TROMBONIST, COMPOSER, TEACHER, STUDENT

HOME BASE
www.jazzconvergence.com

GOT MUSIC?
Modern Man, Convergence, Capri, 2003

"All the great improvisers learned this music the same way."

BACKGROUND AND SOUND
Inspired by his father to continue the family musical heritage, Mark Patterson began his fruitful career at an early age. Throughout time he has played with many groups, including the Maria Schneider Jazz Orchestra, the Vanguard Jazz Orchestra, the Manhattan Jazz Orchestra, and Convergence. Equally strong in both jazz and orchestral settings, Mark has been called to play on movie soundtracks, such as *The Aviator* and *Six Degrees of Separation*, and Broadway shows that include *Spamalot* and *South Pacific*. Other notables who have employed Mark include Barbra Streisand and Tony Bennett. His adaptability as a player will ensure his continued success.

HIS STORY
Jazz has always had a very strong history of being taught and learned aurally, both on the bandstand and from recordings, combined with study

of musical fundamentals, starting even with Bach. But the aural element is indispensable. The idea of absorbing how time feels, how a line flows, by listening, feeling, and standing next to great players cannot be replaced. It's not an exaggeration to say that the melodic and rhythmic ethics are so strong they have become influential to practically all popular music worldwide.

This music is not about books of chord scales and play-along records. One of my favorite things to witness is how a young player takes hold of the soul, the swing, and the spark of how this music is created when they're exposed directly to a great player. I would not be the same player if I hadn't transcribed dozens of Charlie Parker solos and stood next to [saxophonist] Spike Robinson and [guitarist] Dale Bruning to feel how their lines spoke logically and floated over the time. All the great improvisers learned this music the same way. The beautiful thing is that if a young player seeks this type of mentorship, there are a large number of musicians who are passionate and universally generous in wanting to share. It seems that musicians are a very generous lot. This isn't the type of thing anyone takes credit for—it just becomes a matter of the living course of the music.

Nicholas Payton

TRUMPETER, COMPOSER, EDUCATOR

HOME BASE
www.nicholaspayton.com

GOT MUSIC?
Into the Blue, Nicholas Payton, Nonesuch, 2008

"The more open and vulnerable you are, the more life's beauty can pass through you."

BACKGROUND AND SOUND

Surrounded by the five-senses port to the world known as New Orleans, Nicholas Payton delivers strength and heritage-based grooves straight from the bell of his horn to audiences all over the world. He has been the first pick for greats such as Art Blakey and Elvin Jones as well as a firm and kind mentor to the generations following him. Nicholas has told his story through the open books of the masters with an unrivaled power. It's this novel approach to the music of the past and present that has become a gift bestowed upon the jazz world. A legend in the making, Nicholas is one musician who will forever breathe that sought-after spicy local flavor into all life and music around him.

HIS STORY

To define jazz is to lock it into one particular place. This goes against how things should be, but I guess everything is in that constant state of flux. When I initially started out it was for a love of music. I was only eleven years old, and both my parents were musicians. It was really cool to have their influence. My father played jazz bass and my mother was an operatic singer as well as a classical pianist. I remember sitting beneath the piano while my father had rehearsals at the house. Watching those had a profound effect on me. The musicians who are around you have a much bigger influence than those you idolize from afar. It was very important for me to talk and be with those older cats. This helped me get past the "young lions" stage without burning out.

Later on, when I was fifteen or sixteen years old, I seriously got into jazz while playing with Blakey. This is when I knew this was what I wanted to do. Most of the trumpet players I idolized had already played with him. My mentor, Clark Terry, wanted me to come to IAJE and work it out so I could finish high school in New York, but it was then that Blakey passed away and the idea of New York wasn't so appealing to me. The scene changed when Blakey died. Soon after, the club Bradley's in New York closed. Everyone played there, and if you wanted to know what was going on, you went there. . . . There was no place like it in New York. It kept everyone in check. When you went there, you had to deliver a certain amount of respect that seems to be missing from the scene now.

The one thing I always loved about New Orleans is that it had this passing of the torch from the older to younger society. Now everything, everywhere, not just in New Orleans, seems to be geared toward a youthful culture. Older people try to be younger, and there's a lack of respect for aging. People will try anything to negate the aging process. Yes it would be nice to have the energy of a five-year-old, but part of going through life is that you get to accumulate experience. This mentality is backwards. Young people are now the trendsetters. There's no sense of leadership and respect when someone sees a forty-year-old trying act like a fifteen-year-old. It's just downright disrespectful.

This mentality is also encouraged in jazz. The less connected to the tradition someone is, the more they're encouraged. People who go to gigs find that a lot of jazz doesn't feel good anymore. It obscures a pocket or groove for the sake of originality and complexity. The experience can be great making it, but you have to make people feel good. Jazz comes from life, stories of things that have happened and all of our experiences. Through my experiences, I've tried to be an open person. That being said, I also have values, and there are certain things I believe in. The more open and vulnerable you are, the more life's beauty can pass through you. You can put up walls, and people do so for their fears, but being heard through that wall works both ways. No one can come through and harm you, but you can't get through it either. You have to have a mutual respect and keep yourself open. The worst thing someone can do is to come to a concert, whether it's mine or someone else's, and listen with an idea of what they think it should be. Artists change all the time; whatever the artist decides to let come through them is the beauty of jazz. It's art. We're all in a room, whether playing or listening and experiencing it for the first time together. And it's this constant openness that's what I live by and for.

Jeremy Pelt
TRUMPETER, COMPOSER

HOME BASE
www.peltjazz.com

GOT MUSIC?
November, Jeremy Pelt, MaxJazz, 2008

"Jazz is at its healthiest point right now."

BACKGROUND AND SOUND

Jeremy Pelt's career has gained significant momentum since the day he stepped on to the streets of the New York jazz scene. His first gigs included the Mingus Big Band and led to opportunities to play with top jazz personalities Lewis Nash, Frank Wess, Jimmy Heath, Ravi Coltrane, and the Roy Hargrove Big Band, to name a few. Pelt's indigenous and traditionally rooted style steps outside the box in his compositions and solos. He is able to streamline his dynamic  sound into any situation, thus creating a niche for himself. This is just one of many reasons that Jeremy is consistently rated at the top of his field and is a rising star among the legends today.

HIS STORY

Despite what the critics are saying or who's bowing to them, jazz is at its healthiest point right now. There are some famous figures that get a lot of press, and more times than not they're the ones who are stagnant and give this perception of the art being stagnant. But jazz has always survived because of an undercurrent of talent. This is the reason it's still flowering today.

What people want you to hear and what is marketable may or may not be stagnant; it just boils down to what the critics tout as being good or acceptable. This is what shapes the public's perception. It becomes a matter of the public's ability to be able to grasp the music and discern what they like versus what the critics are saying about it. If you're not strong enough in your convictions, then you'll be easily swayed.

It doesn't take a marketing team to tell us that it's good art. It's a lovable music that appeals to a wide audience. As artists we just have to stop caring what people think so much. It's not like I was born with thick skin; your skin has to get thicker with time. After eleven years of being a part of the scene I now know what I'm doing and what I like. This is very important. The layperson doesn't necessarily have to understand this, but if you start giving in to others and the critics, then you're only going to taint your product. After all, this music takes resilience and preparation. You have to prepare yourself for all things that come your way at all times and stand by what you believe in.

Luis Perdomo

PIANIST, COMPOSER

HOME BASE
www.luisperdomojazz.com

GOT MUSIC?
Awareness, Luis Perdomo, RKM
Music, 2006

"The only way I'll know what the future holds is when I'm looking back over what has already happened."

BACKGROUND AND SOUND

Venezuelan native Luis Perdomo moved to New York City hoping to study jazz and get closer to the legends. What he didn't realize is that this experience, combined with the rich cultural heritage of his native land, would push him to the same ground of those who came before him. His dense harmonics and highly rhythmic texture readily break through his soloing and compositions with a healthy and admirable strength. Others who have noticed this power include Ravi Coltrane, John Patitucci, Dave Valentin, Claudia Acuña, and Miguel Zenón. His solo records and collaborations have become a distinct voice among the crowds of pianists today.

HIS STORY

I love being in different parts of the world. You can create music with someone and you don't even have to speak the same language. This is one of the beauties of being a jazz musician. You can play with people you haven't even met and communicate with them without speaking verbally. Sometimes you even get a better insight into their personality this way. I hope at some point others can see this from our point of view. Yet the only way I'll know what the future holds is when I'm looking back over what has already happened.

One of the problems we're having isn't the music—it's exposure. People aren't being exposed to jazz, especially the younger audiences. This music requires a lot of attention when you listen. Some people just don't want to think that hard, and I can see their point of view. You come off work and you just want to relax, so we have to find ways to make music that's easy on the listener while at the same time challenging the musician. But you can't change what people think. I don't sit down with the intention of changing jazz. Sometimes I'm inspired to continue and other times I'm thinking about how out of tune the piano is. It really changes from day to day. But most of the time I just listen and create without worry or expectations. In this way jazz equals happiness, and hopefully I can bring that to others.

Oscar Perez
PIANIST, COMPOSER, EDUCATOR

HOME BASE
www.oscarperezmusic.com

GOT MUSIC?
Nuevo Comienzo, Oscar Perez, Independent Label, 2005

"Be persistent. It doesn't matter if you see the end of the road or not; you must work for your success in this business."

BACKGROUND AND SOUND
Colorful and fluent in all styles, Oscar Perez moves with the times. As one of the top call pianists in New York, his notes have been heard from the city's famed Rainbow Room all the way to Russia. He won a commission from ASCAP/IAJE in 2006 and a grant from the Chamber Music America Grant for New Works Creation and Presentation Program. The creative world he has built is original, while his flair for tradition moves his groove right along. This passion is the essence of the upcoming legends in jazz today.

HIS STORY
We listened to records growing up, and certainly my Cuban and Colombian heritage has influenced me, but my father and mother were not musicians. I was on autopilot, and because of this natural ability, I had to research everything I thought I knew in order to become successful. And even now success is something I work at every day. Nothing happens fast. It's not like

you get a degree in music and the next day you walk into a gig. Be persistent. It doesn't matter if you see the end of the road or not; you must work for your success in this business. Joe Henderson once told me to continue to work and be productive because he worked and worked and one day he said he realized he was that person, the one with the records and name. I still follow this advice. Right now my style is a connective tissue between the postmodern and dance melodies of my influences. I apply what I know and deliver my part in support of others while inspiring them to be their best. The reason those influences were so great wasn't because of their abilities necessarily, it was because they wrote great songs. Composition is the greatest legacy one can leave. Unless we do something to it, breathe life into it, it will die. Jazz is vibrant, and anyone who says jazz is dead, well, they're just listening to the wrong kind of jazz for them. I believe there's something out there for everyone.

Dave Pietro
SAXOPHONIST, WOODWINDIST, COMPOSER, EDUCATOR

HOME BASE
www.davepietro.com

GOT MUSIC?
The Chakra Suite, Dave Pietro, Challenge Records, 2008

"I want to be the eternal student."

BACKGROUND AND SOUND
For more than twenty years Dave Pietro has thumbed through the books of bands in New York. Beneath the undercurrent of fortified sound lies an inner peace. Whether he has been commissioned to write a new work or he is soloing with other groups, he sets his vision straight and delivers consistently fine music. Artists like Maria Schneider, Maynard Ferguson, the Vanguard Jazz Orchestra, John Fedchock, Ray Charles, Liza Minnelli, and Blood, Sweat and Tears have all been a part of his career path. As a composer and performer he has been the recipient of several awards and nominations and a National Endowment for the Arts grant. Currently he

is educating listeners and music students throughout New York at New York University and Hofstra University.

HIS STORY

My dad had a great collection of big band swing records, and I can remember listening to them on the hi-fi when I could barely stand up. I grew up in a small town twenty-five miles from Boston, which was great because I got to hear a lot of jazz, live and on the radio. My junior high jazz band director turned me on to Charlie Parker and had me improvising when I had only been playing the saxophone for a few months. I realize now how lucky I was to have grown up in such a great musical environment.

After attending the University of North Texas, I moved to New York to pursue my passion. Twenty-two years here have tested my resolve, pushed my talents, and challenged me to be a better musician. Music has taken me all over the world. It has defined my life.

For me, everything comes from sound. Your sound is your voice, your vibration, and your song. I am constantly exploring various shades and colors on my instruments, which is why I have delved into playing rare instruments such as the F-mezzo and C-melody saxophones. I find that new sonorities often lead to hearing new ideas and concepts, and that new music often requires new sonorities.

The older I get, the more I look at myself as a beginner. I want to be the eternal student. I want to always be studying something new, something that stretches me, challenges me, and leads me to grow and develop. I'd like to think that my software is still being written.

I try to put my default setting on "discovery," both in life and in improvisation. Staying in the moment, fully present, aware, focused with a calm stillness, is the key. Too much unhappiness and bad improvising comes from worrying about the past or the future and not being present in the moment and listening with one hundred percent of your being. In fact, I find myself focusing on listening more than anything else these days.

I used to struggle with judgment a lot until I learned to distinguish between the healthy judgment that ran parallel to my creativity and informed it and the unhealthy judgment that ran perpendicular to my creativity and blocked it. As musicians we have to interpret our music and ask, is this in tune or not? Is my tone on this note as warm and dark as it could be? The answers to these questions are necessary. But to be self-critical to the point of inhibiting one's own creativity is not a good thing. As a result, I now find myself much more drawn to the *process* of creating and less concerned with judging the creation or the outcome. I've learned that our perspectives and opinions will often change over time.

The world is becoming more and more intertwined, and this is reflected in today's music scene. I think that most "jazz" musicians, myself included, would say that their music doesn't neatly fall into any one category. My playing and composing have not only been influenced by jazz but by my studies of Brazilian, East Indian, European classical, and American pop music. Human beings have this need to label things, to categorize our world . . . people, art, politics, et cetera. Their true nature, however, is to be interdependent, influenced by one another and in a state of flux. Hopefully we'll get to the point one day where labels mean less both in life and in music.

There is no doubt that these are challenging times for improvisationally based music and for the music business in general. However, there are still many incredibly creative musicians out there who are moving the music forward, respectful of where it came from, trying to find their own unique sounds in the universe. I'm happy to be a part of it all.

Jean-Luc Ponty

{LIVING LEGEND}

VIOLINIST, COMPOSER

HOME BASE
www.ponty.com

GOT MUSIC?
The Very Best of Jean-Luc Ponty,
Jean-Luc Ponty, Atlantic/Rhino
Records, 2000

"To feel and write what I feel is where it all starts."

BACKGROUND AND SOUND

Internationally acclaimed violinist Jean-Luc Ponty is considered to be one of the pioneers in modern jazz. Born into a musical family, Jean-Luc was able to dip his hands into the piano, clarinet, and saxophone in addition to his primary instrument, the violin. Once he began playing jazz on the saxophone and listening to the heavy cats of the day, like Miles Davis and John Coltrane, he knew he had to play jazz above all else. Once he focused his career on innovation and not imitation, Jean-Luc started up the path he is on today. By the late sixties the Modern Jazz Quartet, Frank Zappa, and many keynote officials of jazz had already had him on their bills. Since that auspicious beginning he has toured around the world and played in front of hundreds of thousands of fans; recorded dozens of albums on labels such as Columbia, Universal, Koch, and Atlantic; and redesigned the perception of jazz in the public eye. His expressive and vocal-like quality produces a product that is original, accessible, and cordial. Easily listenable, Jean-Luc shines well past the first impression and into the zone of the more legendary creatives in this world.

HIS STORY

I was extremely lucky to start my career when I did. In the sixties and seventies I went through the golden years of the music world, and when I arrived in the US in the early seventies, music hadn't really become a business yet. Artists were still leading the way; in fact, most everyone who was on the business side were musicians or ex-musicians themselves. They respected artists who had visions that opened doors for new styles of music and brought something new to the listeners' ears. Lately, I've seen it decline and change completely. The music world, as it is right now, doesn't encourage young musicians to be different. They have to fit in a special category to find a record deal. I'm even amazed that I'm still in demand around the world and at my age. I'm going to countries that used to be behind the Iron Curtain, and I discover that some people had access to our recordings even though it was illegal and difficult for them to find and to buy this type of music under communist regimes. The fact that I've been so disappointed with so many things in the world doesn't really matter, because music remains a way to live in the world. I can create my own world and as much beauty as I want. In a humble way I want to bring joy and love to people. It's tough to absorb the hard things and take it all in. I wouldn't say music is an escape, though. If we create this music, we have it in our mind and it's there and that's real. I started playing and writing music without analyzing or knowing what was happening. I didn't know why I was doing the music I was doing or the way I was doing it. Then I started analyzing more and more what I was doing and realized that it is an incredible means to understand my emotions. To feel and write what I feel is where it all starts. I hope listeners will share and understand what I feel. I know what I am and what I'm not. I'm a modern musician and improviser who produces music inspired by his numerous experiences.

Dave Potter
DRUMMER

HOME BASE
www.myspace.com/
davepottermusic

GOT MUSIC?
Music Update, Jason Marsalis,
ELM records, 2009

"You'll find a way to do something if you have to do it."

BACKGROUND AND SOUND
There is a little more to life than just keeping time, and this young lion of jazz, Dave Potter, knows it all too well. He has played with Marcus Roberts, Marcus Printup, Jason Marsalis, Kevin Bales, Greg Tardy, and more. But there are a lot of great drummers out there. To find what sets Dave apart takes but a second of listening to his voice both on the drum set and off. There is an intelligent foundation that allows him to extend his solid technique and abilities to hang with the best.

HIS STORY
I listen to influential drummers, and then I take their influence and embody it in my own playing. I ask, is this person playing good music because they love it? I listen for those that have studied in the tradition. You can't go to New York anymore and do a day job and play at jam sessions at night. If you want to learn how to play, you better have one of

the great influences riding over you. I'm doing my damnedest to play and teach people how to show others what jazz is supposed to be. Yet young players must know this is going to be the most difficult thing they've ever tried to do. There's constant misfortune and/or disappointment, but it's also one of the greatest rewards in life. I knew jazz was in the underbelly of music in general, but I had no idea it would be this difficult, and this drives me to continue. I like the challenge. Every time I've been able to reach a milestone in my own playing and I see the joy it brings to the audience, I become a part of the tradition I have so much pride in. This is why I continue with jazz. One doesn't go into jazz because you love it; you go into it because you *have* to. You'll find a way to do something if you have to do it. The human spirit will find a way achieve what has to be done. It's not just a music thing; this should be encouraged for anyone. Love your work. Always.

Noah Preminger
SAXOPHONIST, COMPOSER

HOME BASE
www.noahpreminger.com

GOT MUSIC?
Dry Bridge Road, Noah Preminger, Nowt Records, 2008

"You can't change anything or get anywhere in this field if nobody hears you."

BACKGROUND AND SOUND
A notable strength has emerged from the ranks of the youth in jazz. His name? Noah Preminger. As a composer, he is on fire. He has studied with Danilo Perez and taken note of advice and wisdom from Fred Hersch. His compositions have opened floodgates of creativity. Hanging with the very best, such as Frank Kimbrough and Ben Monder, among others on his recording. Noah easily engages the listener throughout each of his tunes. He is one to keep tabs on as the gateway to the heavy hitters slowly opens to make room for his entrance into the family.

HIS STORY

Some people, from a very young age, know what they want to do with their lives. And sometimes you have to do things you're not so proud of in order to be a musician just so you can do things like eat and live. I was one of them. You have to push yourself very hard as a person. This is true with everything in life. It's been hammered into me to stay away from clichés. This is hard to do, especially when you check out a lot of music. You begin to get obsessed with things you like; you just want to do what they're doing. I try to be open to everything. You can't try to be original, as this music is based on your life experiences and what music you've checked out. It's important to check yourself out and figure out what you need to do. It seems like everyone I know works very hard. There are a lot of people that work on things they don't need to and don't work on the things they *do* need to. It's a matter of figuring it out and moving on from there. The main thing missing from the younger musicians is that they're working on the wrong things. They try to reinvent the wheel and come up with clever stuff in odd time signatures, et cetera. No one wants to hear that. It's ridiculous when they can't play anything and mean it. You can't change anything or get anywhere in this field if nobody hears you. Play with love, that's it. Draw the listener in so they get high off the music. After all, that's why we listen to music and this is why I play. I want to throw my emotions out for other people to get high off of, to show them love.

Lenore Raphael
PIANIST, ARRANGER, COMPOSER

HOME BASE
www.lenoreraphael.com

GOT MUSIC?
Class Act: Lenore Raphael: Live at Steinway Hall, Lenore Raphael, Independent Label, 2009

"Jazz is in my heart, and when I play I'm in another place."

BACKGROUND AND SOUND

Her graceful fingers hit the keys, and you're lost in a myriad of sound and history. Oscar Peterson, Bill Evans, and Bud Powell escape as shadows through her chords and lyrical lines. Steinway artist Lenore Raphael is a known force behind women in jazz. She has appeared on Marian McPartland's *Piano Jazz*, the Jazz at Lincoln Center's Women in Jazz series, her own jazz radio series, and countless national and international appearances. There's an infatuation that extends her love for this music that speaks of refinement and stride and years of respect for the art of jazz.

HER STORY

Even though I had a classical background I was a very unclassical player, fiddling around improvising with Mozart, Beethoven, et cetera. But when I heard Clifford Brown I said, "I'm going to play around with that!" I found it to be easy for me. Yet even after all the gigs that got me to where I am today, when I played across the street at Lincoln Center, I felt for the first time that I was really getting my start—that I'm almost where I want to be. But I don't think you ever really make it. You just have to keep growing musically; you can't judge yourself. Oscar Peterson was very demanding of himself; Bill Evans didn't want the Riverside recording released because he hated it. You're going to be your own worst critic.

Jazz is in my heart, and when I play I'm in another place. There's a space out there where nothing else exists, and it's not cerebral at all; I don't think it ever was. You must feel it. If I think about anything when I play it's the lyrics. Maybe this is where the heart comes in. I don't think anybody is as passionate about any other form of music as jazz because it's such an individual expression. You either love it or you don't, and there doesn't seem to be anything in the middle. There's no reason to discourage anyone from this music, and it may not happen overnight, but it will happen if they just give it time.

Rufus Reid

BASSIST, COMPOSER, EDUCATOR, AUTHOR,
MELLON JAZZ LIVING LEGACY

HOME BASE
www.rufusreid.com

GOT MUSIC?
Live at the Kennedy Center,
Rufus Reid, Motema Music,
2007

"[This music is] at the core of everything I do during every waking moment."

BACKGROUND AND SOUND

Bassist Rufus Reid exemplifies the "ideal" life of a jazz musician. Excelling in all arenas, including composition, education, and performance, Reid has established his legacy as one of the greatest bass players to hit the jazz world. His book *The Evolving Bassist* has been in publication since 1974 and is considered to be a bible for the bass. The International Society of Bassists presented Rufus with a Distinguished Achievement Award in 2001 and the International Association of Jazz Educators bestowed their Humanitarian Award on him in 1997. Accolades and awards continue to roll in for his compositions, including the Sackler Composition Commission Prize and the Charlie Parker Jazz Composition Award. In 2005 he was awarded the prestigious honor of the Mellon Jazz Living Legacy award. He has taught innumerable students in his lifetime at great institutions such as William Patterson University, where he was their director of jazz studies for more than twenty years. His list of achievements is inspiring and the product of diligence in an art he takes unreserved pride in.

HIS STORY

This music is me, it's my life. I've been doing it my entire life, and it's at the core of everything I do during every waking moment. It's not just something I like to do; it's what I am. Throughout my career, I've been around individuals who have been and continue to be an integral part of jazz education. People often forget that just because they learn the music it doesn't mean they're going to be great or successful at it. A lot of people who study and spend tons of money to be doctors or lawyers blow it at their test. There are too many musicians who want to be successful without the work that needs to be involved. But there are still a small percentage of those who want to be a creative musician and *have* to do it. I tell people to do something, anything, else if they can. In order to be successful they must have an unadulterated passion and perseverance to hang in there. Initially, success does not equate to having lots of money. Success means being consistently respected for your abilities in your community. After all, anything worth having is worth working for. I try to instill this in young people. Just because they can get around the horn doesn't mean they can go to New York and survive as a jazz musician. It's a given that you better be good if you expect to take care of your livelihood, your rent, food, and family. There's a lot involved with being a professional musician or professional anything. To me, it really is common sense. Young musicians need to know that if you want to have a decent place to live in, you can't at the outset have all the luxuries that perhaps they were raised with. They certainly can't snort it up their nose or indulge themselves in this way. That's stupid! You have to be truly, painfully honest with yourself. Sometimes people don't want to be told the truth, but being a musician isn't easy. I see young people around thirteen to fifteen years old who want this, and I say, be serious and then go for it. Before they know it, they'll realize their hopes and dreams. Somehow I've made people understand and believe in this. Just being able to be more in control of what it is you do, and with honesty, is the key.

Lee Ritenour

{LIVING LEGEND}

GUITARIST, COMPOSER

HOME BASE
www.leeritenour.com

GOT MUSIC?
Smoke 'n' Mirrors, Lee Ritenour, Peak Records, 2006

"I chose what was closest to my heart, and I recommend this for anyone."

BACKGROUND AND SOUND

Grammy Award–winning guitarist Lee Ritenour is at the top of his game. For more than four decades Lee has collaborated, produced, toured, and performed with the very best in the contemporary jazz industry. His first gigs took place with performing legends such as the Mamas and the Papas, Lena Horne, and Tony Bennett. Since that time he has had more than seventeen Grammy nominations, one Grammy Award, and numerous number one spots on *Billboard* charts and guitar polls alike. As the founding member of Fourplay, the most successful group in contemporary jazz, he brought together extraordinary talents Bob James, Harvey Mason, and Nathan East to light. With more than three thousand studio sessions (including the infamous Pink Floyd album *The Wall* and Steely Dan's *Aja*), forty albums, thirty-five tunes to have hit the charts, and performances with a who's who list of musicians across all genre lines under his belt, Lee continues to be successful in every endeavor he sets out to do.

HIS STORY

I've danced in many musical arenas throughout my career, but I chose what was closest to my heart, and I recommend this for anyone. Sometimes it's the harder road and is one that's not necessarily financially stable, but if you do something you love and are passionate about it will keep you young. I'm grateful for having jazz as the root of all of my music. It's a true international music, and more people are listening to it than ever. Even though the Internet is spawning the music for free and it's harder for artists to get paid for their services, I think it will work itself out. Through YouTube and MySpace people will find the music they want to find. I guess jazz is in good shape in a weird way because of this. At least instrumental music is a common thread around the world. We don't have the problem with language that a singer from Europe or South America would. Instrumentally, if you're a strong player and you remain true, your music will carry you around the world. I've always made room for myself by remaining true to the guitar and this music I love. I don't record something I can't love and be emotionally attached to. If I did this, then how could I expect my fans to attach themselves to it? I never forget what a wonderful gift this is. People remind me constantly that they wish they could be in the position I'm in. I thank God every day for this. I'm always challenging myself on new levels to learn something every day. I've always been a guitar geek, well . . . a complete geek since I was a kid with an amp. I'll always be that big kid. I tend to be a very positive person, and this shows through my music. I hope it's sophisticated enough to get others to think and grow. I guess the fact that anyone gets to this music is a win-win right away, but if they react to it and are inspired to listen to more then I'm happy.

Adam Rogers
GUITARIST, COMPOSER, EDUCATOR

HOME BASE
www.adamrogersmusic.com

GOT MUSIC?
Art of the Invisible, Adam Rogers, Criss Cross Jazz, 2002

"There is no shortcut to mastering music or an instrument."

BACKGROUND AND SOUND
Grammy Award–winning guitarist Adam Rogers has appeared on more than 150 albums and is one of the most critically acclaimed jazz guitarists of our time. Playing with greats such as Michael and Randy Brecker, Cassandra Wilson, Chris Potter, and John Patitucci is just one of the credits that stack up on his charts. He has been praised time and again for not only his playing, but also his compositions and innovative groups, such as Lost Tribe. His voice is clear, concise, and mesmerizing in its beauty. A full plate for any listener to digest, Adam is an intelligent and motivated force in the industry.

HIS STORY
I think a lot of the techniques one learns as a musician in general, and an improvising musician in particular, are things that are so useful as a human being. Extreme sensitivity to one's surroundings: Listening and reacting to what is going on in the music around you as opposed to asserting your internal monologue on that environment. Real humility, which I see as being particularly relevant today, when so much information is available so immediately. As long as I've been playing, there is still so much to learn.

There is no shortcut to mastering music or an instrument. It seems like an endless series of mountain peaks. Only when you reach the apex of one does the next range becomes visible. The elusive nature of the journey can be rewarding and mystifying. I guess my main goal as a musician is to be able to communicate all of the feelings I have about this process, life, music, and discovery to the listener. If I am, even partially, able to do that through my music, I have been successful.

Ted Rosenthal
PIANIST, COMPOSER, EDUCATOR

HOME BASE
www.tedrosenthal.com

GOT MUSIC?
Expressions, Ted Rosenthal, Jazz Impuls Records, 2004

"The compositional aspect, tied in with personal expressive playing, is the way to push this music forward."

BACKGROUND AND SOUND

Ted Rosenthal's career as a pianist spans well beyond the eighty-eight keys in front of him. As the first place winner of the second annual Thelonious Monk International Jazz Piano Competition, he has gone on to play with legends like Gerry Mulligan, Jon Faddis, Phil Woods, and James Moody. His first release as a leader included greats such as Tom Harrell, Billy Higgins, and Ron Carter. His collection of work now contains more than eleven CDs as a leader and a composer. He is in the business of transforming young hands and minds through the celebrated Julliard School as well as the Manhattan School of Music. His lively and off-the-wall compositions and what he calls "derangements" of standards have attracted listeners throughout the world.

HIS STORY

There are many ways to express yourself in jazz. You can play with different strains and styles as long as you play them convincingly and with personal style. You can't just copy. Jazz has to look forward and feel fresh and personal. There should also be a conversational aesthetic while you're creating. It's not a tradition to be chained down. If you have ideas as a composer and you feel strongly about them, there's no reason not to go in your own direction. If you're working with some elements you feel strong enough to weave through the music, then do it with conviction. The compositional aspect, tied in with personal expressive playing, is the way to push this music forward. Most of the great, if not all, jazz masters I look up to have made a big mark not only in their playing but in their compositions as well. If you're a modern jazz musician you can play really good tunes, but you should also have something to say of your own, just like they did. Openness and acceptance are important to have, especially when others are saying their own thing. Ultimately you have to be honest with yourself with this same openness and acceptance. To have an honest, without-ego view of yourself or other matters of life is always important. You can have excuses or "factors," but they don't really matter. If you have this kind of groundedness you'll continue to work toward your musical goals. We all have to learn this. Jazz requires openness and attention as a listener. It's not just a sit-back-and-flip-the-channels kind of music. You have to give something to it to hear it.

Chanda Rule

VOCALIST, COMPOSER, INTERFAITH MINISTER

HOME BASE
www.likewatermusic.com

GOT MUSIC?
I Too Speak of a River, Chanda Rule, Like | Water Music, 2007

"Everyone should always do something because they love it, not because they think it's going to be accepted by somebody else."

BACKGROUND AND SOUND

Rising up from the overcrowded and often clichéd vocal scene in jazz, Chanda Rule is truly a breath that, once taken in, could sustain your life.

Her inner beauty is personified through her song and positive energy. Wrapping her gospel roots and faith in the sheer healing ability of music, she has come out with a sound that is highly nourished through her soul. She runs workshops throughout New York that teach about the African roots of gospel music and has performed or opened for talents such as India. Arie and Regina Belle and the Whispers. The strength in her heart and her desire to sing and spread the message of hope through music has carried her around the world. She can be caught, at any given moment, spreading this message through the clubs and other venues in New York.

HER STORY

I came from a very academic family, and my singing was mostly at home. I guess everyone there just saw me as more of a writer than a singer. It was always like this secret dream I had. When I was older I pursued other things, like journalism and marketing and advertising, but it wasn't long until I decided to say, okay, let's see what'll happen with this dream. Sometimes I'm lucky now . . . this dream world comes together with the real world. Then I step back and say this is what it's going to look like. Maybe it doesn't look like what I thought it would, but the reformed vision I have is still better than anything I could've imagined. I feel everyone should always do something because they love it, not because they think it's going to be accepted by somebody else. You have to follow your own dream.

One of the things I really like to do is take old songs and give them a new spin. It's important for me to do so I can give them to the future generations. Their path is going to be hard enough to follow on their own, so we have to encourage them to use their heart to see and follow their dreams. There's a lot of hopelessness today, and I'm not sure if it's conscious, but it seems that our culture is broken. My friends think I'm so goofy . . . but most of the time when I'm performing this doesn't come out at all. Instead there's this strong person. Sometimes it's uncomfortable, and I have to ask who this other person is and what possessed me to do this . . . but all I can say is that it's a miracle that hits my heart. Whatever story I'm telling in my song, I want you to experience what I'm saying, as it's the essence and spirit of me coming out.

Brenda Russell

VOCALIST, COMPOSER, PRODUCER

HOME BASE
www.brendarussell.com

GOT MUSIC?
Paris Rain, Brenda Russell,
Hidden Beach, 2000

"Music is like food and water: it's something that makes a better human being out of a person."

BACKGROUND AND SOUND

Grammy-nominated vocalist Brenda Russell has enriched audiences with provocative lyrics and melodies. As a veteran of the scene for more than three decades, she has dipped chords in many genres. Her Tony Award–nominated compositions for *The Color Purple* have placed her in the realm of stardom on Broadway, and her hit tunes, such as "Piano in the Dark" and "Get Here," have climbed the Top 40 charts in the past. But her strength lies not only in her ability as a songwriter and composer, but also in her voice. A solid spirit walks beside her as she continues to influence musicians in all genres and listeners around the world.

HER STORY

I came from a musical family. My parents were both musicians. My mother was a writer, and my father was a singer and a drummer. Because of their musical influences I learned a lot about music before I even got here. Whatever they played in the house I learned from, Dinah Washington to Johnny Mathis to Count Basie. The Beatles and Motown sound were also a huge part of me. But I'm self-taught and had a pure love and desire to do what it is that I do. Sometimes you're just born with that desire.

If people thought then the way they think today in the music industry, we'd have never heard of vocalists like Aretha Franklin. They wouldn't have wanted to promote her, and it makes me wonder what we're missing out on now. There are people who don't fit certain images but can sing their asses off, and we're never going to hear from them. That's the problem with the greed that's come into this industry. I like to make pictures with my lyrics and create a visual experience for people. When the music industry came up with videos they put a visual on music that used to be up to a person's imagination. This eliminates a lot of freedom of imagination for the listener. This is why I try to be sincere as possible when I'm writing. I *always* write things that will uplift people. I learned early on that I can't write something that says, "I can't live without you," or whatever. I don't believe in that life. I love to inspire people spiritually or romantically and push a little harder with my lyrics. Even if I think its great I have to take it to the next level and say something that hasn't been said before and not just write down to the common denominator. I'd rather push people upwards.

It's when you have faith and believe in yourself and stop comparing yourself with others, that's when you can write honestly. There's always going to be someone you think is better than you, and we all go there. Eliminate that. Do your own thing. It's important to remember the audience is there to have music they can relate to. Music is like food and water: it's something that makes a better human being out of a person. I can't explain how to understand oneself better as an artist, because the artistry itself should be enough to understand them. Although I try to inspire people and be positive, the music speaks for itself. If you don't have a good idea of who I am after you listen, you're never going to understand me.

Nick Russo

GUITARIST, COMPOSER, EDUCATOR

HOME BASE
www.nickrusso.org

GOT MUSIC?
Ro, Nick Russo, On the Bol Records, 2006

"I'm blessed with the work I have."

BACKGROUND AND SOUND

Nick Russo has led a full life in just a short amount of time. As the winner of the 2004 International Jazz Workshop at Banff competition and the 2001 winner of the JAS Academy in Aspen, Colorado, Nick has gone on to accomplish much in the arenas of performance and composition. As a performer he has played with Jimmy McGriff, David Pleasant, Victor Jones, and Miles Griffith, among others, and made an appearance in the Sam Mendes film *Away We Go*. Nick excels best in soloing and diverse compositions. His work combines a cross-section of Metheny with modern and world jazz, and the product is, without fail, sensational and colorful at its very core.

HIS STORY

This music has brought a lot of joy to me. My uncle Mike is a great guitarist, and my father was on the road with Sly and the Family Stone and played with Chuck Berry. Music was everywhere. Every family gathering was so much fun because of this. But once I started studying it, it really clicked, and sometimes I feel like a chameleon because of all the hats I wear, so I always study each style thoroughly in order to play authentically. I'm just happy to have a voice out there I'm comfortable with.

Some musicians think they should always be on a "bigger" gig. This is an erroneous assumption. There are so many reasons why things happen. I had a roommate who committed suicide. He may have thought he should be in a different place with his career. I think this really affected him deep down inside. It makes me wonder how many others are hurting inside and don't talk about it. Some musicians may feel that they are always "second call," and it may contribute to their unhappiness. This business and art are always going to be a lot of work and a struggle for everyone. There are even days when I still get the feeling that I'm not good enough, too. I'm blessed with the work I have. I'm committed to the music and am honored if at any level anyone thinks enough to listen to me play or invites me to perform with them. I continuously push myself, as it's been through the music that I've been able to learn how to enjoy life. It's just cool to have this healthy element in my life, and one I'm happy with every day.

Jacob Sacks

KEYBOARDIST, COMPOSER, EDUCATOR

HOME BASE
www.myspace.com/jacobsacks

GOT MUSIC?
Two Miles a Day, Jacob Sacks,
Yeah Yeah Records/Loyal
Label, 2007

"Human beings have a natural inclination toward being creative."

BACKGROUND AND SOUND

Pianist Jacob Sacks is turning heads with his engaging and outer-limits style. He can be heard on any given night playing with a range of performers, from traditionalists such as the Mingus Big Band to David Binney's electrified and funkified fusion sounds at the 55 Bar. Surpassing all expectations of a typical youth in the current jazz community, Jacob's talent and ambition do not match his young age. Currently he runs more than nine ensembles as a leader, and they include notable musicians like Paul Motian, Dan Weiss, Jacob Garchik, Matt Wilson, and Mat Maneri. This mature perspective informed his role in the formation of the Creative Music Workshop. This cooperative school run by like-minded musicians encourages young talent not only to seek out their own voice but to defy what today's culture has handed them. Placing his open mind on the forefront of everything he does, Jacob has a clear advantage in today's jazz market. Placing oneself against the tired minds that want to keep everything the way it was, instead of opening their eyes to the way it is, is not a bad place to be.

HIS STORY

People in our culture aren't encouraged enough to be creative. We tend to make it difficult for someone to stand apart from the crowd. Conformity is taught and celebrated at the expense of inventiveness. Too often we discourage creativity in our schools, jobs, government, and daily lives.

Human beings have a natural inclination toward being creative. Our society could foster and cultivate these impulses. Why not? Should we only encourage those things that are measurable by a standardized test, or by how many were sold? I think that we could achieve a healthier and more balanced society if all people had good outlets for their creative energies and weren't always concerned with the payoff.

Monetary concerns can easily get in the way of creativity. This can happen to performers who've figured out how to sell their thing—their growth may lapse at this point. I've witnessed the phenomenon in jazz academies. Programs want to recruit students; they have the students play in a particular, often narrow way; then they sell it to the next class; the cycle goes on. Shouldn't schools that "teach" improvisation have constantly changing results? Imagine what could happen if the obstacles to creativity were removed—and *not* just in a jazz school.

Those of us in the arts have a unique opportunity and responsibility to both demonstrate and recommend a creative approach. I teach and I enjoy it because I get to share with my students how to transform mundane musical building blocks into personal statements. I've seen this sharing of creativity help certain students beyond the music lessons, in other subjects and life in general.

Often we need help, guidance, and encouragement to grow. When I was eighteen and was developing my jazz skills, I remember that a friend of mine invited me over to his place to play me some records. He played things that I had never heard before—twentieth-century string quartets that explored different textures, jazz solos with irregular phrasings and unexpected twists and turns in the rhythms. Listening to these recordings inspired and encouraged me to be more creative with my art. The same thing happened when I was in college; my friends and I challenged each other to learn more, be more creative, take chances, explore, et cetera.

We worry about money now, but perhaps we're all in debt as a result of not enough creativity in the right places. An example might be the person who doesn't check in with their natural creative impulses. This type of person may travel through life convincing themselves that they're happy—they have the job, the family; yet at the same time they're rigid in their sense of self. They pursue what they think is the right path at the exclusion of their own creative needs. It's a drag to live like that. I would hope that a person could be productive throughout their entire life. I feel very fortunate to be a musician. My family and my friends have always been encouraging to me and have constantly inspired me to grow. I hope that more and more people will learn that they too can have a creative life, even if it's not in the arts.

Daniel Sadownick

PERCUSSIONIST, COMPOSER, EDUCATOR

HOME BASE
www.danielsadownick.com

GOT MUSIC?
There Will Be a Day, Daniel
Sadownick, In Time Records,
2008

"Music is the richest occupation you can have."

BACKGROUND AND SOUND

Daniel Sadownick is regarded as one of the world's best percussionists. The intense, high-energy style he is known for has landed him gigs with the best of the best. Regardless of the project he is involved in, from J.Lo to Steely Dan to Michael Brecker, he puts forth every bit of his soul into the music. Through his craft he is able to carry the rhythmic aspects of tunes into another dimension.

HIS STORY

I lived in the Bronx. It was the lower-middle-class projects. My father was a mailman, and my mother was a school secretary. I can remember listening to a lot of popular music in high school. It was more advanced rock, like Jethro Tull, Yes, Emerson Lake and Palmer, et cetera. I was about fifteen years old when a friend of mine handed me a shopping bag with handles. He was older and always looked after me. He said, "check this out." He was different than a lot of the other kids; we were all wearing sneakers, jeans, and he was always in a dress shirt, pants, and a leather jacket. The records in that bag he handed me were Return to Forever, Art Blakey and the Jazz Messengers, Weather Report, and *A Love Supreme*. When I looked at *A Love Supreme*, I didn't know what it was, but I knew it was something special and deep.

It was something I'd never come across before. It was intense. You opened it up and there was this photo and a prayer for God. I couldn't grasp it right away. Then I put on Return to Forever and it blew me away. I started to research everything. There was a radio station called WRVR 106.7 back in the day, and they played every kind of jazz. I had this huge blotter on my desk and I started writing names down, collecting records from the lists they would play. I became a jazz purist despite the fact that I was listening to more fusion than anything else. Art Blakey was instrumental in changing my palate. Then I learned Wayne Shorter was in the Messengers, Joe Zawinul had been with Cannonball, Chick Corea was on *Sonny Stitt Goes Latin,* and an avalanche started, a beautiful avalanche that snowballed from that point on. These guys taught me that jazz can be technical, soulful, thought provoking, and structured. It encompasses all ingredients with emotion.

I just want to represent the fact that I'm blessed to do this. Music is life to me, and more than any other occupation, like a banker, lawyer, doctor, music is the richest occupation you can have. Sometimes we put so much pressure on ourselves and get too intense. This can really be a detriment to your art. For me, I have to make every note count and play with my heart every time. I'm always trying to improve upon myself as an individual and do the right thing by being positive, absorbing, and then reacting. If you carry yourself the right way and are a badass on your instrument, you'll always work. Just put everything in your life in perspective. I'm blessed to be able to play for a living and surround myself with the best musicians.

Arturo Sandoval   {LIVING LEGEND}

TRUMPETER, PIANIST, COMPOSER, EDUCATOR

HOME BASE
www.arturosandoval.com

GOT MUSIC?
Hot House, Arturo Sandoval,
Encoded Music, 1998

"Listen to everything, everybody, and respect everything."

BACKGROUND AND SOUND

Dizzy Gillespie called him "son." The legends that have been a part of his history, the same ones he considers to be mentors and friends, push their way through the valves of his horn and accompany the heritage behind his voice. As an undeniable force of musicianship, Grammy Award winner Arturo Sandoval demonstrates a constant and resolute passion for all music. His abilities on piano and trumpet, both classical and jazz, are astounding. An endearing thrill takes over him the second he walks on stage, and when Arturo is in the house you must live in his moment, as Arturo is joy personified.

HIS STORY

From the moment I put the trumpet to my mouth, I was in love. Before that, I was hopeless, we were so poor. We didn't even have a floor, we had dirt, and I saw no hope in the future. I grew up in the countryside of Cuba and didn't have influences by way of trumpet while growing up until I went to Havana. When I heard the music that came out of America for trumpet and musicians, I thought, this is the mecca for what I was trying to do. I fell in love with the music, and this is when I realized I could do this. This is also when I heard Dizzy for the first time. He became my hero. I could identify with him and was impressed by his playing. He was my obsession. I wanted to learn to play like him, and even to this day I'm still trying to figure it out.

I think back to when I met him in seventy-seven; he was in Cuba and I couldn't speak any English. I had a car, and he wanted to see the city. I was so embarrassed to tell him I played trumpet. Later that night during a jam session he watched me from backstage and said, "No way, that's my driver!" From then on out he would only come do festivals here if I came. He cared about me and loved me. To finally play with Dizzy was a gift from God. He demonstrated his love for me and his appreciation for what I was doing. He gave me a lot of different opportunities to play and pushed me until the day he died. Without him, it would have been impossible to do what I was trying to do.

As a trumpet player you must really make sure you're in love with the music. Respect your career, your instrument. Students of jazz need to listen to jazz as much as they can, all day long. Cover all aspects of your instrument. Prepare yourself to be ready for anything, the amount of effort, discipline, and dedication to get you where you need to go. The only divisions between musicians are the limitations of more or less ability.

We shouldn't discriminate against any style of music. It doesn't matter who wrote it. If it's a good piece of music then it's a good piece of music. The amount of emotion between Dizzy Gillespie and Rachmaninoff can't be measured and shouldn't be. You just have to have the desire to play. I tell my band before each gig that it's my music that gets me high. Yet we all have a little bit of this sadness in our soul. I consider myself a very lucky person. I'm happily married, able to have lunch every day with my mom, and play with my grandchildren. We should listen to everything, everybody, and respect everything. I give a mile of importance to every style. I'm thankful for everything I do and everyone in my life.

Maria Schneider {LIVING LEGEND}
COMPOSER, CONDUCTOR

HOME BASE
www.mariaschneider.com

GOT MUSIC?
Sky Blue, Maria Schneider Orchestra, ArtistShare, 2008

"If you do something in a very personal way it becomes universal."

BACKGROUND AND SOUND
Two-time Grammy Award–winning composer Maria Schneider has created an atmosphere of her own through expressive, cathartic works. Places, passion, and people from throughout her life are relived with every note she pens. She has studied closely with both Bob Brookmeyer and Gil Evans. Through each successive album she has produced Maria reaches deep within that lineage and unfurls tendrils of style and grace. Critics have been unraveled at the mere mention of her name, and *Time* magazine

and the *Billboard* charts have continually placed her at the very top. She has received numerous grants, commissions, and fellowships from esteemed groups such as the Doris Duke Foundation, the Carnegie Hall Orchestra, and the Danish Radio Orchestra. She is heralded for her originality, and her pieces have been performed by hundreds of groups in twenty different countries spanning Europe, Australia, South America, and North America. This profound effect on the jazz community is dizzying. There are no words that can quite explain the intense radiance of her creations. Maria is a gift that guides us as a community, and we must take great care of her, as she is one of the greatest composers that have ever lived.

HER STORY

There were so many influences in my life that I guess it depends on what time of my life we're talking about. Ten years ago, twenty years ago . . . Gil Evans, Bob Brookmeyer, Thad Jones, Charles Mingus, and players like Bill Evans all impacted me. My classical influences range from Chopin back to Hindemith to Ravel. There's a huge scope of material to choose from. Brazilian music, flamenco, in addition to everything else influenced me, too. To some degree I would consider my music pretty eclectic and uncategorizable.

When I sit down to write a piece it sometimes takes a few days or weeks to get it out. Most the time it will patch itself into an experience I've had. Whether it's present, past, or a memoir of sorts, the music inside of me is innately expressive and autobiographical. Creating music is not something I think about, it's what I do, who I am, and there's nothing I regret about what I do. This is for me. It's not ever what others want of me. I record my own music with my own group and with the musicians I've chosen to create a world of my own. I never expected to make money at this. It was never about that. I did it on my own terms and never stepped away from it. This isn't the path everyone is comfortable with. If you do something in a very personal way it becomes universal, it touches people, and I'm committed to doing just that. Success in music only happens if one really pays attention to their voice. This is the great thing about jazz. Jazz is breathing, alive, and in the moment while it's being played. Jazz musicians are most comfortable when they're uncomfortable. This is when the unknown is allowed to happen.

Jazz is eclectic, and the only universal element is improvisation. Jazz is expressive. A lot of musicians have difficult times in their early life, and music becomes a way to escape that life. It creates an alchemy that turns sadness into beauty and allows us to reinvent our lives. I take difficult experiences from my childhood and try to change them somehow through my music. It's very simple on the surface, and the melodies are very simple. When you add all the layers to it, the counterpoint, the harmonies, et cetera, it's the way those elements add to the melody that creates an idea that rubs against its simplistic self and makes it complex. It's a landscape of where I'm from on its surface—flat like the farmland from Minnesota—yet if you go inside, there's so much nature, a huge ecosystem of complex layers. It's my hope that others get swept up in the music as I do and take a ride instead of sitting back and analyzing it. I want them to get involved with it and go inside the music and let it take them wherever they want to go.

Diane Schuur

{LIVING LEGEND}

VOCALIST, PIANIST

HOME BASE
www.dianeschuur.com

GOT MUSIC?
Some Other Time, Diane Schuur, Concord Records, 2008

"I'm so honored to be a part of this history and art."

BACKGROUND AND SOUND

Two-time Grammy Award winner Diane "Deedles" Schuur has brought the house down since she was ten years old. As a formal student of the piano at the Washington State School for the Blind and then an informal but serious student of Dinah Washington, she has knocked on the doors of the blues and traditional jazz for more than three decades. Inhabiting an honest place in each of her songs, she sings of an honest, unbridled passion that has seen it *all* through her words. Deedles has earned a significant following and rightful place at the top. What has emerged for the rest of us is a legend that leaves our awe-inspired tanks full of that fuzzy place deep within the home of our souls.

HER STORY

I've experienced the highs and lows of life. When I lost my mother, I was at the depth of sadness and despair. My mama was really the one who introduced me to jazz. Duke Ellington, Nat Cole . . . all those wonderful people. She wasn't a musician, but loved her jazz. When I had to go to the state school for the blind, I was very lonely at times and was away from the folks I knew. This is when I began to tap into a lot of the feelings that jazz represents. But you bring all of these experiences to the music. This music has taught me, after all, about emotion and feeling, and that it's perfectly okay to access all of these feelings. It's a wonderful instrument. It covers the basic spectrum of emotion while at the same time it's far more complex than other genres as far as structure. There are so many different elements to explore. You have eighty, ninety years to cover . . . just start with Louis and work your way down. Jazz has touched so many. It's my life; it had to be. But it's not a huge moneymaker. You have to be in it a real long time to reap the benefits of it, but there's an upside too. With the pop genre or culture, there's a certain fickleness. With jazz, it stays and stays and stays. I'm so honored to be a part of this history and art. People need to realize there may not be money in jazz, but there's a soul and spirit that's so complete in and of itself it becomes America by its very nature. This is why it's appreciated outside the US more than it's appreciated here. We must keep the tradition going, as we should all feel as I do: honored to be a part of it, as it's this that speaks of every experience we've ever had as a nation.

J.B. Scott
TRUMPETER, EDUCATOR

HOME BASE
www.kellyscottmusic.com

GOT MUSIC?
Just Swingin', J.B. Scott's
Swingin' Allstars, KSM,
2008

"If you're not on the edge, you're not going to experience the best life has to offer."

BACKGROUND AND SOUND

Trumpeter and educator J.B. Scott has renewed his creative license through the traditional jazz scene year after year. When he claimed his stake in the University of North Florida's Jazz Studies Department, his dreams of shaping the future of jazz began to come true. His jovial nature crosses paths with his creative works as a musician and arranger and into the classroom. As the leader for his group, J.B. Scott's Swingin' Allstars, he takes his role very seriously and is a staunch supporter and contributor to the traditional jazz movement. This kind of enthusiasm is echoed in his belief in keeping jazz alive and well, regardless of location and critical recognition.

HIS STORY

None of us get into this for the money. No matter what you're doing, if you're playing jazz, whether you find yourself in a creative setting or not, you're making something new that has nothing to do with finances or the gathering of. It's about a continuous dialog and creation of a world around you. One of the biggest problems we're having in the culture today is the inability to communicate on all levels. In music—and this goes with any style or genre—if you're in a group setting and you don't communicate, you might as well be dead to that group. The music just won't happen. I'm not talking about saying, "hello, how are you?"; instead you're actually having to go deeper than that. This is communication that reaches deeper into somebody's soul or heart. Even verbal conversations need this. If you really do it the right way and delve into their loves, hates, hurts, and idiosyncrasies, and they in turn delve into yours, then you can learn about them. But if either of you fail to do this, you're not creating or learning.

Delving into somebody else's space and learning from and creating from it means that sometimes the chaos that's become of communication can be controlled. My job as a musician is to be a "musical thief," to steal as many musical, harmonic, and rhythmic ideas as possible. Then delve into the soul of the musicians and try to incorporate all of this into my playing and my being. Everyone does this. If you don't . . . you're not playing this music right because you are not communicating with the other musicians nor with yourself. The edge is where the music happens. I know for myself, it is what keeps me fresh, creative, and musically alive. But it goes without saying that if you're not on the edge, you're not going to experience the best things in life.

Marilyn Scott
VOCALIST

HOME BASE
www.marilynscott.com

GOT MUSIC?
Everytime We Say Goodbye, Marilyn
Scott, Venus Records, 2008

"Music is the most magical space there is."

BACKGROUND AND SOUND

With a simple and elegant voice, Marilyn Scott is pinning down the Los Angeles scene. Her influences are more instrumentalists than vocalists and range from Pat Metheny to George Duke to Etta James. She has paid her dues in the blues, R&B, and contemporary jazz scenes as well. Marilyn interprets the emotion in the music and cascades an uplifting love for the craft down to her audience. She is a dedicated and hardworking vocalist, and her voice sings with seemingly effortless and comforting beauty.

HER STORY

I've been singing all my life. Mom sang; my sisters were all musical. I was the only one who made it a career. At fifty-eight years old now, I'm lucky for the most part that I've been able to play with some incredible people. Yet I don't think I've ever had a "break." I just knew this is what I would do. I moved to San Francisco right out of high school and enrolled in college. I played in bands five nights a week, doing four to five sets a night. With that hard of an ethic in singing and then having to sing the things you don't want to sing with club owners dictating the playlist, it's difficult. But that doesn't mean I don't appreciate all kinds of music. It just wasn't an ideal situation. I appreciate all forms, and there's always going to be things I don't latch onto, but it seems as though my tastes reflect whatever I've lived and listened to. I like anything that pulls emotion out of whatever they're feeling.

As jazz musicians we're speaking words we walk around with. We hide so much of this in our everyday lives we have to use music as a way of pulling it out of ourselves. When you do this, you feel the music so much better. As long as you're creating and conversing in the moment, the piece will sound good. Music is the most magical space there is. It makes you want to come back and try it again and again. Your personality has to be a part of the art. As in most art forms, we're never going to make a lot of money as jazz musicians. You just have to be somewhat satisfied with knowing what you feel and what you are and who you are and that you're unique in this place at this moment. Try the best you can to use your music to enhance other people; when you play you're really giving them an act of your love.

Lynn Seaton

BASSIST, COMPOSER, EDUCATOR

HOME BASE
www.lynnseaton.com

GOT MUSIC?
Solo Flights, Lynn Seaton, Omni Tone Records, 2000

"There's music for everything."

BACKGROUND AND SOUND

Bassist Lynn Seaton has walked his groove up and down the stages of masters for more than three decades. His gig roll call is several hundred names deep and includes the likes of Marian McPartland, Jeff Hamilton, Harry "Sweets" Edison, the Count Basie Band, Tony Bennett, George Shearing, Tim Hagans, Mel Tormé, Frank Wess, Nancy Wilson, Diane Schuur, and Toshiko Akiyoshi. Since 1988 Lynn has enthusiastically supported some of the best players in the country through the University of North Texas Jazz Studies Program. As a teacher there he regularly encourages students to reach out to him for guidance, and he, in turn, offers a wealth of experiences and opportunities through which they can grow. Lynn is known to draw his voice upon the canvas of each situation he is in. Through his original works and educational methods, Lynn is a model musician who has laid down the groundwork for not only his legacy but the idiom at large.

HIS STORY

As an educator I try to recreate similar situations that fueled my passion to become a musician. The ones who influenced me didn't just show up magically as complete players. They developed their passion and built a strong foundation by playing standard tunes and technical studies on their respective instruments. Through the study of the history of jazz music, they developed their individual voice. Jazz education provides interaction with those musicians that have "been there, done that." I have been so lucky to live the dream of being a working artist. It's up to us to share that experience with our students and help them live their own dreams. Within the university environment, students are given the opportunity to be forward thinking, try things, and experiment before life's realities take over. With my own students I try to hold up an imaginary mirror so they can see and hear where they are; this way I can help them get to where they want to be. I want to teach them how to get what they want.

My dream was to play music for a living and travel, to be a road rat and see Europe and Asia. Wishes can come true, so one needs to be sincere and work hard to achieve them. I got to play with people I respect and admire and travel around while making lots of recordings. I met my musical heroes, and it's still a dream I guess—there's nothing like it. I always enjoy playing with people that are hungry to play. On a metaphysical level I've been inspired by those masters and the tradition. There's something spiritual about improvising and playing that becomes an amazing connection you feel with other people when you're on the same page musically. Jazz is a lifestyle, a history with a future, and a collection of sounds with individuals interacting on a deep emotional level. It's my social network as well as my musical network. Music is special. I want to listen, and I wish more people would actually listen and watch and recognize the quality they might find in the depth and staying power of the great jazz masters. I hope my listeners will give it a shot and try out a little bit of everything. There's music for everything.

Jaleel Shaw

SAXOPHONIST, COMPOSER

HOME BASE
www.jaleelshaw.com

GOT MUSIC?
Perspective, Jaleel Shaw, Fresh Sound Records, 2005; *Optimism*, Jaleel Shaw, Changu Records, 2008

"I believe exposure is the key to the development of any individual."

BACKGROUND AND SOUND

Philly-raised Jaleel Shaw is one of today's most notable young saxophonists. A graduate of Berklee College of Music and Manhattan School of Music, he has established himself as a sideman with musicians such as Roy Haynes and the Mingus Big Band as well as a leader of his own group. Influences ranging from Charlie Parker, John Coltrane, and Wayne Shorter all the way to A Tribe Called Quest are incorporated into his palette and style. His gift has helped shape him into a model for the jazz community by establishing a mature core deep within him.

HIS STORY

To me, music is therapeutic. Throughout my life it's always been there to enhance or complement almost every emotion or experience I've had. I don't know where or who I'd be without it. Through music I've also learned about different cultures and lifestyles and have been able to communicate with people that don't even speak my language. Most importantly, it has helped me shape and develop goals that have helped develop my character as an individual, which is a lifelong process.

When I think about jazz, I think about the history of not only the African American, but of all Americans. Jazz tells the story of America as well as the lives and struggles of African Americans throughout American history. You can have a better understanding of American and African American history by listening to Louis Armstrong play "Potato Head Blues," Duke Ellington's "Take the A Train," et cetera . . . I could go on for days, but the list goes on from the great jazz masters of the past to the masters of today. By studying the history of this music, I've learned more about my history as an African American than I've ever learned in any American history class.

One thing that concerns me about the future of jazz music is that it's such a definitive example of our history, yet a large percentage of Americans today aren't exposed to or aware of it. When I think of the many styles of music (jazz, hip-hop, classical, R&B, traditional West African, Indian) and food (Indian, Ethiopian, Thai) that I love, I realize I wouldn't know what those foods or musical styles were had I not been exposed to them. I believe exposure is the key to the development of any individual. Through exposure we're able to learn what we like and don't like and develop a better understanding and appreciation of both. This is also how we are able to build our own character and develop strong individual qualities.

I've been composing for the past sixteen years and have always related my music to a personal journal. When I listen to a recording or composition of mine, I'm reminded of what was I thinking or feeling when I wrote that composition . . . or how I was thinking or feeling during the performance. My goal is to continue to be able to express myself and tell my story through my music. It is my hope that my music will enhance and complement the souls and lives of the people that listen to it, just as different artists have enhanced and complemented my life through their music.

Bobby Shew   {LIVING LEGEND}

TRUMPETER, COMPOSER, ARRANGER, EDUCATOR

HOME BASE
www.bobbyshew.com

GOT MUSIC?
Heavy Weights, Bobby
Shew Quintet with Carl
Fontana, MAMA Records,
1996

"I still feel like I'm dreaming."

BACKGROUND AND SOUND

Leonard Feather, one of the great jazz critics of all time, touted him as a "whiplash player" in his early career. His albums have spanned the gamut of Grammy-nominated greats such as *Outstanding in his Field* and soundtracks for *Grease, Taxi, The Muppet Movie*, and more. But what really cooks with Bobby Shew is not his history, but his sound. Whether he is trading solos with the players in the band or leading a jazz orchestra with strings, his glimmering sound shines through. His tireless efforts in educating up-and-coming jazz greats show why musicians from all walks have embraced him for the last four decades. This diversity, excitement, and passion remain as solid as his abilities on the horn.

HIS STORY

When you start playing at ten years old you don't see yourself as a pro. But when I saw Stan Kenton for the first time, then Maynard and Prez Prado, I knew it was something I had to do. I've been fortunate to have played with Horace Silver, Art Blakey, Art Pepper, Bud Shank, et cetera. I've recorded albums with them. They were my idols as a kid. When I was playing with them I had to keep pinching myself saying, "Is this really happening?" It was; I was really playing and hanging with them. The turning point in my life was playing with Buddy Rich. It was a phenomenal situation. I was third chair solo and moved to lead after he threw a temper tantrum about the lead player. First thing I thought was, I can't handle this and he said, "Bullshit; just play it." And I did. When Buddy put me on lead, he played something that wasn't terribly hard and I handled it. Buddy said, "I don't want to hear that crybaby crap. You go home and get your chops and tomorrow come in here. Tomorrow at noon, you're the lead player." He taught me how to play lead by the way he played the drums.

I still feel like I'm dreaming. I've managed to be the most successful unknown guy out there. I don't think of myself as a very good trumpet player; I'm a much better musician than a trumpeter. I'd rather learn music. I'm not taking the time to learn stuff trumpet players learn. I practice what I play at night.

Placing a kid in a classroom to learn jazz is difficult if you can't even get him to be a sincere music student. You can teach him mechanics, but he's going to have to listen to jazz music on his own to get it. I teach because I have a little bit of mother hen inside of me. I'm trying to save this music by saying, "No, no, no, no, no . . . that's not right," and forcing these kids to listen to the right people. But don't get me wrong. I'm happy there's jazz education; it's better than nothing. It's my greatest fear, though, that jazz education will be in part responsible for the demise of the art form. When you try to take something that's so deep, personal, and spiritual as jazz and put it in a classroom, you begin to codify this thing, and that's not what this art is all about. There are always going to be good players who have gifts, and what they do with these gifts is wholly their responsibility.

Matthew Shipp
PIANIST, COMPOSER

HOME BASE
www.matthewshipp.com

GOT MUSIC?
Harmonic Disorder, Matthew Shipp Trio, Thirsty Ear, 2009

"I'm just trying to feed the hungry souls."

BACKGROUND AND SOUND
Matthew Shipp is not merely a pianist; he is a philosopher who happens to pass wisdom from the eighty-eight keys in front of him to the ears of all who will listen. Influenced by some of the very best of our time, such as Cecil Taylor, Lennie Tristano, and Duke Ellington, Shipp's dramatic influence upon the avant-garde jazz scene has reached well beyond accepted idioms. With his prose and music he has creatively spread into the colors of serialism into what he calls a fractured post-Monk school of thought. His artistic statements unwind with an unusual and surreal beauty for all to hear. He Is well on his way to becoming one of the timeless giants of jazz.

HIS STORY
There's a deep sense of discovery when anyone comes to listen to this music. You bring yourself to it. I don't know what's in their head from the past, their conditioning or associations, et cetera, but anyone can listen to it and be motivated enough to want to contribute to it. It's an open energy

field that coalesces with the brain. When I was twelve I heard Ahmad Jamal and felt a deep connection to him. There was something very spiritual, even when he played the blues. Yet I was scared by the darkness of his music. It was a cult of its own. I wanted to be able to do that, put a stamp of my own on this music. Once I got into it, I realized there weren't any alternatives.

There are so many systems that exist to keep people enslaved. Organized religion, education . . . everything. A lot of well-intentioned people seem to be enslaved mentally. It's so pervasive that it's seldom you find someone that can truly surprise you, especially in a nondestructive way. When everyone is looking for an out from this constriction, whether it's with booze or religion, there are very few ways people can look or search for their true selves, and this is the crux of the problem.

As a jazz musician, the only option is to be you. The basic question is how to do this. There's no definition. It's a mysterious process. The mind is an open system of synthesis, and one must approach musical language in that way and have faith in that language. That's when the language will play through you. You can't force anything. Strive to learn everything you can, and don't let materials be your prison. The most important thing is to be yourself, and being yourself, theoretically, should be the easiest thing, as it's the closest thing to you. Paradoxically, being you in this society is completely faking it. The whole society exists to make sure you can never truly be yourself. I just try to get up in the morning and get something done for myself. It's up to the other generations as to whatever they want to do with the language. It's out of my hands at this point. It was never mine to begin with. I'm just trying to feed the hungry souls. You don't have to have a jazz background to play it or listen to it; it either speaks to you or it doesn't. Jazz is just a word and can take on millions of expressions. It's extremely elastic, and I'm so involved with making a living at this that I envy people who sit back and can listen to the music. I get cynical because it's very difficult to make a living at this. As a listener, you get to appreciate the different forms and various different takes on it. This language is a very dynamic life and will never die; it will instead change as it should, because it's part of our structure of our psyche. And it will continue to always do this.

Jen Shyu

COMPOSER, VOCALIST, EDUCATOR, DANCER, ACTRESS

HOME BASE
www.jenshyu.com

GOT MUSIC?
Jade Tongue, Jen Shyu, Chiuyen Music, 2009

"Improvisation is often at the root of music from other cultures. In the most sincere sense, it's a human music."

BACKGROUND AND SOUND

Disillusioned at the expectations others had of her as a vocalist, Jen Shyu broke free from those chains and began to research her ancestors and roots. At the encouragement of Steve Coleman, Jen began to roam the lines and paths that led deep into her cultural heritage. What emerged from this monumental task was a whole new landscape of sound and a foundation for the rest of her days as an artist that echoes into the very depths of her core. Jen's voice can be heard in a gamut of recordings, including those of the great Miles Okazaki and Steve Coleman. What appeals to the listener and radiates through her tone is a haunting yet energetic glimpse at the future of worldly jazz and improvisatory music.

HER STORY

Music was actually the first thing to show me the path to my roots, foundation, ancestry, and identity. Being born in Middle America from Taiwanese and East Timorese parents, I'm not sure if I would have thought about these issues so intensely without that push from music and the questions that it forced me to ask. At some point, I realized everything I did had to come from that identity, and knowing that jazz is an African American music stemming from personal experience and struggle, it just wasn't enough for me to imitate it. If I hadn't gone into my roots, which Francis Wong and Steve Coleman especially encouraged me to do a few years ago, I wouldn't be doing what I'm doing now. Now I feel like I've become part of the Asian American voice in jazz.

Obviously, China has its own music, as does Taiwan, but I am most moved by the music that came out of hardship. What's amazing is that improvisation is often at the root of music from other cultures. In the most sincere sense, it's a human music. People have been improvising in every corner of the world since they've been on this earth. I've had conversations with people who are culturally closer to the source of jazz. They have mixed feelings about others around the world taking it and owning it and making their own means of expression, but what they're seeing and sensing aren't the same things.

There are those who are very sincere about this process, and then there are those who are commercializing it. But most people and even some critics see all of it as "jazz." That being said, I'm now on a mission that's culturally and musically tied together. An example is a piece I wrote based on narratives of Chinese laborers in nineteenth-century Cuba working alongside the African slaves during that time. Routinely, people with ethnic studies and anthropology degrees know about texts that the greater public doesn't, and these voices are often lost in books and documents. What I want to do is get these unheard voices heard in hopes that we don't repeat our mistakes in history.

Bruce Lee said in an interview with Pierre Burton that the idea of the "Oriental" is a perception that's "very out of date." It's so true; maybe it will always be true. I want to be able to offer a new perspective. When people from these cultures—from Taiwan for instance—when they think of jazz, I'm always shocked by their definition. It's like a narrow river. Jazz is what they hear at Starbucks. This is where we get into the difficulty of defining "jazz." If you want to listen to pure jazz, then you have to know that the nature is about people finding and being themselves. Every culture has its blues and can relate. If you go to Lanyu, this little island off the east coast of Taiwan, you'll find that a lot of people aren't even reading music. Instead, there are elders singing what their grandfathers and grandmothers taught them. This music can serve a function in certain rituals or rites or ceremonies. After all, it's lasted this long just by being passed down orally, so there has to be something very potent and powerful inside the music. If you're coming at it from an oral and aural experience of knowing and delivering music, you can then see jazz as an indigenous music that's important to our villages, cultures, and communities. And as musicians, it's on us to get involved with our community. Most of them would be interested if they were only exposed to it in a real way. Besides the pure joy of doing this, I personally just want to make a contribution. Things like racism, equality, and a desire for the underdogs to have their voices heard are my driving forces, and if I weren't a musician, I'd be doing the same thing, just with different tools.

Yotam Silberstein
GUITARIST, COMPOSER

HOME BASE
www.yotamsilberstein.com

GOT MUSIC?
Next Page, Yotam Silberstein, Posi-Tone Records, 2009

"Being a musician is not only about acquiring musical tools, it's about being a human being."

BACKGROUND AND SOUND

Yotam Silberstein has had experiences unmatched by many here in the United States. From birth, Yotam was exposed to a multitude of cultures, their rituals, and more importantly their various forms of art. By the time he decided to pursue music as his passion and career, these influences had already become a part of his DNA. By the age of eighteen he was serving in the Israeli army as a director, arranger, and lead guitarist for three years. Since very early in his career, Yotam has showed remarkable potential as a writer and performer. He has studied and/or performed with greats Kurt Rosenwinkel, James Moody, Jimmy Heath, Frank Wess, and Barry Harris. He has performed on stages throughout the world, including the Umbria Jazz Festival in Italy, and was named as one of the top ten finalists in the Thelonious Monk International Jazz Guitar Competition. Yotam has created an elastic boundary with his original work and group.

His works create a nucleus for the group's expressions while at the same time allowing everyone involved to stretch their creative muscles and interpret and enjoy his art.

HIS STORY

Being a musician is not only about acquiring musical tools, it's about being a human being. The more you experience in life, the richer your personality and musicality. While growing up in Israel, I experienced a different reality that shaped me as a musician. I was exposed to many different kinds of music and cultures by living there. Coming into this country as an outsider gave me a perspective of something that somewhat bothers me. I find it very unfortunate that people, kids even, don't know who Duke Ellington is, or Miles, Dizzy, or Parker. Jazz is the most important thing that ever happened to this country as well as being the best thing this country has to offer. Too many people don't see what's happening today. The style of the music most people refer to as jazz is old and has been done, but there's a continuation that's been expanded all over the world. That someone like me can come from Israel to New York and become a part of it and make my own music is incredible; I see a lot of people do this. They come from all over Europe, South America, and Africa, too, and think it's a great thing. If people from all over are aware of this music, why are the Americans not so aware of their very own treasure?

I've had the chance to perform in Europe many times, as well as Eastern Europe and Russia. As an artist, they treat you with a lot of respect. People look at you like you're a king. There's a lot more emphasis on the culture there, especially when it comes to learning their own country's culture. Russia is not so rich in terms of materials, but somehow they find a way to respect art of all kinds. Here, it's more difficult. There's a certain disrespect for being an artist here. People need to know about what we do. This art form isn't dead . . . it exists. But there has to be a broader change for the whole culture to gain this respect. People can learn things through school and broaden their knowledge of the history, but I think it's going to take a lot more, and it's going to take time. We just have to experiment and take risks to get others into it; that's what I do when I play. Who I am is reflected in this music.

Peter Sommer

SAXOPHONIST, COMPOSER, EDUCATOR

HOME BASE
www.petersommerjazz.com

GOT MUSIC?
Crossroads, Peter Sommer, Capri
Records, 2008

"You are already yourself, so why do you have to 'try' and be yourself?"

BACKGROUND AND SOUND

Saxophonist Peter Sommer cuts right through the edges of modern jazz in both his compositions and performances. A leading player in the Denver jazz scene, Peter performs with the very best groups in the state as well as locally touring national acts. He is an assistant professor at Colorado State University in Fort Collins and is in demand as a clinician throughout the country. His diverse abilities as a performer have led to gigs with the Colorado Symphony Orchestra, the Chie Imaizumi Jazz Orchestra, and the Ninth and Lincoln Jazz Orchestra. As a leader he has produced two albums with his own group on the Capri Records label and proved through his reliable and piercing voice in both his compositions and soloing that he is a force to be recognized.

HIS STORY

John Coltrane was one of my first exposures to jazz. I wasn't quite sure I liked it the first time, nor was it exactly what I expected to be, but over time his music has influenced me a great deal, second only to those musicians I have known and performed with. I try to keep my focus on playing the music at hand, and leave thoughts about "my voice" off the bandstand. I think we all go through a phase where we emulate particular players, and then we break from that and become overly concerned with finding our own voice. By staying in the present moment, focused on the music and my fellow musicians, I try to sidestep the whole issue. We all have something about us that makes us unique. I don't think you have to "try" and be yourself if your intentions are pure. I think that what still makes Coltrane so powerful for me is that focus and purity. We need to encourage young people to reach beyond the most immediate and obvious digestible world. Our solution shouldn't lie in another marketing ploy. Although some great music and some not-so-great music has been made covering popular songs or styles, that alone will not draw large crowds back to jazz. It will require a great shift in our culture's attitude and support for the arts, from the top down and the bottom up. When I'm on a gig, I do what I think needs to be done artistically and then find a way to engage the audience without insulting them by being overly abstruse or insipid. I try to put myself in their shoes as an open and interested participant in the music. Beyond that, my motivation is playing, interacting, and collaborating with all of the great musicians in my musical community. Keeping my sights on the music and the other folks involved in the music keeps me fulfilled and moving forward. I love what I do and am so grateful to the universe for the opportunity to create and perform this music.

Clark Sommers

BASSIST, COMPOSER

HOME BASE
www.myspace.com/
clarksommersbass

GOT MUSIC?
Over Here Over Heard, Dan Cray
Trio, Crawdad Records, 2008

"Jazz has to do with inner will and tenacity."

BACKGROUND AND SOUND

Bassist Clark Sommers may be buried in work behind leaders like Kurt Elling or Dan Cray, but his voice is always there. Clark's intelligent and thoughtful approach to music rings through his sound and ability to pick up even on the slightest nuance or change in the music. Grounding musicians for more than a decade now, Clark has performed and toured extensively with greats like Kevin Mahogany, Tony Bennett, Ira Sullivan, Von Freeman, Buddy Guy, and Diana Krall. He continues to remain at the top of call lists in multiple genres and will remain there through his dogged determination to thrive at this challenging lifestyle and art.

HIS STORY

Jazz has to do with inner will and tenacity. Any person who feels strongly enough about something to pursue it in spite of exterior and popular expectations of the pop culture criteria is someone who does so not without altruism, but does so with a pure objective because they have something to say, not as a reactionary to an industry. Sometimes there's all this other stuff going on in life that seems so shallow and vapid you feel a dire need to chime in. You have to be a voice that's counter and contrary to what's around you. We do this because we feel like we have a natural inclination to do it.

I used to be into sports when I was in high school. I played lacrosse and was being groomed to play it in college. This was great on a primal level, but there was no spiritual or emotional tribal-like connection. When I got serious about music, I thought, oh wow, this encompasses everything. It was apparent to me early on that a spiritual, emotional, and intellectual connection was there, whereas in sports it just wasn't vehicle enough for me. Of course you can have something in your life that helps you tap into these things, but it wasn't until I got into music that I found what worked for me. I just had a natural inclination to do music. There was some will inside of me to get this out. It's the kind of thing that offers a forum, a place that's an alternative to pop culture, a vehicle or means of self-realization.

When you try to evolve as an artist you're simultaneously evolving as a person and assimilating as many different kinds of resources as possible. This will ultimately allow these resources to work for you in spite of external mediocrity. There are just some things you can't compress in the human experience. Immediate gratification and references to pop culture come into play here. We're seemingly built now toward and around sound bites and visuals that offer no real substance. It's a very immediate and instantaneous sort of feedback and gratification. This life, at least in this culture, takes pressure off kids. If you're getting signals from the external world that what you do is strange, overly sensitive, or heady, you're led to think that you can't engage in that activity. We see the fallout of this in art in all its various mediums as they take a back seat to things like *American Idol*. It's not real music; it's a corporate molding of an "artist." We have stopped celebrating artists that chisel away at something and come forth with meaningful work. There are just certain things you can't get in a short amount of time. Every time there's an advent in technology and its released into the culture, there are good and bad sides of it. This is the con of digital technology. All this super-fast information we acquire eliminates the process by which we would naturally acquire opinions of reality. This has a domino affect that hurts us.

This is another, at least for me, impetus to do what I do. Whether you want to call it music or art, I'm just trying to say something that's a projection or expression of my take on this situation I'm in. There will always be support and interest in jazz just for its quality ideas. But it's something that has to develop over a period of time. This forces you to think about things and assimilate information. Then and only then can you figure out how you resonate with it. It's a long, drawn-out process where one has to investigate the history and oneself and then indulge in the self-reflection required.

But just because I think there will be support doesn't mean I don't worry. I worry about being able to work or sustain a lifestyle that allows me to pursue something that's meaningful for me. This is a full-time job. If I have to supplement this in some other way, it diverts the energy I need to be able to do it. As musicians, we're not getting opportunities to perform now. This is forcing us to hunker down on our craft; this is a force that's becoming a form of natural selection. The competitive nature of things . . . keeps me honest and ultra-focused. I find when I'm focused I can get into the sublime, vulgar, sensual, intellectual, repulsive, and grotesque all at once. Jazz is a limitless opportunity to address yourself. This provides me with a mental conduit for whatever emotional or spiritual thing I'm dealing with. There are people I look up to in music who you can tell are not just playing from a craft standpoint, but there is something deeper—an ineffable aspect to their playing that they're tapping into. A lot of music is void of an emotional or spiritual connection. In some way I feel there's a morality issue attached to it when it's this way. We're obligated to do what feels natural, and, for me, this is the foundation of how I put forth my best in all vestiges. Your music has to be the best representation of you in order to be truthful.

Luciana Souza

VOCALIST, COMPOSER

HOME BASE
www.lucianasouza.com

GOT MUSIC?
Tide, Luciana Souza, Verve, 2009

"I've had to keep my focus on the music and not think about success or compare myself with others."

BACKGROUND AND SOUND

Grammy Award–winning vocalist Luciana Souza has one of those seemingly infinite voices. With each listen to her songs, whether they are adaptations of standards or original works, her voice becomes this pliable and multidimensional sound. Her native land of São Paulo, Brazil, cuts through her music today, especially in her original works. She is a master at crafting sophisticated lines and body in her work. Her music and performances as a collaborator have spanned international lines, and she has shared stages with Maria Schneider, Danilo Perez, and Herbie Hancock. As a leader she has had eight solo projects that have earned the attention of the public ear and a critical mass of peers. Luciana is definitely one of the more celebrated and original voices today.

HER STORY

As a jazz musician, I have this desire to create something new each time I go on stage. It's this desire to create that teaches me about humility and gives me the sense to know that this is a pathway of growth. There's no arrival. This idea of humility means I've had to let go in moments of my life. I've had to keep my focus on the music and not think about success or compare myself with others. People tend to get really hurt if things don't happen for them. I try to just live my life and appreciate it every day. I want to make each experience as joyful and creative as possible. As a singer, I don't deal with something on the outside when I sing—everything I do is from the inside, the breath. I have to deal with all kinds of emotions. I walk on stage and am revealing myself and being honest about my singing. I'm taking a breath and giving it to you. I pray every time before

I play, and the musicians on stage know I do this (sometimes we do it together). It's not a religious prayer, necessarily; it's a matter of connecting with what I'm playing and centering myself in that moment—not being attached to what I've done before. I want to greet people with something new and offer the best of what I have inside. One of the reasons we all choose jazz is that we really have something to express that's unique. This is a path of exploration. I can't imagine not being around music. I have a pure love for it, and if I'm not on stage I'm listening to music. The creation of the moment and the excitement (even when failure happens) is what keeps me going. I look at music as if it's an uncharted river and it's mine to discover the new corners, and the fish, and the waves. It's thrilling, the greatest thing. I'm singing on air, from nothing, from the greatest thing I know.

Esperanza Spalding
BASSIST, VOCALIST, COMPOSER, EDUCATOR

HOME BASE
www.esperanzaspalding.com

GOT MUSIC?
Esperanza, Esperanza Spalding, Heads Up, 2008

"The sky isn't even the limit. I have to keep climbing and make sure I'm always ascending."

BACKGROUND AND SOUND
Esperanza Spalding has a full package to offer. Having studied with Joe Lovano, John Lockwood, and Hal Crook, she knows how to serve up heaping piles of euphoric beauty in her words and lines. She is constantly working on the road ahead of her, never looking back but always looking at how she can make the future better not only for herself but for others who want to succeed. Esperanza's fluid vocals and stunning tone have quieted the worried souls in jazz, as she represents all that jazz can be and should be. Branching into the territory of name-brand artists, she has brought an unexpected flavor, audience, and revelation to the genre. This ability to

branch beyond the leaves of even the fringes of the history and family tree in jazz is the very fundamental nature of her art.

HER STORY

Jazz developed in my life on its own. The instrument I chose has more to do with it than anything else. I fell in love with the music itself along the way . . . but, I haven't agreed to be exclusive with it. So many other styles of music influence me. Early on, I read how Ella Fitzgerald said she would study other instruments to learn how to scat and phrase. You learn more about what to play by listening to what the musicians around you are playing. In terms of voice, I'm afraid of sounding like someone else, so I listen to singers for enjoyment and encouragement and inspiration to sound how I naturally sound. The singers who aren't too careful and sound like themselves are the most inspiring: Betty Carter, Dakota Stanton, Maria João, Sarah Vaughn, Dinah Washington. Their instrument is so transparent you don't notice technique; just their spirit and boldness.

For a few decades, I think the word "jazz" was used too exclusively. The music most people conjure up in their minds when they think of jazz is music from the fifties and sixties. For whatever reason the word "jazz" stopped evolving with the music. It baffles me when we call Wynton Marsalis, The Bad Plus, Ray Charles, Weather Report, Norah Jones, and Maceo Parker all by the same title. I don't know yet how to classify myself. I work on bass, voice, and composition. Everything I absorb on any given day is what I imagine kneading into my compositions rather than my bass or voice. But I still need to practice a lot and often to be able to even start to do what I need and want on each and every gig. I know what my heroes in music sound like. I want to reach that level of creativity and execution in my playing. The sky isn't even the limit. I have to keep climbing, make sure I'm always ascending.

Sometimes I imagine I'm as fearless and established as one of my favorite composers, like Stevie Wonder, Wayne Shorter, and Shostakovich, when I feel insecure about a passage in my music. They write so organically. I pretend I'm them so I have confidence to leave the composition the way it wants to be and stay honest about what I'm hearing. I want others to have the same feeling I get when I hear someone that moves me to my core when they're listening to my music. I hope to give that tingle, that "unh!" That sigh. An inhale when you can't even stand how much you're feeling.

But that's something I can't control. I just try and make the best music I can and hope that over the years I'll reach that level of delivery where I can move people every night.

Terell Stafford
TRUMPETER, COMPOSER, EDUCATOR

HOME BASE
www.terellstafford.com

GOT MUSIC?
Taking Chances: Live at the Dakota,
Terell Stafford, MaxJazz, 2007

"I never go into music with a preconceived notion."

BACKGROUND AND SOUND

Rooted deeply in the tradition of jazz, Terell Stafford has risen up from the ranks to become one of the great trumpet players of our time. He has raised his chops in fields farmed by Art Blakey, Bobby Watson, McCoy Tyner, Benny Golson, and Jimmy Heath. He is an avid arranger, composer, and soloist, and his horn has become one of the great transducers of melody in our time. As an educator he is turning the future of jazz into a bright and fully realized show of talent through his role as a professor at Temple University. Terell's joyful attitude in regards to life is conveyed through his music as he lifts spirits of listeners both on and off stage. He is a smiling presence and proof that if you listen to those who take you under their wings, you will indeed secure a place in the same lineage they are a part of.

HIS STORY

I found jazz later in life. The person that made me really want to play the trumpet was Chuck Mangione. His song "Feels So Good" was popular, and eventually it got me a free flügelhorn out of my uncle. But the people who were really influential and I still look up to this day are Kenny Barron and Bobby Watson. They gave me a chance when I had only been playing for a year. To see how passionate they are for the music and how willing to share they are helped me realize where I am in my life and accept it. They'd feed me information as they saw fit. This was a trouble of mine when I was younger, because I was always trying to find myself. My parents moved around a lot, and I didn't have a lot of friends. This really affected me as a person. But it was my mentors and the music that have helped me become who I am. It was the interpersonal relationships that helped me get to where I am. These are a necessity to have before we teach younger generations to do what we did. We also need to keep in mind that we're entertainers. If you watch the Kenny Barrons and Bobby Watsons perform, you hear them speaking to the audience. I see younger players perform, and I see no relationship with the audience. There has to be a trust between the players and the audiences, because that's when they'll totally dig you and hear every note you play and feel like they know you.

Musically I want to continue the tradition with high standards and strong morals. The passion I have for life comes through with a spiritual and melodic energy. I never go into music with a preconceived notion, as what I write and play on the bandstand has to come out naturally. I've had the privilege to perform with great musicians like John Clayton, Jimmy Heath, and McCoy Tyner, and this keeps my fire going. Hopefully you'll hear that love and dedication in my music, for what I do is a blessing and makes me happy.

E.J. Strickland

DRUMMER, COMPOSER, EDUCATOR

HOME BASE
www.ejstrickland.com

GOT MUSIC?
In This Day, E.J. Strickland, Strick Muzic, 2009

"Music is not about technique, even though that's a necessary goal; it's more about creating something beautiful to offer people so they can grasp onto it and be inspired."

BACKGROUND AND SOUND

E.J. Strickland regularly doles out morsels of rhythm through his intuitive and anticipatory guidance on the drums. After all, he is in the business of translating rhythm into digestible blocks before diffusing them out into his audience. Industry professionals who have regularly fed off of his healthy creative cadences include his twin brother, Marcus Strickland, Luis Perdomo, Dianne Reeves, Jaleel Shaw, Tia Fuller, Brandee Younger, Ravi Coltrane, Nnenna Freelon, and Herbie Hancock. On the continuous pursuit of finding the voice within himself and his art, E.J. has become a student of the greats—for life.

HIS STORY

Music has shaped who I am as a person. It's enlightened me. But that's the reward and beauty of being able to work with so many different people, older and younger than you. As musicians, we study those who have come before us. They're our legacy. Yet what we really do to show respect is create our own thing.

It's my hope that future generations look at what's been done before and appreciate it by studying their inspiration and bring it into their own thing, too. Bring in all of the senses, not just some, emulate those before, and respect the tradition by reaching further with growth and exploration. It's important to have one step in the past, one in the present, and look forward as to continue that legacy set before you. It's our responsibility as musicians to make sure our craft is true in all its forms. It has to be something that inspires you; you have to let people who don't know art or music experience it with the world they do know. People are scared of what they don't know and that fear is what keeps them from jazz. They just don't know it.

You have to ask what inspires or captures their interest. What drives them to be honest with themselves? It's hard to relate to someone if they're not open to anything. Being a musician, in this case, means you have to be a kind of doctor. When they're not feeling good, inspired, or creative, they need to go somewhere to obtain that good feeling, and music can heal just like a doctor heals—it's medicine for the soul. Music is not about technique, even though that's a necessary goal; it's more about creating something beautiful to offer people so they can grasp onto it and be inspired.

And as a musician that's what I try to do. I continually challenge myself, practice, and give myself difficult things to do, knowing in the long run it's all for the creation of art and beauty. Jazz is a lifestyle, a way to live your life. It's what keeps me going and what I live for. I wouldn't want to equate it with my creator or anything like that, but to say they're one and the same to a certain extent is true. It's a myth or person I'm waiting to meet at the end of my existence. A character in my life, a religious, spiritual, biblical character I know I'll meet at the end. Trouble starts when you meet this character with discouragement. If any musician were to be truly honest with him- or herself, or anyone else for that matter, they would say they want to be the best. It's when people get satisfied with who they are that scares me. Never, ever give up that want to be someone greater. I never did, and I remember every day what drives me about this music, for it's my life. Someone I want to stand before and be proud to be embraced by.

Marcus Strickland
SAXOPHONIST, COMPOSER, PRODUCER

HOME BASE
www.marcusstrickland.com

GOT MUSIC?
Idiosyncrasies, Marcus Strickland, Strick Muzic, 2009

"The more I play, the more I realize this music is less about me and more about who I'm reaching."

BACKGROUND AND SOUND

Two-time Grammy-nominated jazz saxophonist Marcus Strickland is defining his own voice as a burning force on the modern jazz scene. Even though he has played with the very best, including Roy Haynes, his own aspiration of greatness speaks louder than his résumé. His artful and hip compositions create waves that contain a high-charged electrical current, charring everything its path. With an energy and fervor to change the outlook of not only the music but also the industry itself with his own label, Strick Muzic, Marcus is a resolute channel of hope and light among the next generation of greats in jazz.

HIS STORY

Jazz is a sponge that absorbs and dissects all music. I was brought up on a very wide palette of music, and I have no other choice other than to be influenced by this. Unless I live in a vacuum some jazz musicians live in, of course I'm going to be influenced by those I listen to, like Björk, Stevie Wonder, Miles, Lester Young, Ella, et cetera. My dad was a music lover, and it was just natural for me to gravitate toward jazz because it had everything we listened to in it. But there's so much music out there, and jazz is only a small part of the world. There are many

more facets of life to grab onto as musicians. This is how we create our own sound and make up our own code.

The more I learn about it, the less it becomes about showing off. Jazz is about sharing and giving what you can offer. Jazz is a gift. Some people are only interested in becoming a virtuoso, and I have a certain appreciation for it, but the more I play, the more I realize this music is less about me and more about who I'm reaching. It's so much bigger than me. The generations now should focus on doing what they truly want to do rather than accepting what's safe or what's accepted. Now is the time in their lives to be experimenting and bringing to the table what they feel they can offer. As jazz musicians, we can be our own worst enemy in this way. We hold these paradigms in training and studying icons like Miles Davis, but we need to realize we're strong individuals, too. If we'd just concentrate on saying what we have to say through obtaining our own sound, we'd be better off. I refuse to sit down and let anyone keep me from exposing what I have to say and share.

We all have so much to say. There's a lot of great music that's being overlooked and underplayed. If you're trying to break through, you must understand that your peers are just as important, if not more, than your heroes. Nothing beats having a friend, especially someone that's involved in the same thing you're into. A lot of musicians come to town and focus on playing with certain names. I say no. Play with the people around you, because they're going to be the ones associated with those that are famous or will become famous at some time or another. This is when you'll form that strong and natural bond and become a part of what's going on now. If you're just a musician that's connected through a tux and buttoned up in a very small vortex, you're not going to get people into what you're doing or saying. It's going to alienate you. People in other scenes find jazz musicians condescending because of this. We're not in any position to be this way. Jazz is simply a style of music. There are so many ways and reasons to play. We must understand that the more open we are to our audience, the more open they will be to us. Like every other human being, we want to have fun and be happy. That's what my music is and should be about. Listen to it. It's not meant to be strenuous. Figure it out, as it's meant just for you.

Steve Swallow

{LIVING LEGEND}

BASSIST, COMPOSER

HOME BASE
www.wattxtrawatt.com

GOT MUSIC?
Deconstructed, Steve Swallow,
ECM Records, 1996

"One should only embark on a life as a musician if there is absolutely no other choice."

BACKGROUND AND SOUND

Award-winning bassist Steve Swallow has kept himself busy throughout the last three decades. He has been featured on tours, in innumerable performances, and on recordings alongside greats of the past and the present, including John Scofield, Stan Getz, David Liebman, Chris Potter, Adam Nussbaum, Paul Motian, Carla Bley, Pat Metheny, Chick Corea, and too many more to list. The power of what he delivers regularly fractures the common perception of the electric bass. Subscribing to the thoughts of the musicians around him, he is able to anticipate their moves and thus create a greater voice for groups as a unit. Premiering his evocative original works throughout the world, Steve has been keeping up his dizzying pace for more than three decades and will continue to be the go-to electric bassist for countless musicians throughout the community.

HIS STORY

When I began making a life in this music, I assumed most everything would happen very quickly. I just knew that I'd become a masterful player in a matter of days, if not hours. Of course, it didn't happen this way. I had to learn patience right away. I think this is one of the abiding pleasures of being a jazz musician . . . the music reveals itself very slowly over time. You can safely wake up every morning with the assumption that you're going to learn something. The music is so immensely vast that I've never had the sense that I'm anywhere near the end of what there is out there. It's amazing to me how music in general, despite the fact that there are only twelve notes, has no apparent end to it. I no longer expect to wake up and be possessed by the ability to play everything I've always wanted to play. I'm just happy now to watch it unfold over time.

To this day I'm surprised at what music does for me. I'd like to think that listeners get the same thing I get from it, but my response to music is so subjective that it's unlikely that anyone else perceives music the way I do. Several years ago I attended a concert of a piece by Messiaen, the *Quartet for the End of Time*. I'd heard it on recordings many times, and I greatly admired the piece. I went to a performance of it and, objectively, it wasn't a great performance. As I listened to it, I was in my usual analytical mode and enjoying it while standing back from it at the same time. I guess there's always a part of me that's extracting knowledge from any music I listen to. Then the piece finished and we all got up to leave. I was leaning against the building, waiting, and I was completely, unexpectedly blindsided by an overwhelming sadness. I burst into a deep bout of crying and staggered out of the building and disappeared around the corner to sob uncontrollably. I realized that despite the objective stuff going on, I was having a very deep experience that caught up with me when the piece was finished. From then on, I had a great respect for the mysterious ways music can affect people.

Most of the music I listen to now is so-called classical music. I'm less in touch with the current generation of jazz players than I should be. I made a resolution recently to remedy this and to pay attention to the current generation of guys coming up and making a strong impact. I feel very fortunate, when I think about the guys coming up now, that I arrived in New York City in 1960. The musical environment at that time was very exciting, and the economic climate for the music was relatively benign. It's far more difficult to have a viable life in jazz now than it was then.

Young musicians have to really examine their desire to be a jazz musician. If their reasons for wanting to be one have flaws, then they should, by all means, consider other options. One should only embark on a life as a musician if there is absolutely no other choice. The members of the jazz community are remarkably committed to the music they play. The rewards we get are in the music. If you want to be rich and famous, be a politician or pop star. This is one of the things I love about the jazz community: we all know there's no better feeling than having a great night on the bandstand with a bunch of like-minded players. This feels better than anything else I know. I know I made the right choice when I decided to be a jazz musician.

Ricky Sweum
SAXOPHONIST, COMPOSER, EDUCATOR

HOME BASE
www.rickysweum.com

GOT MUSIC?
Pulling Your Own Strings, Ricky Sweum, Origin Records, 2009

"Music is a lifelong journey of self-discovery and rediscovery."

BACKGROUND AND SOUND

Award-winning saxophonist Ricky Sweum has emerged through the scenes in New York and Colorado as an upcoming master of the craft. He landed on his own two feet with a record deal from Origin Records and tours with the very best in the industry, from solo musicians to Broadway. In the past he has been a member of the BMI Jazz Composers Workshop under the tutelage of Jim McNeely and Michael Abene, toured with nationally touring Broadway companies, and performed with the Tommy Dorsey Orchestra and other greats such as Clark Terry, James Moody, and Terry Gibbs. Recognizing those who have helped him with his initial shove toward the top, Ricky is putting his sweat and earnest belief into everything he does in order to create a journey that will last him a lifetime.

HIS STORY

Jazz isn't a style as much as a way the musicians have learned to play what it is they play. You can't separate playing from listening; you have the ability as a musician to respond to what's around you in a way that's different than every other kind of music. The essence is living, responding, listening, and stretching. Life is about movement and flexibility, and jazz speaks life to me. Focusing music into something greater then the musicians themselves allows their intent to permeate energy to listeners. It has the effect of inspiration within the process of mastery. When I first got into music it was about being excited about something I didn't understand. This was followed by the realization that music is a set of skills, a craft, a model on how one can conduct their life. With it came this feeling of responsibility to master these skills, but that mastery never comes. At that point, it becomes a continuous process of self-discovery. I'm still blown away now, twenty-five years later, the same way I was on day one. I didn't even and still don't know what I don't know.

I think the biggest thrill for me is when someone comes up to me and they know nothing about music and yet they're inspired. Maybe not musically, but the inspiration to repeat whatever process they're into and create something new that couldn't be created by themselves is great. You are your only self, and by bringing two, three, or five people more that are equally inspired creates something that wouldn't be there if you were alone. It's alchemy of inspiration and passion. Jazz is just one form of this alchemy—a microcosm of creative life in general throughout the whole universe. Even if you play something that's been done before, it's not the same—a new, different moment that represents now. For audiences I would hope they appreciate who I am in that moment. This music must be given one's full attention, a worthy chance. Anywhere throughout music, if it's a typical place, it takes on the background role, and this negatively influences musicians. They take on a background role and create that moment to the uninspired and passionless performances. It's a disservice to what it is we're trying to create. The subtlety of everything that's trying to happen is completely covered over. Jazz is freedom within restrictions. Fill yourself with passion, desire—a raw energy you can use. Don't discard anything because it doesn't fit the mold you're trying to learn. Keep it. Save it for later. Music is a lifelong journey of self-discovery and rediscovery. Remain open, as this is allowing whatever is there to be the perfect thing. If you approach what you're doing in music from that standpoint, you'll hear the mood and make it fun for the listener and performer. It's an undeniable force, a visceral experience of combined energies.

Lew Tabackin

{LIVING LEGEND}

TENOR SAXOPHONIST, FLAUTIST, COMPOSER

HOME BASE
www.lewtabackin.com

GOT MUSIC?
Live in Paris, Lew Tabackin Trio, Independent Label, 2008

"Once you accept your own little imperfections, whatever they are, that's when you'll be on your way to accepting who you are and making that person stronger and more profound."

BACKGROUND AND SOUND

Absorbing the world around him in a style that is as distinctive as his aura, saxophonist Lew Tabackin has created and completed a staggering amount of work throughout his career. Lew is highly accomplished on both the flute and the tenor saxophone. He approaches both with a veracity that exhibits an unusually open ear and foresight into the inner workings of his style. In the late sixties he met Toshiko Akiyoshi, and they soon formed their Grammy Award–winning big band, the Toshiko Akiyoshi Jazz Orchestra. Lew has also been a part of numerous other projects, recordings, tours, and productions with greats Lewis Nash, Victor Lewis, Billy Higgins, and Charlie Haden. His talent on both flute and tenor is internationally acclaimed and has influenced countless musicians in the importance of expanding one's horizons in order to be successful in the business. Lew is a major player and has shown no signs of slowing down. He continues today to use his streak of genius in everything he does.

HIS STORY

The first saxophone player I really got into . . . was Al Cohn. There was something about his sound that I loved. After hours and hours on the tenor

I actually got pretty close to imitating what I thought his sound was. Then I checked out Sonny Rollins and Coltrane and became kind of a Coltrane clone. I realized at a certain point that emulating someone else was not the right path to pursue. It was a dead end. So I began to check out Lester Young, Coleman Hawkins and Don Byas. I could feel their passion. Listening to them gave me insight into what it would take for me to eventually find and create something personal. I could listen to Sonny Rollins and hear elements of the players before him, and I realized that this was a clue. It wasn't a secret at all. By listening and keeping my ears and heart and soul open, I was on my way. I've been listening to them since. Finally, when I got into my forties, I began to feel like all those idiosyncrasies I had tried to get rid of as a young person were who I was, for better or worse. Once you accept your own little imperfections, whatever they are, that's when you'll be on your way to accepting who you are and making that person stronger and more profound. Unfortunately it takes a lot longer now to be able to do this. Kids can practice and practice without any idea of what they want to sound like, and this causes trouble. But once you do find that voice, it takes a lot longer now than, say, musicians from the forties to develop it. These musicians were playing six nights a week with sometimes two matinees. Development is accelerated when you can do this. What used to lead someone to find their voice at twenty-five or thirty now takes until they're forty or fifty. Of course, there are exceptions to this, but generally this is the case.

Part of this issue also deals with the schools of jazz. These were supposed to fill in the gap of this, but in fact that scene was getting smaller and smaller and there weren't a lot of opportunities for musicians to play regardless of the schools. So the schools became an industry. It was more for teachers and students who wrote books and made a living creating jazz aides. This in turn created generations of overachievers. There's nothing wrong with being an overachiever if you do it on your own, and most of us do if we're really into the craft. Overachieving on your terms and through your own self-discovery is what you should do. But when you're doing this by way of being told, even with techniques to facilitate your achievement, it can be a dangerous thing. A great teacher is supposed to be someone who will give you the questions, not the answers. As soon as you give a student an answer, you've killed the romance of this music. This whole education system doesn't work because of this. If somebody's really gifted and has the desire, energy, and passion, they'll find a way. But in an academic situation they lose this.

When I was learning how to play, I had to learn one note at a time. There were no serious books or methods to do this. You just listened and played. First thing you learn is how to play the B-flat, and then the B-flat blues, and then you know the shit out of the B-flat. Then while you're playing you all of a sudden begin to feel things and you hear things and play them. This might be the most mundane thing, but it's yours and it's the first time it's ever been played. You'll never forget it. Then you move on to the next note. This becomes *your* musical approach. This way all the notes have meaning to you. They're like your children and a part of you. You don't think of things like a minor ninth moving to a tonic anymore. That will come after the fact. Over the years you'll develop a feeling for how things work. You pick things up by intuition and the actual physical sensation you get when you play those notes, because they're yours. If that teacher tells you what this is and you don't do it on your own, how will you own those notes? Like I said, the romance is gone, and this is such an important part of the music. It's truly sad to see young players losing the essence of this music. When you play, this is what people get, they get inspired through that romance, and there are would-be musicians that will be inspired too. This changes your life. You can become proficient through books and demonstrations, but to be able to play and express something that's you, that has to be discovered on its own.

Ohad Talmor
SAXOPHONIST, COMPOSER

HOME BASE
www.ohadtalmor.com

GOT MUSIC?
Playing in Traffic, Swallow/ Talmor/Nussbaum, Auand Records, 2009

"Music has become a necessary condition of my growth, both emotionally and intellectually."

BACKGROUND AND SOUND

Ohad Talmor is a man of the world. His home base is wherever he is at the moment, and his groups are based out of everywhere from New York to São Paulo, Brazil. Many of the top cats are deeply entrenched not only as influences but also as members of his groups. The undeniably magnetic personality of his soloing, compositions, and general demeanor has attracted greats Chris Potter, Steve Swallow, Russ Johnson, Billy Hart, the Brecker Brothers, Lee Konitz, the Axis String Quartet, Matthieu Michel, and the European Broadcasting Ensemble, among a whole bevy of other players. His compositions have also been featured on media avenues such as NPR, the SyFy Channel, and Random House audio books. There's a peace, light, and positive shield of brilliance that tends to protect and follow Ohad in everything he does. His music is a direct reflection of this light, and as long as he is buried deep in the creation of new works, this light will continue to uplift spirits around the world.

HIS STORY

When I was sixteen I moved to Florida from Europe. What I found upon my arrival was that the jazz in this country was suffering. I guess there's always an entertainment side to art, and that's an undeniable and important aspect of it, but music in the States is exquisitely tied to it. I believe if we only measure success of art through its entertainment value, it can be detrimental. Thus our problem lies much deeper than saying it's all about accessibility. People have access; they just don't value it or know how powerful music can be. But in order to address human beings on the larger scale, music has to be experienced as a truth. When this is done it can be very powerful, almost earth-shattering in its nature. Maybe if we stopped staging our music as a circus act and discontinued the force-feeding of it through academic channels we would actually be able to impact each other through our music and give ourselves up to what we believe in. I have the feeling that even though some of us do believe in this music, in general, people don't relate to what we're doing. This creates a distance between the artist and the audience, and I've experienced it more times than not. Even with the best of intentions I equate my struggles with everyone else's. At least we have that in common. We're all struggling in some form or other to grow as individuals. Out of this struggle, though, is hope. Music can open doors to these difficult feelings and issues and take you through a world created by what you're hearing. As a listener and player, I go back to any strong voice I've heard and that has something to give, as it gets me through my own struggles in life. And this is what music is all about. The more I grow musically, the more I experiment and widen my own personal horizons. I have this inextinguishable hunger that feeds off of itself when I play. Music has become a necessary condition of my growth, both emotionally and intellectually. I see more, experience more, and hopefully create this need to see more in others.

Chris Tarry

BASSIST, COMPOSER, EDUCATOR, NOVELIST

HOME BASE
www.christarry.com

GOT MUSIC?
Almost Certainly Dreaming,
Chris Tarry, Nineteen-Eight
Records, 2008

"The inquisitive people will always find their path."

BACKGROUND AND SOUND

Three-time Juno Award–winning and internationally acclaimed bassist Chris Tarry has filled his plate with success. With eight critically acclaimed albums and appearances on more than one hundred various recordings, with such greats as John Scofield, Henry Hey, and many more, Chris is not only playing the field, he is harvesting the fruits of his labor. His compositions stand out like a barbed wire fence against the more traditionally rooted vines of his peers, owing to influences such as Radiohead. It is this ability that transforms the ethereal and distinct sounds of jazz into color. Chris is one musician who paints a story with his song and colors it with hues of exquisite rhythm and lifelines from his soul.

HIS STORY

I lived in Canada a long time before moving to New York. The local guys were not only my influences but they helped me learn and break my career into two different sections: one, as a professional bass player, and, two, as a leader and composer. My initial influences were David Binney, Dan Weiss, Ben Monder, and Miles Okazaki. Listening to them makes me wonder if I can do something similar. I love to hear what they're doing and be a part of it while being influenced at the same time. The fact that we all hang out as friends is also very important; in a way, being friends and working together makes us feel like we're a part of the music—contemporaries of the same art. My music represents the people who are in the trenches, slugging it out and doing their own thing. It's supposed to invoke a good vibe and feeling. We have to, as musicians, find that path for others to get to the music. The inquisitive people will always find their path, and it's unfortunate that most people are told what to listen to. We have to look at what value each piece of art takes on.

When I'm eighty years old, I want to be able to say I did everything I wanted to do. This keeps me going. Most people talk about what they want or should do—I'm about doing it. In reality I work twenty-four/ seven; it just doesn't feel like it. Success looks better from the outside than it is from the inside; it's more of a combo of what I should have done and the reality of what I have to do. I try to be a good person and treat everyone fairly and be happy with what I have and keep my head down. But there are always people willing to help out if you're willing to take it at the right time. Just follow their lead and how they make a living and keep it going. It's a journey of hard work and working harder than others. You just have to trust yourself with your art.

Jason "J.T." Thomas
DRUMMER

HOME BASE
www.myspace.com/jasonjtthomas

GOT MUSIC?
The RH Factor, Roy Hargrove, Hardgroove, 2001

"Since God blessed me with the gift of music, I feel it's my responsibility to bless others with that gift."

BACKGROUND AND SOUND

Entrenched in the heart of the Texas and international jazz scenes, drummer Jason "J.T." Thomas is wildly energetic and as entertaining as they come. He has toured, performed, and recorded with jazz, R&B, and gospel groups. While establishing his career among his local peers, he was discovered by Roy Hargrove and Les McCann. Eventually he went on to tour with them, and his career hasn't been the same since. He has played for Grand Hyatt Hotels, the Intercontinental Hotels Group, and the club Jamz while in Jakarta. Gospel vocalist Natalie Grant and jazz bassist Marcus Miller, among others, employ his talent on a regular basis. Not only is J.T. feeling blessed because of his talent, he is certainly reciprocating that blessing to not only the jazz world but the communities around him.

HIS STORY

Music, especially jazz, is very personal to me. Since God blessed me with the gift of music, I feel it's my responsibility to bless others with that gift. And with jazz I feel the most open, creative, and capable of musically saying whatever He wants to say. Music is so powerful, and there are so many things it can do without having to say one word. I've gotten through some very emotional times by playing and have even gotten over the flu and many other illnesses by playing. For me, being a part of something that can touch on so many different emotions, make someone smile or cry, and, in some cases, change people's lives is sometimes indescribable. This is also the reason I give everything I have when I play. You never know who's listening and what they may be going through and who might need that touch.

As for me, I'm living my dream. I'm extremely blessed to be able to do what I love for a living, and it's even more of a blessing to be able to share this gift. I have a lot of fun, and I get to play all styles of music. Jazz, to me, is just the purest and most honest way of making music, period. It *is* what you make of it. Pro Tools isn't going to make tracks that make everything perfect, there aren't going to be multimillion-dollar productions with dancers for you, and certainly there's not going to be a big light show . . . it's just God, you, and your instrument. Open your mind, open your heart, let the music flow through you, and play, but have fun and remember to share the gift of music with someone today.

Kim Thompson
DRUMMER, EDUCATOR

HOME BASE
www.myspace.com/
ktmusicproduction

"Through the art of creative expression I've been inspired to change minds and touch souls around the world."

BACKGROUND AND SOUND

Kim Thompson's short but productive career has taken her around the world several times over. As the drummer for icons like Beyoncé, she has learned what it means to be a hardworking musician. Her impeccable ability to anticipate the next move by other musicians in the group is a skill that takes years of sweat and persistence to hone, but Kim does it seemingly with ease. Her future as a musician is bright, and she is highly respected by her fellow musicians and looked up to by drummers from all over the world. Kim's take-no-prisoners approach to playing has helped her engage the crowd and give her a closer listen before dismissing her as just part of the backdrop.

HER STORY

Digging deep . . . a familiar sense for who we as individuals truly are. Everyone has a story as we all walk under the same sky and lift our head as the sun rises together. It is an honor to respect the journey. Life has made me stronger. I could only be humble enough to share my own tales of treason, love, light, and vulnerability through such an imaginative lover: the music!

The anchor is here for all boys, girls, men, and women to enjoy selfishly. It's true intention and responsibility is the spiritual expression of us. Together we produce love, create life; we work a little harder; we walk with our heads held high. We become family through the music. Artists, how do we sustain the high level of sonic intimacy? The musical schooling on the jazz scene circling the inner cities not only depicted value, intelligence, but also morals, always encouraging to respect our elders.

I'm grateful to have worked with some of the most iconic artists who have contributed to my career. Through their hard work and dedication they have reached a destination of peace and harmony that one day I hope to achieve. They have earned the respect and acknowledgement of their audience and each other. They to continue to hold on and further describe its new language in this moment, in this lifetime. We must be humbled to the means of vibrations. The quality, the behavior, the intention—everything changes. Jazz is a huge part of our history. The openness of creative expression and freedom is vital, and supporting the arts is the only way for it to reach the hands that desire such spiritual conquest.

Steve Turre {LIVING LEGEND}

TROMBONIST, SEASHELLIST, COMPOSER, EDUCATOR

HOME BASE
www.steveturre.com

GOT MUSIC?
Rainbow People, Steve Turre, Half Note, 2008

"We can't go backwards and recreate what once was."

BACKGROUND AND SOUND

Steve Turre is an outstanding voice in the jazz trombone world. Innovation has always been incorporated into everything he does, and the word "imitation" isn't a part of his vernacular. After researching his ancestral history he began to incorporate seashells into his repertoire. Many in the business have made note of his notes. He has been a long-standing member of the *Saturday Night Live* band, has led his own groups, and has played with folks like Lester Bowie, Herbie Hancock, Horace Silver, Woody Shaw, and more. Transforming his thick knowledge into a transmittable "oomph" through his music, Steve Turre is definitely one of the most interesting and pioneering players to have entered the jazz community.

HIS STORY

My mom and dad met at a Count Basie dance. They were from the generation where big band music was the popular music of the day and not only went to listen to Ellington, Basie, or Herman, they danced to it. When I was in the fourth grade they began to take me to hear Duke and Count; that's when I saw Coleman Hawkins and Johnny Hodges play . . . man, what a beautiful sound. I've never heard a sound like that. It was incredible. That blew my mind and made me want to play this music. Over time I saw Monk, Bill Evans . . . Sonny Rollins. Sonny blew my mind, I never heard anyone play like that. But I saw the fusion thing come in and the change of the music happen. My first gig was with Ray Charles, and then Art Blakey. Art was the one though who brought me to New York. After that followed Woody Shaw, Dizzy, and then McCoy Tyner.

We can't go backwards and recreate what once was. You have to incorporate what once was and then build on that. As far as I'm concerned the level of music was much higher back in the sixties, and not just with jazz but also pop, R&B, et cetera. The spirit motivated it, not the get-rich-or-die-trying attitude we have now. Instead, it was motivated by the signs of the times. That's when we had the civil rights movement and fought for political change and freedom. It wasn't just the black power or hippies or latinos doing this, it was like a whole consciousness had taken over us. But everything has a cycle.

These kinds of things are manifesting themselves in totally different ways now. I believe the human consciousness is starting to cycle around again to the old way of thinking. It's almost as if people have to have somebody to hate. I call them haters. It's not about politics or anything else; it's this whole way of thinking that just doesn't work anymore. If we keep dealing with life in this way, we're going to destroy civilization and our planet. It's just a militant solution to everything and demonstrates a lack of respect for other cultures and people and races. It's also a lack of respect for the planet. This attitude that nature is only here for humanity to exploit is wrong.

We're not above nature; never have been. We're, in fact, a part of it, and we should respect it as such.

Music is on another level of discussion than politics. Although there are some who are political with their art, I'm not. It's just not the way I express myself. In the middle of the civil rights movement in the sixties, which was a brutal time in history, with lynchings, murders, et cetera, there were some musicians like Mingus that would play tunes like "Fables of Faubus." He was clearly a reactionary. I don't disagree with his point of view, but it was purely reactionary. I went to see Mingus one time in New York in the seventies. It was a great set, everyone was killin'. Then at the end Mingus grabbed the mic and said, "Ladies and gentleman, fuck you very much, it's been a pressure." He said this just to shock people. This is superficial. Coltrane was much deeper. He talked about a love supreme instead of killings or shocking stuff . . . I like this approach. He let that negative crap go and didn't get sucked in.

That's what I'm about. My music is even for the haters because it hopefully brings them love. We all have different paths in life, and no two people are the same. But . . . we can learn lessons from each other. We have to find our own way, and there isn't one answer to anything. It's patience, discipline, and dedication that go into making one's art valuable. In turn we have to see life as valuable, too, because in the end your art is just an expression of your life.

McCoy Tyner
PIANIST, COMPOSER, NEA JAZZ MASTER

HOME BASE
www.mccoytyner.com

GOT MUSIC?
The Real McCoy, McCoy Tyner, Blue Note Records, 1967; *Guitars*, McCoy Tyner, McCoy Tyner Music/Half Note Records, 2008

"Jazz is music, and music is what I do."

BACKGROUND AND SOUND

Only once in a lifetime does a musician like McCoy Tyner drop down from the sky and paint the world a different and more brilliant color just by playing the piano. McCoy's prolific career has produced more than eighty albums, four Grammy Awards, and the distinguished honor of being named a National Endowment for the Arts Jazz Master. He has covered almost every creative talent in the business with his influential style that emphasizes the use of rhythm and dense harmonics with the left hand while decorating the melody with the right. The beginning of his climb to the top started with his collaborative efforts with John Coltrane when he was featured on the monumental release titled *My Favorite Things*. His solo works and albums that were recorded with him as a leader further cemented his status early on in his career. He has performed and toured the world many times over and continues to impress with his ability to stay with the times in his soloing and compositions. Although McCoy has always been successful, the greater effect on the genre is just now fully being realized.

HIS STORY

I've always loved the piano. It's really just an orchestra laid out in front of you. There's so much you can do with it. Jazz was just the music I gravitated toward. Jazz is music, and music is what I do. It's a personal feeling and will have a different effect on everyone. But I studied classical music when I was a kid, thanks to my mother. We didn't have a piano, so I used to go to her friends' houses, and they would let me play. I just couldn't wait to get home from school so I could start playing it. My mother, who had a beauty shop in town, eventually put a piano in the shop. Women would be getting their hair done next to a saxophone player taking a solo! It was a wild scene. Growing up in Philadelphia, I got to be around some of the greatest jazz musicians of all time, like John Coltrane, the Heath Brothers, Bud Powell—people like that. Bud was like a hero to us kids in the neighborhood. Some of the great musicians would stop by at the beauty shop from time to time and listen to us. Great musicians continue to come out of the Philadelphia area—there's just something about that city!

I feel very blessed to have been able to do what I've done so far, and I'm always looking forward to what's going to happen next. It's important to do this. It's nice to have success and be appreciated and look back at what you've done, but it's much more important to be thinking about the next project or the next gig.

Manuel Valera
PIANIST, COMPOSER

HOME BASE
www.manuelvalera.com

GOT MUSIC?
Vientos, Manuel Valera, Anzic Records, 2007

"I love this country and am very fortunate to be here."

BACKGROUND AND SOUND

Manuel Valera has a gift in his ability to forge new sound by combining the traditional sounds of his native land of Cuba and that of his new home in America. Crafting and sculpting a career is one thing, but building a new world into and out of your craft is something that takes a lifetime to master. Manuel is well aware of this and persistently works at his personal growth and potential as an artist. His sound reflects this tenacity in its mature and resolute panache. Arturo Sandoval has recently plucked him out of the streets of Manhattan to tour throughout the world. As a leader he retains musicians like James Genus, Seamus Blake, and Antonio Sanchez to bring out the very best in his music. His original works garnered the attention of Chamber Music America; in 2006 they granted him a commission for new work. Manuel continues to surprise and bestow his gifts upon the scene.

HIS STORY

Growing up in Cuba meant that Cuban music was all around. It's a way of life there, and you can't get around it. If you're from there and you don't know or feel it, people think there's something about you that's strange. Even the people who aren't musicians can generally play patterns or know how to play a percussion instrument. It's a part of our lives, and in many cultures—not just Cuba—it's the same. If you go east, it's very common to find this in India, Nepal, and Africa; even in Europe it's common and dates back to a couple of centuries ago. This kind of community art has been lost though. I think this is mainly because it's become so easy to make music now. In general, it's now like a game or something: everybody and anybody can do. It doesn't take much. There's a vibe that's become more of an American way of making music. Hip-hop guys and the DJs say they're making music, but it isn't that they've made music; they've only put it together. This isn't to say that there aren't guys that are DJs or whatever that aren't doing some interesting stuff. It just seems to me that Americans generally like everything to be easy. This can sometimes be a good way to learn, but most of the time it's not the best way. This isn't only in music. It's in everything. "Learn to play guitar in thirty minutes . . . have abs of steel in only eight minutes . . ."

In Cuba we have more of an Eastern European way of learning music. It's taught like medicine and law and those things there. Our way of learning music is very hard-core: no games, no little songs to teach you how to do certain things . . . it's straight up. But this doesn't mean that the way they teach in Cuba is always good either. I love this country and am very fortunate to be here. This country has so many incredible things that whatever is "wrong" with it doesn't even come close to anywhere near the amount of the good. Regardless of where anyone lives, the artists have always struggled with society to be taken seriously.

Justin Vasquez
SAXOPHONIST, COMPOSER

HOME BASE
www.justinvasquez.com

GOT MUSIC?
Triptych, Justin Vasquez,
Independent Label, 2009

"I want to be a part of this flawed, stream of conscious current."

BACKGROUND AND SOUND

ASCAP Award–winning composer and saxophonist Justin Vasquez is an artist who highly values the storytelling abilities of instrumental music. Every nuance and spread of color is penned in an attempt to realize his vision as an artist. As one of the youngest and more talented saxophonists paying his dues, he is making every effort possible to ensure his success. Realizing these goals may be a lifetime pursuit, but he is clearing the path early on by playing with other peers and greats like Adam Rogers, Aaron Parks, Tom Harrell, and David Liebman. He is savvy, driven, and continually reaching for that next inspiring moment.

HIS STORY

When people find out you're a musician, the first thing you want to say is that you're a jazz musician. But . . . this word has so much baggage attached to it and covers such a broad spectrum you soon realize that even you can't accurately describe it. The public needs to be more exposed to it. The only reason I got into jazz in the first place is because at a fairly young age someone gave me a jazz record. I was handed a CD, and at first it was strange to me, but then I became intrigued. I wonder how many young people today have even heard what we do? If you're not exposed to it, then you don't stand a chance to make a decision one way or the other. It saddens me to think that people think of music as this static feeling in the air that makes people comfortable when they can't think of anything to say. How did we get to this point? It seems that everything we're a part of in this country has nothing to do with where we were. Now we're just about fast-food entertainment, and music has been, unfortunately, relegated to this as well. Think about the person who has a nine-to-five job. They get up an hour before they leave then they're home by five or six in the evening and go to bed around ten or eleven, sometimes earlier. This leaves them with only three hours a day to see family and take care of personal business and eat and get ready for that next day. Whatever last slice of the pie that's left is supposed to be for your personal interests. This doesn't leave room for music.

I like to ask the people sitting next to me when I'm waiting in an airport to name their favorite singers. Most of the time they'll say a pop singer that's new or popular today. Then I ask them, if they found out that singer didn't write any music or lyrics and in reality can't even sing because they digitally enhance their singing to make it sound good for the record, would this affect their purchase of their music? Most of the time they say they don't think about that, and it wouldn't affect anything anyway. It seems that anything that's creative isn't valued in America. I guess any competent or real creative output is going to be flawed and looked down upon. For me, I want to be a part of this flawed, stream-of-consciousness current. I'm still a blank canvas when I play that's having to slowly tear my pieces off and reveal myself to be heard.

Will Vinson
SAXOPHONIST, COMPOSER

HOME BASE
www.willvinson.com

GOT MUSIC?
Promises, Will Vinson,
Nineteen-Eight Records, 2008

"Music has been a central part of my life for as long as I can remember."

BACKGROUND AND SOUND
London native Will Vinson has done well for himself since moving to the States. He has recorded, toured, or performed with a wide array of individuals and groups, including folk singer Sufjan Stevens, the Ari Hoenig Quartet, Geoffrey Keezer, and the Mingus Big Band, among others, and

he has led his own group, consisting of Lage Lund and Aaron Parks, in performances and recordings. Although he validates his muscular strength on the horn through his performances, the subtle glow beneath it all speaks of his depth and his rapidly developing maturity as a musician.

HIS STORY

People used to tell me that being a musician meant living a tough life. What I would add to that, when addressing budding musicians, is that it's really important to just concentrate on what it is that you have to do, to do what you want to do. Music has been a central part of my life for as long as I can remember. I'm not really sure who I'd be without it. I really want people to know about this music they way they know about all the other music that's around them. Jazz is cool and expressive, but it's also quite complex a lot of the time, and, depending on who you're playing with, this complexity combined with the spontaneity can cloud the important aesthetic and end up smothering the audience with an excess of abstract information. This can make it difficult to understand the emotional message. Whenever I think about the people I've listened to or loved the most, I realize they're the musicians who speak with an uncompromising, unashamed sense of beauty and pure melody—the ones who send that emotional message. Early on, I was absolutely in love with the playing of Stan Getz . . . almost obsessed with his restraint. He didn't really flaunt his chops at all, although he certainly had them. Another musician, but from this generation, is Seamus Blake. It doesn't seem to occur to Seamus or Stan or people like them to play something that isn't beautiful.

I hope, in my own playing, that I'm able to always communicate something so concise that the person who listens to it can decode within it the same spirit I played it with. I guess, though, that I'll never know how in touch I am with the audience. Sometimes I'll play shows and feel like there's no connection, or I see that the audience looks bored. This makes me miserable about the way the music is being received. But I don't know what's going on under their skin. I just want them to be as absorbed in the music as I am. This level of appreciation fuels me. It reminds me that I don't have to wake up each morning and wonder what it is that will keep me going. But for the most part I hope just to play well. I definitely have a long way to go in every area of my life, but I've also come a long way.

Doug Wamble
GUITARIST, VOCALIST, COMPOSER, PRODUCER

HOME BASE
www.dougwamble.com

GOT MUSIC?
Country Libations, Doug Wamble,
Marsalis Music, 2008

"Experience your life as much as you can, listen to all of the music you can, but always be focused on what you want to sound like."

BACKGROUND AND SOUND

Having begun his career with some of the best in the field, including Cassandra Wilson and Branford and Wynton Marsalis, to name a few, Doug Wamble is far from singing the blues. His Tennessee roots seep through his solos with an emotional trail that leaves the listener humming his tune long after the music is finished. With one smothering glide after the next, he holds a quiet assuredness close to his soul. Ken Burns picked up on this and employed his services for the background of his documentary *The War*. It is this diversity and love for the art that has earned him a seat among the hardest-hitting players of his time.

HIS STORY

After I graduated Northwestern with my master's, I went straight to New York. Within days I was playing with Madeleine Peyroux. Before I knew it, I was recording with Cassandra Wilson. But then the bottom dropped out. It's not that easy. I was lucky, then broke. I ended up as Cassandra's personal assistant just so I could stay in town. I was so dogmatic and purist back then. When you're in it, it forces you to be so strong, tenaciously strong. But this is why I came to New York. To play with different musicians and to play my own compositions. I even used to be worried when I started singing that people would stop taking me seriously as a guitar player. I wanted to be the one everyone talked about, emulated. But I'm not a guitarist's guitarist. It used to be important to me, but it isn't anymore, thank God.

Jazz hardly exists in the jazz world. People who play on the scene today favor a highly intellectual music that's focused on technical perfection, rapidly paced harmonic progressions, and elimination of all traces of American music history. The blues is viewed as a quaint artifact rather than a bedrock of the foundation of jazz. Sometimes there's a need to call things "jazz" as a form of validation for those great musicians, but I just find it unnecessary. The most important thing is deciding who you want to be and sound like. Practice all day; devise a system based in math algorithms allowing you to penetrate every harmonic. Dress like your favorite musicians, smoke their brand of cigarettes, and be them. But be prepared to be isolated and neglected. This is the path of the righteous. Experience your life as much as you can, listen to all the music you can, but always be focused on what *you* want to sound like. Be willing to sound good even when you don't play well. Anyone can be a master instrumentalist; it just takes time. Artistry only finds you when you open yourself to it.

Greg Ward
SAXOPHONIST, COMPOSER, EDUCATOR

HOME BASE
www.gregward.org

GOT MUSIC?
South Side Story, Greg Ward, Independent Label, 2009

"Despite the struggle, frustration, and challenges that have met me along the way, I haven't given up."

BACKGROUND AND SOUND
Saxophonist Greg Ward is emerging as one of the rising star household names in jazz. With a versatile and contagious groove, his soulful magic is in high demand. In his short career he has earned some of the highest accolades possible, including recognition by critics and peers for his fierce and cutting skills as a soloist. He tends to indulge himself in the realm of the classical and world in his compositions, and experiments through commissions for groups like the Peoria Ballet. He has studied, performed, and toured as a soloist with a number of musicians not only in Chicago but throughout the country, like Von Freeman, Frank Wess, Al Jarreau,

and Brian McKnight. With honors Greg is graduating from his time as an apprentice of the art into a full-fledged artist.

HIS STORY

A lot of people on my father's side were musicians; some were professional, but they all had talent. My dad and uncle were both gospel musicians in the church, and that's the scene I grew up around. I began singing in choirs and listening to them play, and I knew I wanted to do that. My dad already had a sax, and since that was the most affordable thing for him to give me, that's what I started playing on. But once I heard Charlie Parker I knew that this was what I wanted to do the rest of my life. Parker broadened me by giving me direction and focus. I'm lucky to have this focus and that I don't have to be one of those wandering around life wondering what I'm going to do with it. I know this is what I want to do. Jazz is everywhere and everything for me; it's at the forefront of my life and has helped me develop something I can really dig into. Despite the struggle, frustration, and challenges that have met me along the way, I haven't given up. There are moments of beauty that happen through this music, and I've found myself beginning to work for those moments. This is has given me perspective on life . . . as now I know nothing worthwhile is going to be easy.

When I'm playing I want others to hear boldness through my ideas and this perspective I have learned through natural curiosity. They shouldn't be sitting back, as I don't want things to seem so clear. I want people to think about things they believe are real. You can work all angles and make your music go to a place where it makes your audience develop and come to you. You have to plant seeds in hopes that they'll grow. I think people relate and understand this kind of curiosity for life. Especially now, we have to, as artists, create a culture for ourselves so we can begin to internalize what it is we're doing. This will keep this tradition alive. Anybody who wants to embrace this and learn is a responsibility for me. I get total fulfillment through knowing that I'm able to share my knowledge and ideas. I'll always work with someone who's ready to learn and shows that they're hungry. I want people to know what my experiences have been with the masters and how I got to where I am today so I can pass down my tradition . . . these are the opportunities I embrace. If you're here to dedicate yourself to the craft and find out how to express yourself through this craft, you'll be happy no matter where you are or what you're doing in the art.

Derico Watson

DRUMMER, EDUCATOR

HOME BASE
www.dericowatson.com

GOT MUSIC?
Palmystery, Victor Wooten,
Heads Up, 2008

"Natural ability is only going to take you so far."

BACKGROUND AND SOUND

Derico Watson's source of undeniable skill and love for music is not of this world. He serves a greater purpose through sharing the infectious spirit he has inside of him with listeners around the world. Credits to his name reach from steamy studios in Nashville all the way to world tours with folks like Victor Wooten, Marcus Miller, Stanley Clarke, Jeff Coffin, Spyro Gyra, and Earth, Wind and Fire. Derico is open and resourceful in all areas of performance. He is more than enthusiastic to lead others through his experiences and knowledge to fulfill his intention to bring joy to others through his art.

HIS STORY

You have to have the same skills to play music that you do to survive life. It's just like growing up in a way. You can teach kids how to live, but then they have to depart from you and develop their own way of thinking and acting. They start to form an opinion and learn how to make it in the world. The same goes for jazz or music in general . . . you have to strive for your own voice. I have a strong belief in God, and I know he gave me the ability to play music; however, I had to grow up and learn how to use it. Everybody's born with a natural ability at something . . . could be music or fixing cars. Whatever it is, that natural ability is only going to take you so far. Then, you have to start nurturing that gift so that you can contribute to the art form. This is what I call developing your own style or voice. Now, you have to go out and start interacting with others. I love playing music. It's my calling.

Walt Weiskopf
SAXOPHONIST, COMPOSER, EDUCATOR

HOME BASE
www.waltweiskopf.com

GOT MUSIC?
Day In Night Out, Walt Weiskopf
Octet, Criss Cross Jazz, 2008

"This music is my religion."

BACKGROUND AND SOUND

Since the age of twenty-one, saxophonist Walt Weiskopf has made a lasting mark as a performer, arranger, composer, and sideman throughout the international jazz arena. Walt is considered to be one of the best unknown musicians in the modern scene. And although listeners may not readily recognize his name, his sound is renowned and instantly distinguished as one heard on countless albums and in commercial media. He has performed with Steely Dan, Frank Sinatra, and Steve Smith's Jazz Legacy, among many others. His octet and smaller groups have been signed by the Criss Cross label and have received serious accolades from critics. Walt has been the recipient of several performance grants through the National Endowment for the Arts and a commissioning grant through Chamber Music America. His career is a testament to the fact that although you may not have heard of someone, it doesn't mean that they're insignificant in their contributions to the culture at large.

HIS STORY

When I first had the idea of being a jazz musician I didn't even know what it meant to be one. Now, this music is my religion. It's one of the things I care about most in this life, as it's been my constant companion, a family member. Since I can remember, I've always felt more comfortable playing rather than talking, as there are personal aspects of my life that give me reason to play. If artists in general were always so happy-go-lucky, I don't think we'd have anything to say when we play. My music is who I am and what I choose to express about my life. I know it's not necessarily going to be a bowl of cherries. But I do know that the more you invest in it, the more you'll get out of it. Unlike sports, this music is something that keeps going in your life. I have to do more of what I've done, and I'm not sure how much more there is to do. As artists though, our creative arc rises and falls. It's very rare for us to sustain that curve throughout our lives. This is why I'm constantly looking for the next chance to play. I get a bang out of it; it's the way I choose to communicate. There's no turning back now. At a certain point we all just have to play the hand we're dealt and stay happy and make the best of what we have.

Dan Weiss

DRUMMER, TABLA PLAYER, COMPOSER, EDUCATOR

HOME BASE
www.danweiss.net

GOT MUSIC?
Now Yes When, David Weiss Trio, Toap, 2006

"Music is my bottom line."

BACKGROUND AND SOUND

It has been said that if Dan Weiss is going to be on the gig or in the session, that musicians will painstakingly write their music around his voice. Dan Weiss is a man of many surprises. There is not a single technique or beat that speaks of cliché. He is influenced by many experiences beyond music and the world of jazz, and there's an inner tranquility to his voice that takes on many forms while he plays. He is a master at the tabla and other world music devices, and he has the right words to convey what the role of a drummer truly is in this art. He has played with myriad musicians who sit at the top of their game in all fields of music, including metal. This renaissance approach to his career has brought about a following and immense respect from all in the field.

HIS STORY

My biggest influence in jazz would have to be John Coltrane. His music was always evolving, and he was always pushing himself and his music further.

This was a good model for me to follow. Nikhil Banerjee was a sitarist from India. His musical legacy and his musical work ethic along with his total his devotion to music has been a very profound influence on me as well. I've got so many influences, thousands maybe. Through music I've been taught self-awareness, compassion, discipline, and how to be grateful for everyday things. Music is my bottom line. I no longer even see a division between cultures, and I have learned how to take away fragmentations of ideas or thoughts at times because of music's power.

There are higher places one can go when immersed in music. I keep working hard at going deeper in the sound. I try to let music lift me up, as well as others. This is an attribute that I have learned from many people, but most importantly from my guru, Pandit Samir Chatterjee. I know a lot of musicians get frustrated, but it's important to persevere and always keep reaching for that higher level. If you have an openness and willingness, the musical path can become clearer. I will bring this openness and willingness to whatever musical situation I am involved in. I'm always going to try to be open to whatever happens and go wherever the music wants to go. If I'm going to be a successful musician, it has nothing to do with exposure or money or the number of gigs I have. It has everything to do with working hard every day and pushing forward so I can do the best I can for myself and for other states of mind. This is what success means to me. We all have to figure out at some point what it is that we want out of music. That is part of the pursuit.

David Weiss

TRUMPETER, COMPOSER, PRODUCER

HOME BASE
www.davidweissmusic.com

GOT MUSIC?
The Mirror, David Weiss, Fresh Sound/New Talent, 2005

"Although some have tried to avoid having their music labeled as jazz or themselves as jazz musicians because of the connotations those labels had, I find myself defiantly saying I am a jazz musician."

BACKGROUND AND SOUND

Holding up a wall of tradition through his own definition of jazz, David Weiss has found a way to not only expand but also cultivate and breed new hybrids of the seeds that fall from the tree. Greats such as Freddie Hubbard, Charles Tolliver, and Frank Foster used his talents on their bandstands. Weiss has also toured internationally as the leader of several original groups, such as Point of Departure and the Cookers. Weiss demonstrates on a regular basis a keen and solid knack for taking what was once tired and old and making it new and exciting through his compositions. This has helped him stand over and above the players' and listeners' favorites. Anyone who is interested in keeping the tradition of jazz viable and fresh will surely enjoy David Weiss and his artistic journey.

HIS STORY

It's been such a long journey to find my way to jazz, more specifically the style of jazz I play, that I have to assume that jazz is the ultimate challenge to me as a musician and composer. The first records I bought in junior high school were by groups like Led Zeppelin, Aerosmith, and Black Sabbath. I grew up in Queens, New York, and that was the music of my neighborhood. From those records I moved on to more progressive rock like King Crimson and Gentle Giant, and from there I moved on to European avant-rock, then fusion, and then to free jazz, then finally to where I am today. It's where my ears and mind sent me, and I got there because I loved music and was curious to discover new things. It's this love of music and my diverse influences that have driven me to be the best possible musician I can be. The great variety of music I've played has also shaped my vision as a bandleader. There's no other feeling like when your band gets to that place you've been striving for. There's a higher plane where the magic happens, and this sometimes sends shivers up my spine.

I've never quite defined jazz because it's a combination of elements that I can't entirely put my finger on or should; although lately I've felt more of a need to decide what it's not. I listened to the next batch of supposed great artists that have been hyped to death and have found myself starting to get a little defensive. Maybe jazz needs to be defined a little more these days. The good thing is that jazz is open-ended and can have all sorts of elements to it, but the flip side is that these days, a lot of it seems to get too far removed from anything resembling jazz. I'm hearing a lot of music lately that's being sold as jazz, but I don't hear anything in it that I would consider jazz, not even in the broadest sense. I'm not sure why they would even want it to be considered jazz. I have to ask, why did jazz have to inherit this? It's a weird place for it to go, I suppose, just to get some hype and sell some CDs. I find myself taking somewhat of a purist stance because of this, and this is a place I never thought I'd be, as it's not how I approach my music. I don't have a problem with bringing elements from other types of music into jazz, but when the music becomes only about those other elements, then why is it still considered jazz? I've listened to and played pretty much everything at one point or another, and I bring those experiences into the music I create. Although some have tried to avoid having their music labeled as jazz or themselves as jazz musicians because of the connotations those labels had, I find myself defiantly saying I am a jazz musician. This is great music, and I should be proud of it, and I don't think this label should have any implied limitations or confinement to it anymore.

Paul Wertico

{LIVING LEGEND}

PERCUSSIONIST, COMPOSER, PRODUCER, EDUCATOR

HOME BASE
www.paulwertico.com

GOT MUSIC?
Impressions of a City, Paul Wertico's Mid-West/Mid-East Alliance, Chicago Sessions Ltd., 2009

"A large part of the beauty of doing this is the journey itself."

BACKGROUND AND SOUND

Seven-time Grammy Award winner Paul Wertico has been throwing down the pulse of life behind jazz legends and as a leader of his own group for more than forty years. His extensive list of credits includes an eighteen-year stint recording, touring, and performing with the Pat Metheny Group and a seven-year gig with the eastern European rock band SBB. Mingling his expertise with a boundless and tireless imagination, Paul is able to draw fully realized pictures of the music around him through the set. Offstage, he is chiseling the features and ethics of a successful experience and career into the minds of the next few generations. As the head of jazz studies at Chicago's Roosevelt University and an avid clinician and workshop leader, he has authored numerous books and instructional media to spread his word. His on-edge approach to the body of work he has yet to do promises an even greater look into his highly inspired and open-ended expressions through rhythm.

HIS STORY

Some major objectives of this music are to realize and accept who you are at any given point, to learn how to truly express yourself by continually striving for excellence and artistic growth by seriously studying your instrument, and then to share what you find with others. A large part of the beauty of doing this is the journey itself. So many people in this culture always seem to want to arrive "there" immediately, without fully understanding and appreciating the process of actually getting "there." A lot of things nowadays are about instant gratification and quick fixes, and that is not what jazz is about at all. As an artist, you have to have patience and dedication to hang in there. I look at my personal journey through my art and use it as a gauge for my life.

Great musicians like Art Blakey, Elvin Jones, and Roy Haynes are a part of this journey and have influenced the way I play. They also continue to be influences, as I continually get a deeper appreciation of their musical contributions, and this is what's so beautiful, this process of constant growth and understanding that never finishes and thus can never become boring. Plus, if you realize and accept the fact that along the way there are always going to be "mistakes" and bumps in the road, then you can learn and grow from those things, too. Just make sure to never give up. The older I get, the better it is. Nowadays, I just want to inspire people to do similar things with their lives. As a teacher, I always want my students to "find themselves" through their instrument. I also don't want them to be a carbon copy of me, since everybody's strengths, weaknesses, goals, and dreams are different. I want them to find their own voice. I give them my guidance and share my experience and let them run with those things as they wish. I want my students to know how good it feels to be "alive" while living an artistic life.

I remember an extraordinary thing that happened once when I was playing with the Pat Metheny Group in Italy. At the time, there were a lot of kidnappings going on in that country. A young man came to one of our shows and he told us about how for two years he was held for ransom in a cave and didn't know if he was going to survive. He said that what got him through that unimaginable ordeal was thinking about our music. It's amazing to think that the music we make can have that powerful of an effect on people's lives. When you're playing live, or in the studio, you have no real idea of whom you're affecting, or whom you'll affect in the future. But, unlike the people that are building bombs, killing, stealing, and doing of other types of horrible things that destroy others, what musicians attempt to do is to inspire and lift the human spirit. It's a valiant cause. Most musicians I know are smart, and often brilliant, hardworking people, and they just want the chance to honestly share their talent with others and give something back to society. And although it's a shame the generally pop-oriented mass media and the non–artistically friendly economic structure make doing that so difficult, in many ways that helps make us stronger, too. If this was easy, anybody could do it.

I turned fifty-six this year, and I still feel like a kid. This music has kept me young, in shape, and sharp. I'm doing what I've always wanted to do. Plus, in life, we're always going to find ourselves in new and unfamiliar circumstances. As jazz musicians, I feel that we often adapt much better to different situations than most average folks that are used to a certain type of "stability" in their lives. By taking an improvisational "jazz attitude" to life in general, a person can learn how to actually embrace the unknown and make something out of nothing. And even though change can be frightening to a lot of people, musicians learn to deal with things as they come. Whenever I perform my music, I liken the experience to having a full tank of gas in my car, and even though I'm never quite sure where I'm going to be headed on any given night, I'm confident I can take the audience, the other musicians, and myself for an interesting, and hopefully enjoyable, musical ride, and I'll get all of us back safely. Every day is a new experience, and as artists and educators we're doing what we can do to add some beauty and substance to the world. I'm extremely proud to be a musician!

Kirk Whalum

SAXOPHONIST, COMPOSER, EDUCATOR

HOME BASE
www.kirkwhalum.com

GOT MUSIC?
Ultimate Kirk Whalum, Kirk
Whalum, Mosaic Records, 2007

"By overanalyzing this living, breathing thing called jazz, we risk doing violence to the spirit of it."

BACKGROUND AND SOUND

Emphasizing the spirit, essence, and grace that jazz can be, saxophonist Kirk Whalum has not only promised but delivered time and again a buffet of provocative material, sounds, and thoughtful works of art. For years in the beginning of his career, he toured and performed with greats such as Bob James, Whitney Houston, Quincy Jones, Al Jarreau, Nancy Wilson, Barbra Streisand, and more. Branching off into his own creative space, he harnessed what he loved about music the most and brought it to the forefront of everything he did. This was a soulful and sincere craft, and listeners around the world responded. Today Kirk has many Grammy nominations and various other awards and merits to his name. But if you ask him, he'll say that he gets the biggest reward from using his music to help others. As a true philanthropist, he has gone on to facilitate many programs that help children in need or young musicians looking for a guiding light for their path. Driven by a spirit that's largely untapped and much needed in the music community, Kirk Whalum's potent message speaks volumes through his powerful music.

HIS STORY

We have to harness this technology in order to have our story be seen and heard. In order to compete with programs such as *American Idol*, we have to tell it in a very compelling way, and this is a huge undertaking, but I'm hopeful. In spite of this culture, I think these programs are working to our benefit. They're creating a void in the culture, leaving young consumers (as well as older consumers who may be young in technology) wanting more.

They need more substance in order to be discerners of the superfluous. Once they are able to discern the substance from the emptiness, they'll see that many of these types of things really don't speak to them as altruistically.

There's also hope in groups, like Dave Matthews, who can captivate an audience made up of a demographic that covers everyone from the age of fifteen to sixty-five. My buddy Jeff Coffin is up there on stage with them blowing like Sonny Rollins. He is out there playing jazz, and not just any jazz—this is an avant-garde player who's played with lots of folks, including Béla Fleck. Then we have a stadium of thousands and thousands of people and they're all jamming to improvised music. This is an example of what's at the end of the rainbow for us, but to get to that pot we have to harness this technology and use it so we can captivate imaginations again. We want them to be able to say they didn't know it existed, but they need it now. This is a whole generation that's primarily written off an entire genre of music by saying they don't like it. We have to get them to pay attention.

By overanalyzing this living, breathing thing called jazz, we risk doing violence to the spirit of it. We tend to think we're doing someone a favor by explaining it, but really we risk killing it. As artists we're compelled to elevate this music to the academic environments because we know it deserves to be there as well as the premiere *legitimate* concert halls. But we have to be careful. There's an organic element and infrastructure to this music that relates it to God. He's the owner, proprietor, and creator of this art form, and we dare not ignore this connection by overanalyzing it in an academic setting. This is when the light will go out, and this is not a small thing. It's up to us to be both creative and fearless so the story gets told.

Matt Wilson
DRUMMER, COMPOSER, EDUCATOR

HOME BASE
www.mattwilsonjazz.com

GOT MUSIC?
The Scenic Route, Matt Wilson, Palmetto, 2007

"We should all take the time to realize and celebrate the creativity around us."

BACKGROUND AND SOUND

Although he is considered to be one of the more serious drummers alive today, Matt Wilson is one artist who finds the humor throughout every phase of his life. Being hyper and easily excitable in any other profession would label him as outcast material. But these characteristics can lead others to deem you a brilliant talent if you play the drums. His offbeat humor and encouraging positivism are just two devices Matt has used to help him weather the ups and downs of the business. As a leader he has hauled hot players like Gary Versace, Terell Stafford, and Martin Wind onto stages throughout the country. His groups continually receive rave reviews for live performances and recordings because of their overtly flared versions of jazz. This panache for entertaining and taking art to an accessible level comes from greats who mentored him, including Dewey Redman. Other highlights of his lengthy résumé include working with Jane Ira Bloom, Lee Konitz, Ted Nash, Ted Rosenthal, and more. Matt's mind is one of those turbocharged forces running with a full tank down the superhighway of the creative life. The jazz world should be utterly thankful to have this personality among them as he brings the humor out of any absurdity that comes his way.

HIS STORY

Jazz has taught me to appreciate and accept not really knowing what it is. I'm still incredibly mystified that musicians can gather and allow new music to emerge before our very eyes and ears. Even though I do this all the time, it still amazes me. We should all take the time to realize and celebrate the creativity around us. I love that I haven't even gotten to the surface of what to do with my instrument. This liberation lets me approach music in a way that dispels judgment and allows vulnerability. These elements welcome honest music that is alive in the moment.

When I play with younger generations, I find purpose in their energy and approach, and I want to experience it. They also give me someone to tell the stories I have collected to. I come from a family of storytellers and collectors. We would sit around the table and listen to relatives tell tall tales about events and people. Although we often heard the stories a million times, it was really important to hear. I believe this is really suffering in jazz. To the younger artists, the "art of the hang" isn't as important as it should be.

I want to say to them that I expect more, that they have to be around people who've done this before them. This is how we learn to deal with others, and hearing these stories teach us in so many ways. Older musicians have helped me, and they sometimes didn't have anything to say to me; it was just enough to be around them and have them as friends. Life is a constant learning experience, and I cherish these relationships with folks who are and were characters of the music, not just players. I am doing my best to encourage the hang because I love to sit around and visit and *laugh*!

Remember that you're there for the unexpected moment—we all are—and for no other reason. There's an honest energy that cycles if you invite listeners to be a part of the music. You can play anything and make them feel welcome in the sound. This is when they'll hear something that may sound in them. The technical aspect of music is the least of my worries. I'm there to play with people totally in the present and for that moment. This is why I feel connected to people from the bandstand, both on and off. We get to know each other and talk about everything, maybe even argue some, but we always create bonds that are strong, like a family. What we learn about being a person through this music is very much that you have to be flexible, confident in what we say and do and how we approach it. Great musicians allow their fellow musicians to go places and discover themselves in the music. I avoid trying to control music and having a concept of how it should go; I just try and get out of the way and allow what's supposed to happen to happen. This is when it is genuine, gratifying, and really fun!

Phil Woods

SAXOPHONIST, COMPOSER, PRODUCER, NEA JAZZ MASTER

HOME BASE
www.philwoods.com

GOT MUSIC?
The Children's Suite, Phil Woods,
Jazzed Media, 2009

"Jazz is an American invention that defines our country better than anything else."

BACKGROUND AND SOUND

National Endowment for the Arts Jazz Master Phil Woods is well known in not only the jazz arena but also many other commercial areas, including pop, country, television, radio, and film. Credits for his performances throughout his lifetime are extensive and impressive. Phil is a philanthropist at heart and is an active participant in many local and national groups that support and uphold the importance of the arts within communities. He is the founder and advisory board member of the Delaware Water Gap Celebration of the Arts and on the board of directors for the Al Cohn Memorial Jazz Collection at East Stroudsburg University. His generous nature and kindhearted work have come through in every aspect of his career. Recognized as one of the more important figures in jazz saxophone and doubling, composition, and education, Phil Woods has spent most of his life preparing to be cast for his role as a mentor for artists everywhere.

HIS STORY

Jazz is an American invention that defines our country better than anything else. It embraces all other cultures and is a mélange of diversity. It's about loving each other and giving space to each other to express oneself. But, it's the universality of this language that's the most important thing. You don't have to know the language I speak to play; you can just make up your own language immediately and get to know the other person speaking to you by how they handle themselves. As for the situation I'm in, I think my life has gone by fast. It does this if you're getting paid to do what you love. Music is truly for those who have no choice. I was never dissuaded from it.

It's fire in the belly and commitment to playing art that has to take over you. We have to all be sure of our dreams and very, very, very strong, and this fire must burn forever. It's not about a bottom line or corporation; it's about the pursuit of a dream no matter what it entails. If you don't like the idea of bringing joy to any note you play, then you're in the wrong business. A note doesn't care what style you play; it just wants to be given life, and you have to do that regardless of the style. I've been playing for well over sixty years and I still have an awful lot to learn. Even if you're the type that gets famous at the age of twenty-five, you still have to learn that this is a journey and voyage. It's about making music every day and learning every day. I still haven't met anyone who knows everything. This is a full-time commitment, and you have to be prepared for the sacrifice that comes with it. It's never cut and dry. I'm just fortunate. I may not be getting any better, but I'm certainly not getting any worse. I don't take myself that seriously. I was doing a gig once, and a young sax player came backstage. He stopped and said to me, "you're that guy on the Billy Joel record . . . have you done anything on your own?" Ha! I keep this on my humble wall every day. I'm truly blessed to do this.

Eli Yamin

PIANIST, EDUCATOR, COMPOSER

HOME BASE
www.eliyamin.com

GOT MUSIC?
You Can't Buy Swing, Eli Yamin,
Yamin Music, 2008

"Music really does bring people together and save lives"

BACKGROUND AND SOUND

Eli Yamin has one of the most positive attitudes in music. He has established himself as a forthright and visible voice in jazz education. As the artistic director of the Jazz Drama Program and Middle School Jazz Academy through Jazz at Lincoln Center, he is breaking ground for kids everywhere. His jazz musicals for children have been performed for thousands of kids around the world. He has also performed with notables Kate McGarry, Mercedes Ellington, and Wynton Marsalis. His revelation as an artist and educator has yielded a fresh body of work among the tired wasteland of materials available for children today. Combine this with a confidant and distinct strut throughout his compositions and it becomes clear why he is in such great demand on all fronts.

HIS STORY

Someone once told me that in India, people study music, not so much to have a career, but to learn more about themselves. This has dawned on me many times through my journey in music. When I was in high school, the arts were such a savior for me. My school day started at two-thirty in the afternoon, when school officially ended and I got to participate in band, radio, choir, and theater. These experiences throughout my life were what really touched my spirit. I often felt frustrated and uncomfortable in the rest of the school day. This taught me that being an artist is valid. It's important and valuable. Now I go around as an arts advocate saying that the arts are not a frill; they're something that's really necessary. This isn't rhetoric. I've experienced how the arts save people's lives. You have kids who don't talk in class and you put some jazz or blues on and suddenly they're singing. This transforms their ability to express themselves the rest of the day. This isn't a dream. Music really does bring people together and save lives. It's totally necessary for our survival, and there's something about jazz that is perfect for this. Perhaps because it is born out of music that helped African Americans survive slavery. I've seen its healing power over and over again all over the world so many times I have to believe how powerful music can be and believe in my path through music. It's this path, which at the outset seemed like an unusual one, that's really my true path, and I'm sticking with it and following it the rest of my days.

Raya Yarbrough
VOCALIST, COMPOSER, LYRICIST

HOME BASE
www.rayayarbrough.com

GOT MUSIC?
Raya Yarbrough, Raya Yarbrough,
Telarc, 2008

"Jazz is just a sponge for other music."

BACKGROUND AND SOUND

Award-winning vocalist Raya Yarbrough's voice is supple and gorgeously undefined in its boundaries. There's a certain West Coast tranquility that comes out of an underlying strength. She has won esteemed awards, such as the Betty Carter Jazz Ahead Composition Program as well as the Quincy Jones Award and Herb Alpert Scholarship at the University of Southern California's Thornton School of Music. There's an inherent and organic talent that stems from deep within her voice and a lifetime of being submerged in this music's soil. Her maturity is well beyond her years, and the fortitude she demonstrates is respectable and honest.

HER STORY

My house was musical when I was growing up. I remember hearing a Brazilian guitar player and Scott Joplin records. It's coagulated weirdly in my head, and everything since has been a progeny of that. My father was a stay-at-home parent who was his own traveling soundtrack. We listened to music constantly in order to feed ourselves. He took me to the clubs, even when I was seven years old, on Friday and Saturday, even the ones I was way too young to be in. He put me on stage right away and I began to sing. I had five tunes, and I didn't even know they were grown-up songs. I sang them, liked them, and wanted to be Jessica Rabbit. I learned how to communicate with an audience and perform. But people were nicer to me then. I think it was because you didn't see many seven-year-olds on stage. After I was through singing my father would sit me in the front row and hand me a screwdriver—not the drink, an actual screwdriver—and say, you know where to stick this if anyone bothers you. So that's where I started.

I didn't get to have the childhood I wanted until later, and I think it's only now that I'm beginning to get an inkling of who I was then and who I am now.

What I do now comes from a place outside this spectrum. I walk a fine line between jazz and other flavors I'm into. It's been a blessing artistically to straddle this broad line. Jazz is just a sponge for other music. Everyone who's immigrated to America has to put their stamp on it. Jazz has enough of a path now we know where it started and where it's gone and its phases, et cetera. Where jazz is, though, is without boundaries. The more tightly we bind it, the less it can breathe and live. It has to have that spirit of experience alongside the willingness to pull in elements of different genres and musical traditions from all over the world. Jazz throws things together with some new reckless abandon. Mutations of it bring about interesting harmonies and melodies that are lyrical and challenging.

When people hear me and see me I want them to feel that I can make something beautiful out of life's comedies and tragedies. I want to give my listeners bookmarks that capture the importance of what's going on today. Without music we can't own things that would be too difficult to deal with otherwise. I can never write about the wholeness of a situation, but it helps me own a little bit of that experience. Instead of feeling it's too big to handle, I'm better. Everyone deals with these things. We have to put it all into perspective and get lifted for a bit. But in order to find strength in our vulnerabilities we have to drop them at the end of the day so we can see that our hands are free. When you give in to the stuff that sucks and makes you feel vulnerable, it's only then that you can own it and feel free and justified in their saneness. My role is to empower this in some way. If you're empowered in your own experience, no matter how it came about, then you'll get what you want and understand yourself.

Brandee Younger

HARPIST, COMPOSER, EDUCATOR

HOME BASE
www.brandeeyounger.com

GOT MUSIC?
Of Song, Marcus Strickland,
Strick Muzik, 2009

"It's important to live a disciplined life with a healthy dose of faith."

BACKGROUND AND SOUND

Rarely is there such beauty displayed in music as when a jazz harpist enters the picture. Influences like Alice Coltrane and Dorothy Ashby may have given Brandee Younger a light for her current path, but she has also carved her own niche as the go-to gal for not only jazz but also R&B, hip-hop, and pop. Despite the sheer difficulty of the instrument, her ability makes it sound seemingly effortless. Ravi Coltrane, Charlie Haden, and Kenny Garrett not only have taken notice but have called upon her to contribute to  their own works. Younger is also an in-demand educator throughout the northeast. Her intuitive rhythm and insatiable drive coupled with grace and style are but complements to the often unforgivable and male-dominated scene of modern jazz.

HER STORY

When I began studying harp I was only given classical music, and at the time I couldn't really relate to it. Throughout my studies I did what I had to do to advance but didn't find it fulfilling. One day while in high school my father came home with the CD *Priceless Jazz* by Alice Coltrane. The first track on it was "Blue Nile." I don't even think I went to track two before I broke the disk from overplaying it. I said, "Wow, I want to do that."

It wasn't until years later when I was in graduate school that things began to come together for me.

The great Alice Coltrane passed away in January 2007. Four months later Ravi Coltrane called me to play her memorial at Saint John the Divine here in New York. During the rehearsal, I took a moment to look around the cathedral at many of the living artists who had worked with and were so heavily influenced by the Coltranes. It was that night that I finally felt comfortable, like I had a place.

Harpists like Dorothy Ashby have set an example for me to follow as well. She wasn't the very first jazz harpist but possibly the most influential. Her discography was extraordinary. She played with musicians like Roy Haynes, Freddie Hubbard, Jimmy Cobb, Art Taylor, and Frank Wess. To have her and Alice Coltrane as my examples is a huge source of motivation for me. Just when I get to the point of complete frustration I pull out one of their records and they remind me that it's very possible to do this. If it weren't for them, I'm not sure I would be doing this now. Yet with every step I take I'm creating a path that represents me.

Oh, and as a self-employed musician, you know, no one is going to call you to wake you up every morning to go out and find work . . . you have to get up and create work for yourself. This music isn't a secretarial nine-to-five, and to make a good living takes a tremendous amount of self-discipline. It's important to live a disciplined life with a healthy dose of faith.

I've created this world around me with my instrument. I'm a woman, an African American in what is dominantly a white community of classical harpists, yet I was raised around jazz, hip-hop, funk, and R&B, and that is what I am. I guess I'm part street, part book, and part chic. This music is more than a means of expression, but it's God's purpose for me. I'm inspired every morning. There's no better feeling than to know God's will at such an early age and to have the means to carry it out. It's an obligation I'm thankful to fulfill.

Miguel Zenón
SAXOPHONIST, COMPOSER

HOME BASE
www.miguelzenon.com

GOT MUSIC?
Jíbaro, Miguel Zenón, Marsalis Music, 2005

"It's the energy and interaction from an audience that makes this all worthwhile."

BACKGROUND AND SOUND

Award-winning composer and saxophonist Miguel Zenón is originally from San Juan, Puerto Rico. Miguel has provided confirmation for many who feel the need to have proof that there's new talent meticulously working to revive the spirit of jazz. Miguel is a part of the San Francisco Jazz Collective and has been awarded several commissions and fellowships, including the coveted MacArthur Grant, which is also known as the Genius Grant. Many artists, including David Sanchez, Charlie Haden, and Steve Coleman, recognized the potential in him early on and to this day continue to push Miguel in new directions so that he may become one of the very best players in the present day.

HIS STORY

I moved to the States from Puerto Rico when I was nineteen. I was already a musician then. For a long time I only thought about music as a hobby, and I honestly never thought it would be an essential part of my life. But then ... it took over. Being a musician became everything to me. By the time I turned sixteen or seventeen I was completely immersed in it, especially once I discovered jazz. Charlie Parker, Miles, and Coltrane had a profound effect on me when I listened to them. But there were also a lot of latino musicians I could identify with, including Paquito D'Rivera, Arturo Sandoval, and Danilo Perez. They all were purely jazz players but had totally different backgrounds, and this inspired me. I guess people like this always stay with you. Yet my biggest inspiration today is when I see my peers and young people making great music. I'm motivated to get better when I see them push themselves to do creatively.

Unfortunately, there aren't many places for musicians to get the opportunity to grow like they should. Most states, if they have a big city, will only have three to five clubs. How will we grow as artists and others know to listen to us if we don't have venues that allow this kind of exposure? It seems that for a while people didn't see jazz as a serious form of music. To them it was like something you hung out to dry or some kind of lifestyle instead of art. But to me, music is so essential in my life, I can't imagine thinking about it in any other way. My life has fallen into place, and I've been able to hold regular gigs as a player. Of course I deal with the challenge of staying creative enough to move forward, but I think we all do from time to time. It's easy to get stuck when you find one thing that works. I just have to keep moving forward and challenge myself daily, even if that means doing what I do without regard for what others have to say about me. Of course I want others to like my music, but I try not to think about it. If what I do cuts through to people, then good. After all, it's the energy and interaction from an audience that makes this all worthwhile. But I have to make this music as personal as possible so that same audience will know it's me. I just hope to have this kind of support so I can go on playing forever.

Sonny Rollins
LAST WORDS

I learned jazz as a little boy. My guess is that I was about two or three years old when I heard people like Fats Waller and jazz bands on the radio. They'd be broadcast from the Apollo Theater and around the country with other guys, but it was basically Fats I listened to. He was also from Harlem. I was born there, and I gleaned a lot from there. It was in the air somehow. There was so much jazz in that community it rubbed off on me. That's how I became attracted to jazz. Over time I kept at it and got involved with mentors. When I realized I wanted to play sax, Louis Jordan became my idol. He had a popular rhythm and blues band at the time, and although I used other shoulders to stand on to learn, Fats and Louis were the ones who introduced me to the sound of jazz. The people I came up around didn't have the contrast in life we have today. They lived in a very negative world and had to make their music despite that negativity. Hopefully things are better today, but jazz has always been a sort of stepchild. Musicians have had to steel themselves against the indignities I'm sure they get by playing jazz.

But we all got through it. The next generations, they'll get through it too. It's a part of life. We all have personal battles, these everyday little battles. This is what makes the difference between life and death. Whatever it is, a person should have the inner strength to overcome anything that's out in the world. Jazz musicians have been suffering for a long time, and life is about suffering, so there's a correlation there. To me, music is like a neutral force. It has nothing to do with the style of music. This is where the individual comes in. If you're trying to be a certain kind of person, the music should express that and they should go together, they have to go together. I've had a sense of wanting to be positive in my approach to life despite this.

I've played everywhere over the years, and a long time ago I decided jazz should leave the confines of clubs. I made a career decision some years ago to not play in clubs anymore and only do concerts. Plus, I thought maybe jazz would be more appreciated and accepted by the American public if it was seen more in concert halls than nightclub atmospheres. Regardless, a lot of people still look down on jazz, although not as much as before. The American people have become much more educated about jazz, making it possible to have jazz in concert halls and universities. There's more respect for it as an art form. It's native born, and there's always a tendency to not appreciate things that are right in front of you. But we all need hope that it's changing, for our biggest challenge in life is life. The rest of life, or since I'm still alive, I have to work at and survive out here in that negative world. It's about staying positive, taking care of my health, eating right, and having a moral center. Trying to live like that is a challenge because you're going up against forces that are out there.

However, I'd like to see people feel more optimistic so young musicians can come along and feel they have a platform. Be encouraging. They should feel optimism around them.

It's good to be encouraged and to know your music means something. Maybe, when people listen to me—at least I've been told this by my fans— what I play gets them through the drudgery of their everyday life. This is wonderful and helps me realize I'm not playing for my own edification, as in vanity. This is important to me. They say it's a positive affirmation and hopefully something not negative in a very negative world. At least some people do. I'd like that to be more, of course. I'd like to reach more with the jazz message of love, affirmation, and goodwill. I'd like to be the person who spreads that message, but I can only take credit for improving upon my gift as I'm woefully inefficient in some things. Of course, I tried to develop it. What I try in my everyday writing, practicing, is endless. I haven't felt I've accomplished . . . well, I'm sure I've accomplished something, but I don't feel I've established my musical legacy yet. That's why I practice and I'm still in the middle of it.

I haven't done what I was put here to do.

I'm still improving myself to be a better and more realized person.

I just want to do more, and hopefully with jazz I can do a little more to affect the world, but I realize I'm not going to turn the tides. It's extremely difficult to get more converts to jazz. But as far as doing something with the human condition by way of jazz, it's a losing proposition. So I have to do more. I don't think I've done everything I can do.

I'm practicing and hearing music in my mind that I want to bring out, and if it does any worldwide good, great. My life is consumed by this. All I can hope for is that somebody will always get something out of my music and that it's never just for myself, otherwise what's the point? If it's for yourself then it hasn't served or had a purpose. This purpose is my reason for living. I'm just trying to be a better person. It's what we all have to do as long as we're alive.

APPENDIX A

Got Jazz?

I encourage you to visit our website at www.newfaceofjazz.com for a revolving resource of jazz organizations, live music venues, artists websites, and other educational and supportive resources.

Today, jazz is largely held in place through the artists and significant contributions of communities around the world. Below is a sampling of these contributors from record labels to nonprofits to jazz cruises. Each and every person involved on this side of the business has one goal: to see jazz continue on as a living, breathing art form.

EARSHOT JAZZ SOCIETY

www.earshotjazz.com
General Information: jazz@earshot.org
Jazz Calendar: jazzcalendar@earshot.org

Founded in 1984, the Earshot Jazz Society is one of the most prominent jazz nonprofit music, arts, and service organizations in the United States. Earshot ensures community involvement with its diverse selection of programs and opportunities offered for the aficionado to elementary kids who are just learning how to swing.

JAZZ CRUISES LLC

www.thejazzcruise.com

A no-nonsense luxury cruise line offering opportunities to listen to music by and mingle with artists like Herbie Hancock, James Moody, Roy Hargrove, Eddie Higgins, Clark Terry, Regina Carter, Wycliffe Gordon, and Arturo Sandoval.

THELONIOUS MONK INSTITUTE OF JAZZ

www.monkinstitute.org, www.jazzinamerica.org

The Thelonious Monk Institute is your place for all things innovative and new in jazz education. With countless Internet curriculums, videos, and other resources to satisfy the needs of every level of student or teacher, they are able to present this music in a light that is easily understood and obtainable by even the most foreign ears.

SMITHSONIAN JAZZ

www.smithsonianjazz.org

The Smithsonian jazz site is a great place for everything jazz. You will find an endless support system, a log of jazz societies around the world, and various other educational resources, not to mention a huge wealth of facts and historical research on our national treasure.

ALL ABOUT JAZZ

www.allaboutjazz.com

All About Jazz remains one of the best sites for interviews, articles, and CD reviews, and also serves as a guide to the scene throughout the country.

APPENDIX B

Reading List

Would you like to read more great books or publications on jazz? Check out the following works:

Cook, Richard and Brian Morton. *The Penguin Guide to Jazz Recordings*. 9th ed. New York: Penguin, 2008.

Cook, Richard. *Richard Cook's Jazz Encyclopedia*. New York: Penguin, 2006.

Gioia, Ted. *The History of Jazz*. New York: Oxford University Press, 1998.

Griffith, Farah Jasmine, and Salim Washington. *Clawing at the Limits of Cool: Miles Davis and John Coltrane and the Greatest Jazz Collaboration Ever*. New York: St. Martin's Press, 2008.

Hentoff, Nat, and Nat Shapiro. *Hear Me Talkin' to Ya: The Story of Jazz as Told by the Men Who Made It*. New York: Dover Publications, 1966.

Koenigswarter, Panonica de, Nadine de Koenigswarter, and Gary Giddins. *Three Wishes: An Intimate Look at Jazz Greats*. New York: Abrams Image, 2008.

Ratliff, Ben. *The Jazz Ear: Conversations over Music*. New York: Times Books, 2009.

Shipton, Alyn. *New History of Jazz*. London: Continuum, 2008.

Taylor, Arthur. *Notes and Tones: Musician-to-Musician Interviews*. New York: Da Capo Press, 1993.

Wilmer, Valerie. *As Serious as Your Life: The Story of New Jazz*. London: Serpent's Tail, 2000.

More Schools of Thought

The schools listed here are the most notable schools for jazz around the country. They offer bachelor's and, to a limited extent, master's and doctoral degrees in jazz studies. All of them offer scholarships based on need and ability, and all of them have world-class musicians sitting at their helm, waiting to pass their knowledge to you. Ready to become a member of the house of swing?

CALIFORNIA
California State University, Fullerton
www.fullerton.edu/ARTS
musicinfo@fullerton.edu

University of Southern California, Thornton School of Music
www.usc.edu/schools/music
uscmusic@usc.edu

COLORADO
University of Colorado, Boulder
www.colorado.edu/music/departments/jazz
davisj@colorado.edu

University of Denver: Lamont School of Music
www.du.edu/ahss/schools/lamont/index.html

University of Northern Colorado
www.arts.unco.edu/uncjazz
jazzstudies@arts.unco.edu

FLORIDA
Florida State University College of Music
www.fsu.edu/~music/jazz-studies.htm

University of Miami, Phillip and Patricia Frost School of Music
www.music.miami.edu

University of North Florida
www.unf.edu/coas/music/jazzstudies

University of South Florida, College of Performing Arts: School of Music
www.arts.usf.edu
info@arts.usf.edu

GEORGIA
Georgia State University School of Music
www.music.gsu.edu
music@gsu.edu

ILLINOIS
DePaul School of Music
www.music.depaul.edu
music@depaul.edu

Northwestern University, Bienen School of Music
www.music.northwestern.edu/programs/jazz.html
musiclife@northwestern.edu

Roosevelt University, Chicago
http://ccpa.roosevelt.edu/music.php
music@roosevelt.edu

University of Illinois Urbana-Champaign
http://www.music.uiuc.edu/acadPerfJazzStudies.php
musicadmissions@illinois.edu

KANSAS
Kansas State University
www.k-state.edu/music/jazz/

KENTUCKY
University of Louisville
http://jazz.louisville.edu

MASSACHUSETTS
Berklee School of Music
www.berklee.edu
admissions@berklee.edu

New England Conservatory of Music
www.newenglandconservatory.edu

NEW JERSEY
William Patterson University
www.wpnj.edu
musicadmissions@wpunj.edu

NEW YORK
Eastman School of Music
www.esm.rochester.edu/jazz
admissions@esm.rochester.edu

Julliard School of Music, Jazz Studies
www.julliard.edu/college/music/jazz.html

Manhattan School of Music
www.msmnyc.edu/jazz/

New School for Jazz and Contemporary Music
www.newschool.edu/jazz

OHIO
Oberlin College
http://www.oberlin.edu/con/divinfo/jazz/

Ohio State University
http://music.osu.edu/node/58

PENNSYLVANIA
Temple University, Boyer College of Music and Dance
www.temple.edu
music@temple.edu

TEXAS
University of North Texas
www.jazz.unt.edu
jazz@unt.edu

VIRGINIA
Virginia Commonwealth University, School of the Arts
www.vcu.edu/arts/music/dept
music@vcu.edu

ACKNOWLEDGMENTS

More than I will ever have to give is owed to the following people: Ned, it can always be said again—thank you for your love of the art and for always making me laugh. Ryan and my girls, Ella and Margo, thank you for understanding that one day I'd return to my normal state of insanity. Thank you to my parents for teaching me how to have good taste in music and encouraging me to always pursue what I love. Gary Heidt—without your faith and seemingly endless supply of affirmation speeches, I'd still be wandering the streets looking for Oz. To my editor, Amy Vinchesi—thank you for taking a chance on me. Whether you know it or not, you've been welcomed with love and open arms into the giant family of jazz musicians by ensuring the reality of this book. Shyrel and Peter, thank you for introducing me to the Mile High City. I honestly couldn't have finished this process without both of you. Donald, Tyler, and the rest of Dazzle, thanks for feeding my mind, body, and soul at all times. Thank you to Convergence for not laughing. Chie, thanks for being my one and only groupie. Chris Tarry, thank you for having a killer distraction at NAMM and forcing me to be who I really was through all the noise. Doug, Nancy, LeeAnn, Suellen, Ted, Cheryl, Dwight, and Russ, thank you for making sure the seatbelt of rationality was tight at all times. Thank you to Jason Frost and Spencer Kwit, for taking time to pull me out of the quicksand. Cassandra Davis—your hard work kept me sane. Deb Courtney, thank you for listening and providing more hugs than one person should. For Carrie Morris—forever. For John, this time was the next time, not the last time. To the rest of you who lent me your tunes, souls, and love…I'm not sure where I'd be without you, nor do I want to imagine what that place would look or sound like.

INDEX